M000306905

'This is a "must read" book for anyone in leadership, including those who wonder how they got there! In her perceptive examination, Kate Coleman uncovers what so often lies hidden in this area, and places it firmly on the agenda. It's rare to find such careful research, gripping narrative and positive mentoring all in one book. I loved it!'
ELAINE STORKEY, AUTHOR, SPEAKER, BROADCASTER, PRESIDENT OF TEAR FUND

'If you need a push to step up your leadership skills, this book will encourage you in a thought provoking, relevant and practical way. Kate Coleman's experience and insight furthers our understanding of leadership and the recognition that, as women, we have a responsibility to lead. Kate's perspective on a consensus leadership style hit a particularly powerful chord in my heart.

I would recommend this book to all women, at any stage of their leadership journey, knowing that God can use us in extraordinary ways, if we are willing to respond. This is a contemporary, breezy read, compelling in substance and style.'
KAY CHALDECOTT, MANAGING DIRECTOR CAPITAL SHOPPING CENTRES PLC

'Thank God for 7 Deadly Sins of Women in Leadership! I am convinced that this book will equip women in leadership to hone their craft, enabling them to "swim" rather than "sink" as leaders. It is a timely and essential resource for women leaders across all sectors.'
GRACE OWEN, CAREER COACH, SPEAKER, AUTHOR OF *THE CAREER ITCH*

'A clear and timely tool for women leaders and for the men who celebrate them. To get the most out of this book, approach it as you would a panoramic fitting room mirror: you may not like what you see, but you're in a good place to put it right.'
KATEI KIRBY, WESLEYAN MINISTER AND FORMER CEO OF ACEA UK (AFRICAN CARIBBEAN EVANGELICAL ALLIANCE)

7 DEADLY SINS OF WOMEN IN LEADERSHIP

OVERCOME SELF-DEFEATING BEHAVIOUR IN WORK & MINISTRY

KATE COLEMAN

next**+**eadership

PUBLISHED BY NEXT LEADERSHIP
PO Box 15502, Birmingham B9 9GQ, United Kingdom
www.nextleadership.org

Unless otherwise stated scripture quotations are taken from the *Holy Bible,
New International Version* © 1973, 1978, 1984 by International Bible Society. Used by permission
of Hodder & Stoughton, a member of the Hodder Headline Group. All rights reserved.
'NIV' is a trade mark of International Bible Society. UK trademark number 1448790.

Scripture quotations taken from the *Holy Bible, Today's New International Version* © 2004
by International Bible Society. Used by permission of Hodder & Stoughton Publishers,
a division of Hodder Headline Ltd. All rights reserved. 'TNIV' is a registered trademark
of International Bible Society.

Scripture taken from *The Message* ©1993,1994, 1995, 1996, 2000, 2001, 2002.
Used by permission of NavPress Publishing Group. A CIP catalogue record for this book
is available from the British Library.

ISBN 978-0-9565572-0-9

Julia Lloyd Design
Printed and bound in the UK by the MPG Books Group, Bodmin and King's Lynn

2 4 6 8 10 9 7 5 3 1

© Mixed Sources
Product group from well-managed
forests, controlled sources and
recycled wood or fiber
FSC   www.fsc.org Cert no. TT-COC-002303
© 1996 Forest Stewardship Council

In loving memory of my mother who was promoted to Glory shortly before the completion of this book. She raised an army of wonderful women leaders. I have the privilege of calling them all… my sisters.

Contents

Acknowledgements

I am deeply indebted to the many significant women and men in my life, without whom this project would not have been completed.

I am particularly grateful for the insistent and persistent encouragement of my friend and colleague Cham Kaur-Mann (your surname may look different but it certainly sounds the same as mine!): I count you among my own sisters. Thanks for your commitment in staying up late, talking over and painstakingly reading through my notes (again!): you definitely went way beyond the second mile. Thanks to Grace Owen who has been a wonderful sister, friend, cheerleader and an awesome coach. I am extremely grateful to Elaine Storkey, who has mentored me through some very 'sticky moments' in my own leadership journey. Thanks Elaine for your effort to get the book out of my head and into print by 'subtly' encouraging me to avoid getting knocked over by a bus! Thanks also go to Kay Chaldecott, Grace Owen and Katei Kirby, three wonderful leaders, who together with Elaine have provided the initial endorsements for this book. Thank you Tracy Cotterell... I love the way you think and how you constantly challenge me to stretch my own thinking! Jane Day also provoked me to greater levels of faith through her unstinting support and unwavering belief that I 'have something important here'. Thanks Jane, your role has been pivotal.

A huge thanks to friends, Kay and John Chaldecott, Jane and Steve Day, Mark and Shernell Durrant, Kate Hutton, Cham Kaur-Mann, Grace and Simon Owen, Sandra Nicholas, Lynn and George Patterson, Christine Richards, Jacky Storey and my 'anonymous donor', who all gave sacrificially, so that this book could move to print and beyond.

Special thanks to the W'men Core Team: Jo Bagby, Cham Kaur-Mann, Grace Owen and Sandra Thomas. Together, we have worked on a programme through which many women have found their voices and are fulfilling their potential. God is good!

Thank you seems an inadequate way of acknowledging the hard work of our support team, especially those of you who have been with us from the beginning and have embodied all that we have taught and modelled. You often 'saved the day', practically speaking (sometimes very late at night/early morning) with your wonderful gifts and dedication. (Unfortunately, I can't mention you all by name without writing yet another chapter!) The same could be said of my women mentees and the many women participating in the 7 Deadly Sins programme in various parts of the country. Having said how inadequate it sounds, 'thank you…' many of your stories are represented in these pages. May God continue to take you from strength to strength! Nearly last (but certainly not least!) I want to thank my editorial team, Leda Sammarco, Julia Lloyd and Jane Collinson who worked 'beyond the call of duty'. It has been a privilege…

It all begins and ends… as we say in Ghana, Gye Nyame, 'Only God'.

Foreword

Sin is a serious issue and a deadly sin is the most serious of all; most of the time we think of it as something personal, degenerate, wilful and deliberate. We think of it in relation to God and our violation of God's standards for human life. Sin is something we shun and strive to avoid.

But in truth sin is more complicated even than all that. Sin can also be passive, unwitting, or habitual. It can be something of which we are wholly unaware, part of a mindset which we have inherited. Sin can also be something built into the very structural background of our lives which has become so normalised that we don't notice it is there.

Kate Coleman's approach to the 7 Deadly Sins might seem somewhat unusual. She is not offering a diatribe of offences against God for which we deserve punishment. Nor is she cataloguing our moral ineptitudes in order to make us feel wretched. On the contrary, Kate identifies the nature of sin with the destructive patterns of thought and behaviour that thwart the leadership God calls us to exercise. She looks at the way we can allow wrong attitudes, blind alleys and conventional patterns of behaviour to hold us up from serving God better and more faithfully. This in itself is certainly serious.

It is particularly serious in relation to the essential theme of this book – effective leadership. Women leaders in particular can too easily allow their direction, vision and strategies to become thwarted by false perceptions of themselves and others. But this need not be so. This book offers other ways forward.

Kate knows and understands leadership and in every chapter of this book, speaks with wisdom and personal experience. We should be grateful that she has done so much reflection on that experience for the result is a probing and insightful piece of writing that leaves few stones unturned. It would not surprise me if many readers find themselves described in these pages, and are taken aback by the accuracy of description! But Kate gives us every encouragement that we can stretch up, reach out and move on. Given the current climate and the increasing numbers of women in leadership both within and beyond the church, I have no doubt that this book will help many. I hope it might help you.

Elaine Storkey

Introduction My Journey into Leadership

I blinked again, struggling to understand the implications of what I was reading. Here I was, staying in a flat, in what could only be described as the middle of nowhere, somewhere on the west coast of Scotland. I had arrived on retreat two weeks earlier and still had another week to go. I had come here in response to a deep sense of conviction that God would clarify my life's calling and work to me. Some friends thought I was crazy and I must admit I was beginning to wonder about this myself…

For the past few days I had been reading the Bible, allowing myself to be 'led by the Spirit' and so far, every verse I had looked up related to leadership. Many of the passages were unfamiliar to me, as I had only been a Christian for three years. There had also been a number of 'incidents' and compelling 'coincidences' which all seemed to point me to one inescapable conclusion: God was calling me to leadership! Not as simple as it sounds… there were two problems: firstly my church was totally opposed to placing women in leadership roles, secondly… so was I!

Although I now mentor men and women leaders from across the public, private, charity and church sectors, my own leadership journey emerged from within the context of local and national church life. The church environment poses distinctive challenges for all leaders, particularly women, and therefore generates some unique insights. Historically, perceptions of women in the workplace, at least in the Western world, have frequently emerged from unhelpful views promoted by the church. This has often been at variance with Jesus' disposition and behaviour toward women. If we advocate Jesus as the supreme model for leadership in every sphere, church leaders are better placed to offer insights on leadership discussions beyond the borders of the church. Unfortunately, we have regularly compartmentalised Biblical leadership principles and values in ways that have been wholly unhelpful to the rest of society. It is my desire to contribute to the process of dismantling this unhealthy divide particularly at a time when there is an obvious need for greater integrity and ethically based leadership everywhere.

Leadership in every field is tough. Within the church, leaders seek to motivate a predominantly volunteer force, who frequently view church involvement as a mere 'leisure' pursuit. It is also a context where people frequently and liberally project and transfer painful emotional baggage in ways seldom replicated within paid 'working' environments. Therefore, leadership 'success', within church life, relies almost entirely upon 'good will' and the skilful (not to mention prayerful!) exercise of influence.

During my early years of ministry, I learned principles of good leadership largely by observing poor leaders! Please don't misunderstand me, I was privileged to interact with some great leaders but I also witnessed some spectacularly unhelpful ones. Consequently, I learned from 'the good, the bad and the ugly'. However, those who remain indelibly etched in my memory were frequently insecure, fearful or characterised by unresolved personal issues. These leaders were the ones I determined never to emulate.

I began my leadership journey in the early 1980s. It was a time, in some church circles, when the language of leadership was rarely in use and questions regarding the leadership of women created even greater levels of tension and anxiety than they do today. Outrageous behaviour was justified and significant ministries discounted, on the basis of what sometimes masqueraded as doctrinal 'conviction' but more often resembled personal preference or plain bad manners! As a result of this 'mis-education', many of the unhelpful (and helpful) leadership examples I encountered were from men.

I intuitively knew that there were lessons about leadership only other women could teach me, however, I was unable to articulate these thoughts at the time. For example, I now notice divergences between male and female preachers, particularly in relation to the illustrations each share from the pulpit and the emphases each place on specific issues. I find both perspectives unique, yet equally powerful.

Although women leaders were in short supply, I intentionally sought them out whenever I could. I am profoundly grateful to God for the privilege of meeting so many extraordinary women leaders along the way. I am fully aware that in a world in which 'different' treatment for women seldom means 'equal' treatment, this small group of women helped to ease the challenges of my journey into leadership. I wish to honour and thank them, for mentoring me, often unknowingly and from a distance. It is my conviction that the leadership and ministry of women has much to teach us all.

The formation of leaders is not a momentary encounter but an ongoing process of reflection, development and execution. My earliest days taught me the value of learning from the experience, wisdom and insight of others. The stories shared within the pages of this book reflect many of the leadership challenges that we face, particularly as women. This book aims to express all that is unique and wonderful about women's leadership, while also seeking to identify areas that may be problematic and in need of scrutiny.

There is increasing recognition that men and women bring different gifts to leadership and that both experience significant leadership challenges. Yet while men have been working on their leadership 'downsides' for decades through attending conferences, mentoring, exposure to role models and relevant reading, women are only just beginning to consider what their unique 'issues' might be.

Empowering Women Leaders to Excel

This book is committed to the task of empowering women already exercising leadership within the church and/or the marketplace to recognise and understand what may be unique about their leadership. It is primarily dedicated to promoting leadership development wherever women happen to serve as leaders. In this book, my intention is to enable women who are already in leadership, to lead well. These women inhabit every arena of leadership. They may include CEOs, directors, line managers/middle managers, women running businesses alone or in partnership with others. Women leaders who serve within the church may be responsible for some area of ministry such as evangelism, pastoral care, children's or youth work. They are sole leaders or part of leadership teams accountable for small groups, missions and churches. These women sit on boards or work with committees in large, medium and small organisations and churches. They are women of influence but sometimes fail to recognise their significance.

I want to encourage all women to affirm what is good about their leadership, while addressing what is potentially destructive. I aim to identify solutions to behaviours, rehearsed knowingly and unknowingly, which effectively sabotage women's leadership and may even undermine their best intentions!

I have identified at least three major challenges that continue to face all proponents of women in leadership. The first is *Education* (or perhaps more accurately, 're-education'). This involves the task of revisiting what we think we know, concerning the contributions of women leaders to both Biblical and Christian traditions, as well as social and global advancement. The second major challenge is *Empowerment*. Here the concern is related to how we might actively inspire, equip and train women who already hold strategic positions of leadership within churches and/or the marketplace. The final challenge is related to the task of *Encouragement,* particularly of emerging leaders who may not have been introduced to, or even considered the role of leadership.

Elements of this book will address all three concerns. However, I do not intend to present extensive theological arguments that advocate for women in leadership (although I make specific references when appropriate). Others have more than adequately addressed the debate on women's leadership in church and society, elsewhere. Instead, I *assume* the normality of women's leadership for the sake of those women already engaged in leadership roles! Rather than being concerned with the issue of whether 'women's ways' are innate or environmental, my interest lies in the fact that these 'ways' are specifically identified with women. Some of these characteristics possess a potentially destructive shadow side that frequently goes unrecognised by the women in question.

> I want to encourage all women to affirm what is good about their leadership, while addressing what is potentially destructive

Researchers and writers on the subject of leadership, agree that the hidden internal and personal factors pose the greatest dangers to leadership. If indeed, 'self-knowledge is vital to effective performance as a leader',[1] it becomes imperative to identify and address these negative factors. Christian leadership trainer Jeanne Porter writes, 'an essential ingredient of leadership success is the capacity to assess your own strengths and areas that need development – and make changes to your course when called for'.[2]

Many men will also benefit from the leadership advice provided within these pages, in addition to gaining insights into the challenges experienced by the women leaders around them! After all, principles surrounding leadership are of value to both men and women. While some women leaders exhibit more traditionally masculine traits, some men will discover that they display more traditionally feminine leadership traits. As a result, some men will find the discussions surrounding deadly sins far more applicable to their own experiences, than some women.

This book does not assume that the nature versus nurture debate has been exhausted, as scholars remain undecided on the question of whether we are primarily products of our parental DNA or our environment and upbringing.[3] Neither does this book assume that views on women's roles are no longer contentious, particularly within church contexts. However, I do not intend to specifically focus on either of these areas. Although these questions are important, the main priority for women already engaged in leadership roles, is the practice of leadership itself. For women working within particularly challenging circumstances, survival is also a necessity!

My early experience of church leadership was energising yet exhausting, instinctive yet challenging, profound yet lonely, exhilarating yet depressing. Almost every week, I vowed to resign on the grounds of personal mistakes, disappointments, discouragement, intense spiritual attack[4], opposition and resistance. All were compounded by overt expressions of sexism and racism.

Although I consistently received support and input from some remarkable men and women, as a woman in leadership, a single black woman, no less, I often felt that I was clearing a path through challenging terrain, without a map or compass. Quite frankly, it was just as well I had faith! Although I had over five years theological 'training', what I'd been 'taught' still didn't make sense of my actual experiences or my personal challenges. My confusion about leadership continued.

Leadership Development: the Necessary Key

This was Lisa's first experience of participating in a Christian leadership development programme, specifically designed for women and she was glad she had come. However, some of her friends at church had been sceptical about the conference, until they began to notice changes in her attitude and disposition. Someone even commented on Lisa's increasing display of confidence in her work and ministry. Her contributions were more considered and focused. Lisa was beginning to feel and behave like a valuable member of the team. In fact, many were preoccupied with the concern that she would seek to explore more attractive ministry opportunities elsewhere, now that she was flourishing. 'Thank God for leadership development,' she thought…

The idea of 'leadership' is becoming increasingly important in society. Yet in some contexts it is still viewed as another 'NEW' concept, initiative or bandwagon, threatening to place additional demands on already limited time and emotional resources. From a Biblical perspective, the notion of leadership goes back as far as the creation of humanity (if not further), with the mandate to 'rule' or 'steward' the earth's animate and inanimate resources. While it is true that the term 'leadership' itself is not found within the pages of the Bible, it is everywhere alluded to and assumed. Writer Steven Croft reminds us that, 'the Judeo-Christian tradition provides the longest continuous source of reflection on questions of leadership in the whole of human history'.[5] However, whether we want to get on or get off the leadership bandwagon, we cannot ignore the profound impact that leadership is currently having on all our lives, for better or for worse.

There is an increasing expectation and pressure on those in positions of influence to accomplish more with significantly fewer resources. These leaders are also expected to adapt to rapidly changing environments and to navigate their way through a wide variety of situations with relative ease. All of this requires a certain degree of equipping. Subsequently, governments, corporations, educationalists and some churches rightly endorse the significance and/or importance of leadership. Public and private sectors invest hundreds of thousands in hard currency and time, providing leadership training programmes in an effort to maximise the productivity of their employees and to ensure their competitive advantage in the marketplace. Meanwhile, charitable and church agencies invest in the hope of making their leaders more effective. Therefore, any attempt to avoid the subject of leadership unwittingly promotes poor leadership.

> We must know who we are, who we are following and where we are going, if we wish to make a positive impact

While such training is vital, Christians must attend to another essential matter. Just as every leader needs to be equipped to get things done, keep things going, organise well and help others in the process, we must simultaneously integrate who we are as spiritual beings into every aspect of our daily lives and work. In short, we must know who we are, who we are following and where we are going, if we wish to make a positive impact on the people we are privileged to influence and lead. Unfortunately, none of this happens 'by accident'. Leadership mentor Reggie McNeal, confirms this in his book, *Practicing Greatness*, 'Great leaders don't just appear, they are crafted over time. They practice being great. Extraordinary character and exceptional competence develop over time. Leaders must make countless good choices and right calls to fashion greatness.'[6] Therefore, men and women must become responsible for intentionally cultivating and developing their personal leadership. However, this is not quite as straightforward as it sounds...

Although the role of women and men in leadership is identical i.e. to lead, leadership experts are increasingly identifying both masculine and feminine facets to leadership. Ironically, much leadership development, training, literature, conferences and advice is largely, albeit often unconsciously, tailored by men for men. While all leadership advice should be welcomed, attempts at so called 'generic' training may fail to meet the specific needs of women leaders in particular. Such needs are only just beginning to receive due recognition. Therefore, many women continue to remain unaware of the specific nature of the unique challenges they face in leadership and often, how to address them.

The Changing Face of Leadership

Wendy climbed into her car and let out an audible sigh of relief. The final interview was over. She had been offered the post and she gladly accepted. 'Training manager', she smiled as she said it out loud. She was now one of only two senior women leaders in the whole company. Her experience, expertise and innovative approach to leadership, had greatly impressed the company, making her the obvious choice. She was pleased, things needed to change, old management models were simply not working. Wendy felt that what she had been doing recently had suited her temperament and personality better. She couldn't really explain it, she simply felt much more 'at home' in her own skin using her own distinctive style...

Leadership is not only incredibly important, it is also highly complex. Like many other disciplines it involves a variety of models, styles and schools of thought. The very word conjures up a variety of images for many of us. Inevitably, leadership means different things to different people. Whether a leadership issue is prioritised or a particular style considered valid, is primarily affected by gender, culture, age or ethnicity. Our background, history, class, and friendships determine the leadership preferences we have and the conferences we choose to attend. For Christians, even our interpretation of the Bible, our understanding of the Holy Spirit's role in our day-to-day activities, our sense of God as immanent or transcendent, our vision and mission, all affect how we believe leadership should be applied and who should be allowed to exercise it. For those who sincerely choose to embrace the mandate to lead, there is much to think about.

However, in the leadership debate, it has become apparent that 'traditional' models and approaches to leadership are increasingly unpopular with both women *and* men. People from all sectors are rejecting traditional male models that focus on independence and the need to command and control. It is recognised that this approach promotes the unhelpful view that 'one size fits all'. Consequently, people are turning to models, more often associated with women, that promote consultation and collaboration rather than competition (although this is seldom recognised or acknowledged). Such models tend to be less conscious of hierarchy, emphasise the big picture, encourage relationship-building and attempt to incorporate the ideas of others before final decisions are made. Rosie Ward states, 'Leadership is changing. Old dualistic and hierarchical models are disappearing in favour of egalitarian and holistic ones. The trend is towards leadership as team, and the idea that a leader is more like the conductor of an orchestra than the commander of an army.'[7]

Clearly a transformation in thinking is occurring around contemporary expectations of what makes a good leader. Lois Frankel captures the mood, 'Leadership in the twenty-first century is different from leadership in the mid-twentieth century is different from leadership in the pre-twentieth century. What makes leadership different through the ages are the needs of the followers.'[8]

Women and younger people, who for so long have been relegated to the sole role of follower, are now emerging as key influencers in reshaping leadership thinking and practice. Almost simultaneously, some arenas, traditionally viewed as the domain of male leaders, have been experiencing an increase in the numbers of women entering leadership roles.

Interestingly, women are coming to leadership at precisely the time that the culture of leadership is experiencing some of its greatest changes. It is difficult to say whether expectations of leadership have altered 'because of' or 'in spite of' the increasing influence of women leaders in the work place. Whatever the case, the essential but often missing aspects of leadership, namely women's perspectives, are at last beginning to experience an awakening!

Internationally acclaimed leader and advisor to four presidents, David Gergen states, 'today… command and control leadership has given way to a new approach, often called an influence model of leadership… the new leader persuades, empowers, collaborates, and

> '…The best leader, we are finding, is one who identifies top talent and nurtures them to become leaders in their own right …'

partners. The best leader, we are finding, is one who identifies top talent and nurtures them to become leaders in their own right – a leader of leaders.'[9] He adds 'Women leaders, as it turns out, seem perfectly tailored for this new style. Think about the words we use to describe the old-style leadership: aggressive, assertive, autocratic, muscular, closed. When we describe the new leadership, we employ terms like consensual, relational, web-based, caring, inclusive, open, transparent – all qualities we associate with the "feminine" style of leadership. One can argue whether this feminine style is in women's genes or is created by socialization. It doesn't matter much. The key point... is that women are knocking on the door of leadership at the very moment when their talents are especially well matched with the requirements of the day.'[10]

Research shows that women entrepreneurs are growing in number, while those in executive committees and church leadership are increasing in the UK and around the world.

Although it is reported that twice as many men as women in the UK start their own businesses, according to the Department for Business, Enterprise and Regulatory Reform (BERR formerly the DTI), a record 34.1% and 41.2% of UK small businesses are currently owned or at least co-owned by women.[11] In the US, these figures are closer to 30.4% and 48%, with women-owned businesses growing at twice the rate of all US firms.[12] A similar phenomenon is occurring in boardrooms across the Western world. According to the 2009 female FTSE, 'the percentage of companies in Spain with at least one female director is 55% (up from 40% in 2006)...'[13] In 2007, the then Deputy Leader of the Labour Party, Minister of State, Harriet Harman reported:

> **'When I helped launch the FTSE female index in 1999, I found that many of Britain's boardrooms were a no-go area for women... Since then, we have made progress. Eight years ago 36% of FTSE 100 boards had no women – today that figure is down to 24%.'[14]**

The proportion of female ministers across all church denominations in the UK stood at just 12.3% in 2005, up from an estimated 7.9% in 1992.[15] *The Church Times* reported that just 12 years after the first woman priest was ordained in 1994, more than 50% of ordained Anglican priests in 2006 were women.[16] Many were non-stipendiary and seldom in senior roles, however, this increase still represents a remarkable achievement.[17]

Sally Morgenthaler is rightly cautious, recognising that although US society (among others) increasingly favours relational paradigms,[18] leadership among Christian organisations, including churches, is still predominantly, and perhaps ironically, hierarchical 'command and control'.[19]

However, as mentioned earlier, it is women and younger people intent on expressing an alternative vision of leadership who are often the 'face' and the driving force, of the new paradigm.[20]

Whose Face, Which Women?

Raj was annoyed but she managed to calm herself down. Once again her quietness throughout the discussion had been misinterpreted as deference and passivity. She had listened intently to the debate and had smiled encouragingly as each speaker presented their perspective but her decision had been clear and considered. Yet certain members of the committee were visibly shocked by her vote against their proposal and now they appeared to be shunning her. She was beginning to realise that they had simply 'misread' her behaviour as acquiescence and expected her to approach things in exactly the same way that they did...

The subject of women in leadership is frequently perceived from the vantage point of one particular group of women, usually white and middle class. This approach implies that women leaders are monochrome and devoid of diverse experiences. It also suggests that all women face similar barriers to their leadership. In reality, the face of women in leadership is not confined to a particular race, history, class, culture, ethnicity, education or formal title.

All women face a variety of social expectations and many wrestle with prevailing stereotypes. The following examples may be overly simplistic but they represent the kind of 'thinking' that continues to impact different kinds of women in debilitating ways.

From around the 18th Century, *white Western upper-middle class women* were placed on a pedestal from which there was virtually no way down (at least, that didn't involve the trauma of falling!). However, this was not necessarily the case for white working class women. The former were viewed as too pure and too fragile to work within or beyond the home. Although they were idealised and idolised by their husbands and children, they were not necessarily respected as human beings in their own right. These women were expected to model morality and purity for their children within the principal role of a homemaker (often with the support of servants or hired help). They were expected to serve their husbands and provide them with an heir. In contrast, husbands were viewed as income generators and permitted to enjoy limitless freedom and liberty. This social expectation was initially destabilised by the Industrial Revolution. However, it was only truly altered by the demands of two world wars that effectively propelled women into the general workforce. The result has led to a reconfigured but similarly related stereotype where men still retain the dominant role in the workplace.

The social history of *black women in the West* cast them in the role of 'natural' labourers. Ironically, in contrast to white upper-middle class women, black women were fully expected to work outside their own homes. They were also expected to be highly sacrificial and totally deferential toward the (white) ruling classes. Typically cast in supporting roles, black women seemed destined to care for other people's homes and families (whether children or the infirm). Therefore, it was deemed socially acceptable to deprioritise black family life (a state of affairs that arose partially as a by-product of slavery and servitude). Consequently, black women were penalised for 'neglecting' their children *only* if they went 'off the rails' and disturbed everyone else's peace! In Western society, black women are still expected to have children (but not necessarily husbands), with an emphasis placed upon motherhood (i.e. having babies) rather than mothering (i.e. raising children). They are expected to 'labour' but certainly not to exercise leadership over others.

South Asian women, like Raj, on the other hand, are frequently stereotyped as passive, accommodating, silent and invisible. How surprising then, to discover the presence of at least four 'glaring anomalies' in South Asian political history. [21] These include a Sri Lankan, Sirimavo Ratwatte Dias Bandaranaike, who also enjoys the distinction of being the second woman prime minister in modern history,[22] long before any female heads of government existed in Western Europe! Indeed, two of the world's best known and most powerful global leaders happened to be female; Indian, on the one hand (Indira Gandhi), and Pakistani, on the other (Benazir Bhutto). Within the realm of work, it is often expected that Asian women will engage in primarily home-based occupations and will accommodate both work and family in equal measure. There is a general perception that Asian women focus upon finding a husband, having children and caring for their in-laws to the exclusion of all other personal interests.

Work is perceived as secondary, entered into only with the permission of others and principally for the greater good of the extended family unit. Although this thinking contains partial truths, in that cultural expectations emphasise both family and community, it is often a misrepresentation.

Such social expectations are often presented as prescriptive rather than descriptive of *some* women's lives and effectively limit women's opportunities for leadership. For example, white middle-class women who long for fulfilment both within and beyond the home are severely penalised (or taught to chastise themselves) for entertaining desires for work beyond a partner and children. Many African and Caribbean cultures raise black women to be more socially assertive and to have a more direct style of interaction than white women. Yet Western society interprets such behaviour as aggressive. Perhaps unsurprisingly, leadership researchers report greater levels of resistance to the leadership of black women. Consequently, these women are also more likely to start their own businesses. Openly assertive, ambitious and highly visible South Asian women can prove to be an unexpected surprise (or shock!) to a society blinkered by its own prejudices and conditioned to expect only passivity, invisibility and accommodation.

Thankfully, there are many examples of culturally diverse women engaged in leadership activities who do *not* conform to stereotype. In spite of the dissimilarities between culturally diverse women leaders, I believe there is sufficient common ground in our social experience to enable us all to identify with many aspects of the 7 Deadly Sins addressed in this book. Although challenges faced by different groups of women are unique, many share common strategies in their approaches to leadership.

The Unique Impact of Women's Leadership

Jackie was elated ... not only had her company won another major contract but they had also been recognised as ethical leaders in the marketplace. This 'success' reflected particularly well on her and on the changes she had insisted on implementing throughout the organisation. While she was glad it had reflected on the 'bottom line,' she was far happier that she had taken a stand that had honoured her Christian commitment. While the congratulatory emails continued to appear on her screen she silently prayed and thanked God for making her who she was ...

Women in leadership positions in today's world are often unaware of the unique gifts they exercise, these have transformed the very nature and understanding of leadership. In early 2009, the Bank of Scotland

Corporate's Women in Business programme partnered with *Real Business* to profile and celebrate Britain's 100 most entrepreneurial women. The profile revealed that women's distinctive approaches to business and leadership have been chiefly responsible for changing the rules for business success.[23]

> Women in leadership positions in today's world are often unaware of the unique gifts they exercise

Research reveals that women, on average, lead differently to men.[24] It is also recognised that organisations and nations who promote the full and equal partnership of male *and* female leaders tend to be amongst the most humane, economically vibrant and environmentally friendly.[25] For example, Fortune 500 Companies committed to the development of women and their promotion to senior leadership perform better financially than those that have lower female representation.[26]

There is widespread acknowledgement that the involvement of women within national, regional and corporate government has led to beneficial shifts in political behaviour and priorities. Nordic countries such as Finland, Sweden and Norway which have a critical mass of women legislators, sometimes in excess of 40%, are outstanding examples. According to the UN human development reports, these nations rank ahead of wealthier nations such as the US.[27] These once poor, famine-ridden nations have been transformed into prosperous, peaceful nations with a high quality of life as a result of the presence of women, where care-giving and the protection of natural resources is prioritised. In the arena of peace-building, women often pursue refreshingly non-violent approaches to conflict resolution. Former US president Bill Clinton commented, 'If we had women at Camp David, [during the talks between Palestinians and Israelis in 2000] we'd have an agreement.'[28]

Researcher and professor Scott Page notes, 'There's a lot of empirical data to show that diverse cities are more productive, diverse boards of directors make better decisions, the most innovative companies are diverse.'[29]

Unfortunately, resistance to female leadership has been particularly strong within church organisations. It is often argued that female ministers send churches into numerical decline. However, a report produced by Christian Research in 2005 agreed that although 'female ministers are often associated with declining churches' this is primarily due to the initial state of the churches they inherit.[30] The overall proportion of women in church leadership currently stands at no more than 13%. As more women embrace the call to church leadership, the overall quality of leadership actually appears to have improved. Bob Jackson explored the ideal leadership requirements for church growth amongst the UK Anglican churches and concluded, 'women incumbents and younger incumbents are more likely to have growing churches. The ideal candidate profile for a church that wishes to grow would appear to be young, female and willing to stay in post for ten to twelve years!' He adds, 'Such findings do not of themselves affect the theological arguments for and against the ordination of women, although there may be a certain force in the "by their fruits ye shall know them" argument.'[31]

It is my conviction that male *and* female were designed by God to *co-steward* his resources, in order to achieve his purposes in every task or human endeavour. When either is missing from the leadership task so is a distinct aspect of the nature of God.

It is worth stating here, that I am using the term 'he' because it is the most often used grammatical designation for God and not because the Bible portrays God as male. Indeed, 'he' in the Bible is a generic term and therefore nonsexual. Although God is revealed as the source of all gender, God transcends gender because God is Spirit and has no form, male or female (see Isaiah 40:18 and 25). As one scholar has written, '…God has no sex. God is in God's own class'.[32] However, I will be referring to him/his etc in this book for simplicity of style.

The Unique Leadership Challenges Facing Women

Caroline was still struggling with the outcome of the meeting. Although she had been affirmed in her leadership by her church overseers, there was still considerable unrest and complaint from a few of the church members. A number of them continued to struggle with the idea of having a female minister, 'it just isn't right!' she'd overheard one woman say. To be honest she couldn't blame them, she struggled with it herself, she knew all the arguments and that what she was doing was right even though it felt so strange. Unfortunately, some of the congregation had now dropped the facade of politeness and had become increasingly hostile towards her. She could see that this transition was not going to be easy for any of them…

Unfortunately, women continue to be shaped by powerful cultural, social, educational and familial forces that act to contain and constrain them. In relation to the US, Marie Wilson writes, 'when it comes to women's leadership, we live in a land of deep resistance, with structural and emotional impediments burned into the cultures of our organizations, into our society, and into the psyches and expectations of both sexes.'[33]

This reality is not limited to the US nor indeed to Western Europe. In 2005, the World Economic Forum undertook research to determine the relative status of women in 58 diverse nations, entitled 'Women's empowerment: Measuring the global gender gap'.[34] The authors discovered that even within the most progressive contexts, women continue to be significantly disadvantaged, 'the reality is that no country in the world, no matter how advanced, has achieved true gender equality, as measured by comparable decision making power, equal opportunity for education and advancement and status in all walks of human endeavour'.[35] For example, women's political representation in the UK is currently ranked at 58, ahead of the US which holds joint 70th position with Turkmenistan. Interestingly, both are outperformed by Rwanda, Afghanistan and Iraq![36]

In spite of recent advances, opportunities for women in leadership are still relatively scarce and progress, although steady, continues to be painfully slow. The reality is, 'Most women still report to male bosses. Ninety per cent of the top leadership jobs in the UK are still held by men. This statistic has changed little during the last thirty years… "Women's work", particularly in the teaching and caring sectors of the economy, is still undervalued when compared to other more male-dominated occupations. Average wealth and income remains much lower for women than for men.'[37]

Women often report having to work twice as hard as men, to be considered half as good. The 1982 cartoon by Robert Thaves expresses this paradox in the following way: 'Ginger Rogers did everything he [Fred Astaire] did, backwards… and in high heels!'[38]

There is also a growing recognition within the corporate sector that women are more likely to be offered opportunities to lead as a last resort and often when a project is most likely to fail.[39]

The average woman in leadership has to deal with a vast array of negative factors not necessarily encountered by men. For example, women are often minorities within leadership cultures that feel alien to their way of working; this may partly explain why women who begin life in large corporations and institutions eventually opt for self-employment opportunities.[40] Commonly, women who pioneer leadership roles are exposed to fewer role models, subsequently many feel that they have to reinvent the proverbial 'wheel' as they go along!

Interestingly, in circumstances where opportunities for advancement are limited, women are more likely to be viewed as a threat by other women, as well as by men.

Life is frequently lived at the sharp end for women in leadership, leaving them more vulnerable to negative experiences, emotional backlash, spiritual attack, resistance and even 'friendly fire' from those closest to them. These women seldom receive sufficient understanding, support or encouragement.

Figures on leadership burnout within churches and businesses are sobering. These figures include the countless number of women, who together with men, experience isolation, anger, fear, loneliness, the absence of anyone to talk to and extreme discouragement. Women may also be tempted to give up because they frequently carry the burden of care for their family and are often over-stretched or simply 'running on empty'.

However, it would be misleading to suggest that external factors alone impede the progress of women leaders. There are other more disturbing and potentially devastating factors to contend with. These 'forces' are of greater concern to me and make up the major themes of this book because they remain unaltered by changes in equality legislation or improved working conditions. These often 'invisible influences' are what I describe as the *Deadly Sins of Women in Leadership*.

> Deadly sins are essentially self-defeating, undesirable and ultimately destructive behaviour patterns that undermine leadership potential and our relationship with God

These deadly sins are essentially self-defeating, undesirable and ultimately destructive behaviour patterns that undermine leadership potential and our relationship with God. On average the particular 'sins' identified also appear to present a greater threat to women in leadership than they do to men.

The Importance of Personal Leadership Development

I first started out in church leadership over 23 years ago. Like most women in leadership, the demands of work and ministry left little time and space for me to reflect on what I was doing and the unique factors hindering my own service and leadership. Only when I intentionally decided to put time aside for my personal leadership development, and that of others around me, did the many insights contained in this book emerge.

In order to serve to the best of our ability, women leaders must make time to identify and overcome the self-defeating beliefs and behaviour patterns which threaten to derail our leadership journey.

This challenge, together with other factors too numerous to mention here, has prompted me to write this book. I wish I knew 23 years ago what I know now. I also wish I'd experienced the level of intentional mentoring from great men and women that I value so highly today, it could have saved me a great deal of heartache, time and energy. Put simply, this is not just the book I have always wanted to write, it is also the book I have always wanted to read!

It is my prayer that women leaders, in particular, within and beyond the borders of the church, will find the contents of this book liberating and inspiring as they seek to understand and develop their own leadership capabilities.

Much of this book was shaped through interaction with many wonderful women during the pilot of our innovative leadership development programme, *7 Deadly Sins of Women in Leadership*, and through our network, *W'men in Leadership* (Women's mentoring, equipping and relational network). The stories contained in these pages are a mixture of personal accounts and third party narratives. They represent the experiences of many women I have met along the way on my own leadership journey. I have sometimes combined two or three similar stories belonging to different women in an attempt to conceal their identities! If these stories resonate with your own experiences, it is because they represent challenges real women have faced.

In the following chapters I will explore the nature of *7 Deadly Sins of Women in Leadership*, not because there are only seven issues to contend with (if only!) but because, for those who appreciate such things, seven is the Biblical number of completion. In other words, I wish to identify foundational themes that often lie at the root of the many additional challenges we face as women leaders.

Each chapter will include an analysis in relation to each theme, theological reflection and mentoring advice to enable leaders to take practical steps forward. I will conclude with coaching tips aimed at encouraging further personal reflection, setting goals and generating momentum.

How to Get the Most Out of This Book

This book is best read in bite-sized chunks, rather than in a single sitting. If you are like most women leaders you won't have time to read the book all the way through anyway! This introduction sets the tone for understanding the remainder of the book. After this, you may wish to simply access the chapter that addresses your immediate need first and then return to complete others that may seem less pressing. I have produced each chapter to build on the insights of the previous one however, each can be read independently.

7 Deadly Sins of Women in Leadership is a leadership tool, so please make good use of a highlighter or pen to highlight the sections, stories and passages that particularly 'speak' to you. This approach will also allow you to put the mentoring advice into practice and encourage significant reflection and goal setting when working on the coaching tips. Record some of your own thoughts in the margins and if you have time communicate your reflections about the whole book to me via my web site, I would love to hear from you (www.nextleadership.org).

Reading the *7 Deadly Sins of Women in Leadership* will enable you to radically transform your leadership capabilities. It is my prayer that many of your expectations will be met and your resounding declaration upon completing the entire book will be 'Amen!'.

1st
DEADLY SIN

LIMITING SELF-PERCEPTIONS
Adjust how you see yourself

Here, I'll encourage you to revisit how you see yourself, so that you can become more assured as a leader, able to bring about effective transformation with everyone and everything you encounter. It is very common for women to establish their own internal road blocks to progress as well as having to deal with those created by others. I will help you to identify your limiting beliefs and replace those with empowering ones.

2ND
DEADLY SIN

FAILURE TO DRAW THE LINE
Establish appropriate boundaries

At this point you will be enabled to identify your specific boundary battles so that you can become a more efficient leader. Many of the leadership (not to mention relationship) challenges faced by women in work and ministry are boundary issues. Subsequently, it may be particularly challenging to establish appropriate and healthy boundaries. I will help you to draw your boundary lines in healthier places by learning how and when to say 'yes' *and* 'no'.

3RD
DEADLY SIN

INADEQUATE PERSONAL VISION
Develop and maintain a God-inspired vision

Clarity of vision is perhaps the single most important characteristic of a great leader, yet it can be one of the greatest challenges that women in leadership face. I will encourage you to move beyond the mundane in order to discover the very purpose for which you were created. You will discover a more adequate personal and ultimately God-given vision based upon your unique gifts. This focus will inspire and sustain you even through your toughest challenges.

4TH
DEADLY SIN

TOO LITTLE LIFE IN THE WORK
Establish a healthy work-life rhythm

Getting to know yourself and your own rhythms will enable you to discover your God-given drives and passions. You will be invited to discover ways of feeding not only your body and your intellect but also your emotional and spiritual life. Women leaders frequently do one job at 'work' and then another at home. It can be difficult for them to ever truly stop, even while on 'holiday'! I will help you to define what the Biblical imperative to *work*, *rest* and, yes, even *play* looks like for you.

5TH
DEADLY SIN

EVERYBODY'S FRIEND, NOBODY'S LEADER
Defeat the 'disease to please'

Here, I will demonstrate how you can excel at relational leadership, without succumbing to its dangers. You will be introduced to some of the benefits, pitfalls and challenges involved in relational leadership. Such an approach to leadership is characteristic of women leaders. I will help you to identify whether you suffer from 'the disease to please' aka 'approval addiction'. I will also equip you with leadership skills that will ensure that friendship, whether in the work place or ministry environment, never compromises your commitment to provide good quality leadership.

6TH DEADLY SIN

COLLUDING AND NOT CONFRONTING
Deal with men (and women!) behaving badly

You will be helped to recognise the leader's primary responsibility in the face of conflict. Until the *idea* of leadership is both male and female, women leaders will inevitably face greater misunderstanding and often greater conflict than men in leadership. Whether you are dealing with conflict between others or on a personal level I will equip you with peace-making and conflict resolution skills that will enable you to confront and 'face' your challenges, rather than colluding with them.

7TH DEADLY SIN

NEGLECT IN FAMILY MATTERS
Be intentional with your nearest and dearest

Whether you are married, single, have children or not, family members may be a very significant part of your 'inner circle', your circle of influence. In this section, I will help you to achieve 'success' with your inner circle. These are the people closest to you, who determine your ultimate accomplishments as a leader. I will enable you to see how the principle of total reliance upon God can empower *you* to lead yourself in ways that release your inner circle to operate at their best.

1ST
DEADLY SIN

LIMITING SELF-PERCEPTIONS

Adjust how you see yourself

'Know who you are or someone else will tell you!'

ANON

Leadership: Am I or Aren't I? Do I or Don't I?

Sue was a highly sought after consultant and trainer. However, she couldn't understand why she felt so uncomfortable about the way the organisers had represented her in the promotional literature for their weekend course. 'Sue is a fantastic communicator with some great insights for leaders. We are privileged to have her with us for the day, so be sure to make the most of her outstanding leadership gifts and skills.' It wasn't an inaccurate description but Sue was uneasy about the emphasis placed on her 'leadership gifts and skills'. She kept thinking, 'but I don't really think of myself as a leader'.

I frequently hear similar sentiments, expressed by influential women in many different settings. Often these women are remarkably gifted, some are even positioned at the forefront of their particular profession.

Having faced my own doubts and challenges in this regard, I can understand the dilemma many women face when confronted with the 'truth' of their 'leadership'. I can even appreciate why women, unlike their male counterparts, are often unwilling to embrace the title 'leader', even when they clearly exercise 'leadership' roles. However, the fact remains that we effectively undermine both our influence and giftedness by expressing such ambivalent behaviour toward our own leadership.

For years, numerous women have struggled, and in some cases, 'battled', for the right to be formally recognised as leaders. However, some continue to feel uncomfortable with the term itself. Even when leadership is conferred upon them, there are those among us who vigorously insist, *'I'm not really a leader',* or *'I don't really think of myself as a leader'.*

Women unable to identify the source of their discomfort continue to wrestle with mixed emotions, or worse, simply ignore them! However, further exploration frequently reveals issues seldom recognised or even articulated by the women themselves.

For example, we sometimes feel alienated from the prevailing culture of leadership. At times this is simply a result of having been marginalised by those with the power to exclude us. On the other hand, we may simply feel 'different', as if we don't really belong to the 'leaders' club. This is hardly surprising when what often passes for the culture of leadership is little more than the culture of a particular type of masculinity. Many women struggle to identify themselves with approaches to leadership that are based on go-it-alone mono-myths or adversarial political, sporting and military heroes. The imagery of leadership is often designed by men, sits better with men and makes much more sense to men. Basically, men have had the advantage of developing and shaping a system in which they are not newcomers. This only serves to heighten the irony of Margaret Atwood's comment and others like it, 'We still think of a powerful man as a born leader and a powerful woman as an anomaly.'[1]

Women can learn a great deal from masculine imagery and leadership styles. However, we do not have to act like men in order to work as equals, or to be recognised as leaders. In a society where women are given subtle and not-so-subtle messages about 'where they belong', it is important to understand that, as leaders, we often 'think outside the box' because we are, quite literally, 'outside the box'!

Women do not easily imagine themselves engaged in the activities described by some leadership 'gurus'. They seldom recognise themselves in 'roles' based on competition or winning and losing, particularly as women generally prefer collaborative, win/win encounters, as I noted in my introduction.

Other women shy away from the term 'leader' because of associations with negative leadership encounters from their past. They recall personal experiences, or those of female friends and relatives, who have been on the receiving end of an abuse of power. They also remember leaders who directed power for their own benefit rather than on behalf of those they were leading. Faced with such incidents, many women simply do not want to 'become what they hate'. However, some women who struggle with the concept of leadership often do so because they still find it hard to accept that they *can* lead and that leadership, among other capabilities, is a gift that God has empowered us to express.

However, there are women who fit in all of these categories or none, who simply lack the confidence to wholeheartedly embrace the designation of 'leader'. They wrestle with inappropriate thinking and unhelpful beliefs about themselves and fail to take themselves as seriously as they should.

Many women of influence often conclude that because they neither resemble nor behave like their perception of 'a leader', they are therefore not 'a leader'. Of course they are absolutely right, they are not *that* type of leader at all. Women make extremely powerful leaders however, we are often simply leaders of a different kind.

Our struggle to embrace the concept of leadership can be traced back to a number of roots. Often beneath these roots, lurk some misconceptions regarding the meaning of leadership as it relates to women, who we perceive ourselves to be and what women believe they are capable of accomplishing as leaders.

What You *See* is What You'll Get

Although Kemi ran a very successful business and had a remarkably broad range of experience in her field of expertise, she still felt like a failure. She felt as if she didn't really know what she was doing or how she had managed to become so 'successful'. In fact, Kemi secretly dreaded the moment when 'the truth' as she saw it, would finally surface. She'd never spoken to anyone about her fears, after all who would believe her? Others were often telling her just how amazing and inspirational she was as a leader. For her part, she just wanted to be left alone in her small corner to do her own thing...

Self-perception is essentially the way we *see* ourselves. It encompasses what we believe and how we come to understand who we are. It is rooted in a number of factors, including our general competence as leaders, the messages we absorb from society at large and also what friends, family and colleagues communicate to us. For Christians, it also includes our understanding of God's perspective of us.

> Self-perception is essentially the way we *see* ourselves

However, the influence of society frequently overwhelms all other factors and we often choose to believe irrational and unreasonable social expectations and/or personal fears. Like Kemi, we wrestle with what we think we are not, rather than celebrate what we are. Consequently, we often fail to validate or fully appreciate who we really are. Studies show that when a woman fails, she's likely to blame herself. When a man fails, he's likely to blame others.[2] Such behaviours emerge from limited perceptions of our leadership capabilities and direct us toward choices based on low self-esteem, rather than our many accomplishments and achievements.

Anne Dickson, psychologist, educator, a leading authority in assertiveness training and author of *Women at Work: Strategies for Survival and Success*, describes how many women struggle to believe in who they are and the value of what they bring to leadership. She explains, 'This paradox can be found in academic, health, educational or commercial settings in England, Scandinavia, Eastern Europe or Japan. On the one hand is the high level of academic or professional qualification and experience of these women, their intelligence, their talents, their commitment and dedication; while on the other is a vivid picture of internal doubts, misgivings and anxieties stemming from an abiding, and sometimes disabling, *lack of confidence…* Sometimes this relates to specific situations, but often it is a more generalized lack of confidence that permeates every interaction.'[3]

Such themes emerge not only in 'secular' contexts, they also prove to be a challenge for church women. Rosie Ward voices the concern of women's leadership mentor Gretchen Englund, 'Even the most confident-appearing women can struggle with a sense of low self-esteem. Stemming from one's skewed view of God's acceptance and delight in her, she questions her own worth and doubts who she is. She is a called woman leader who is clearly called of God, but who inwardly struggles with questions of self-doubt, personal shame, and quietly wonders whether God's delight in her is really true… Women leaders – again because of the many layers of a woman's life – need to address their inner anxiety before they can freely move to the next level… Women can have an internal tornado, full of questions and unfinished business: Am I okay? Am I really competent? What about being single? Are my kids doing well? Does my husband find delight in me? Am I doing life right?'[4]

Self-perception is the atmosphere in which we conduct our leadership development and it can often prove toxic. Lois Frankel describes the condition, 'Like air pollution, if you live in it and breathe it long enough, you come to believe that that's just how the air is supposed

> Self-perception is the atmosphere in which we conduct our leadership development

to be. It's not until you see the beautiful blue skies of some unspoiled territory that you realise things can be different. We come to believe that our possibilities are limited, when in fact they're limited only because we allow them to be.'[5] Eleanor Roosevelt captures it well, 'Nobody can make you feel inferior without your consent.'[6] Women are often waiting to be 'found out' or to trip up and fail. Many times it becomes little more than a self-fulfilling prophecy.

Some women in leadership are totally unaware of how their self-perceptions limit their progress as leaders and they continue to make choices that negate their sense of self. Subsequently women hold on to mental habits and familiar but faulty self-understandings, that inevitably prevent them from exercising the full spectrum of their leadership gifts.

When we unwittingly foster inaccurate self-perceptions, we grieve the heart of God who loves us and delights in us. We limit ourselves in innumerable ways and when we believe inappropriate things about ourselves, we end up fostering dysfunctional relationship and leadership paradigms. The following are some examples of this phenomenon.

Shrinking to fit!

When we underestimate ourselves and downplay our own significance in our own minds and in the minds of others, we embrace invisibility and fail to do justice to our many gifts and abilities. In other words, we 'shrink to fit' an extremely limited view of ourselves. Although this 'playing small' may appeal to our low self-esteem, it can have dire consequences for our leadership.

Shrinking to fit can prevent us from taking a lead in a project or putting ourselves forward for exciting new opportunities. It can inhibit us from taking the initiative, or leave us paralysed by a 'fear of failure'. Shrinking to fit causes us to doubt our experience and our skills, so that we believe our progress is the result of 'fluke' theory[7], rather than sheer hard work! Research shows that most women attribute their failure to lack of ability and credit their successes to good luck, while men do the exact opposite and tend to ascribe their failures to bad luck and their successes to their abilities.[8] While men tend to overestimate their abilities, many women underestimate their abilities. Nancy Badore observes, 'I find it often takes a woman ten years longer than men to realize how good they really are. I don't think you can make a contribution until you've moved *beyond* wondering if you're good enough.'[9]

Many women worry that despite their role and title, they don't really belong in the ranks of the successful. They deflect the confidence that others have in their abilities and perceive their successes to be accidental, incidental and probably not repeatable! The list is endless. Anne Dickson adds, 'We also shrink ourselves in our manner of speech: we hesitate, we over-apologize, we put ourselves down, we understate the importance of matters. We keep silent instead of raising points we want to raise; we don't challenge pretence; we don't challenge criticism. We hesitate to be clever, to be brilliant, to be outspoken; we don't dare.'[10] Yet the willingness to take risks and to 'dare' is a leadership skill that requires our utmost commitment if we are to improve as leaders.

Confidence deficit

Limiting self-perceptions rob us of the related leadership virtue of confidence, particularly the kind that enables us to launch out beyond our comfort zones. This explains why women who have done well in one sphere may be unwilling to take even calculated risks in unknown territory. Rosie Ward reflects on how this affects women's willingness to explore new job opportunities, 'Men tend to look at a job advertisement or job description, see that some of it is outside their current experience and think, "Oh, I'm sure I could do that". Women are more likely to look at the same information, realise that there are a few things beyond their experience and think, "I couldn't possibly do that".'[11]

Growth in confidence is vital to leadership, without it we become prone to procrastination and avoid, rather than engage with, situations that make us feel anxious and uncomfortable. There is a perception, often backed by available evidence, that in certain contexts men are more likely than women to confront difficulties and embrace challenges.

> Growth in confidence is vital to leadership

Early in my experience of leadership, my supervising pastors came to visit my church on a day I happened to be leading a meeting. After the congregation had left, they gave me advice I found difficult to hear at the time but fully appreciate now. They pointed out that when I prayed, I did so with great authority, passion *and* volume but when I spoke in a meeting, my voice was so soft I could barely be heard. They advised me that if I was going to be a leader I must learn to speak with the same confidence and certainty with which I prayed! To be fair to me I'd just been through a particularly difficult time with my church and I still felt raw and vulnerable. I was very aware that a number of people vigorously opposed my leadership, on the grounds of my gender (although they were quite happy for me to exercise my gifts while no title was attached!). Many of these individuals had been personal friends, who subsequently distanced themselves from me and I was still mourning the loss of these relationships. Overall, I still felt hugely unqualified for the task of leadership. However, the level of frankness and honesty offered by my supervising pastors, enabled me to make valuable progress in my growth as a leader. I quickly realised that my lack of confidence did not only affect me, it also affected those who depended upon me for clear leadership in the midst of difficult circumstances.

I now understand that my sense of confidence has less to do with me and more to do with what I believe God is capable of doing with what He has given me.

Striving for perfection

Having been led to believe that we are totally flawed, imperfect beings, women often overcompensate by striving for perfection. Intellectually we know it's impossible, but emotionally we go there every time we feel insecure or less than competent. In leadership terms, this behaviour is often a huge waste of time and energy. Women trapped in paralysing levels of perfectionism continue to seek the unachievable 110% on every detail and drain physical and emotional reserves that would be better spent elsewhere.

False humility

There is also considerable temptation for women to indulge in a false humility that expresses itself through self-deprecating talk, 'I'm *just* a teacher, I'm *only* a housewife, I *kind* of run a business. It *really wasn't* anything!' This may develop further into a tendency to denigrate ourselves and our abilities.

Rather than emphasise our many accomplishments or recognise the significant roles we have played, women often minimise their successes focusing on what they perceive to be their negative attributes. Rather than promoting a sense of 'sober judgement' concerning ourselves, this disposition fuels self-defeat at best and self-negation at worst. Women regularly underestimate their potential and their abilities and proactively minimise their capabilities, for fear of being accused of 'behaving like a man' or in an 'unfeminine' way.

Women who struggle with limiting self-perceptions are often in danger of giving up their personhood. They fail to value themselves, thereby failing to honour one of the many gifts God entrusts to us unreservedly, the gift of 'self'. The deadly sin of limiting self-perceptions daily erodes our identity and sense of purpose. Women consequently become a fertile breeding ground for 'approval addiction'. In other words, we abdicate our responsibility to seek affirmation in God-honouring ways and place unreasonable demands for validation and definition on others that they can never deliver. Such patterns of behaviour sabotage our attempts at leadership.

Since both women and men are capable of oppressive and controlling behaviour in leadership, both should seek to address unhealthy mental and emotional beliefs and habits that may affect each in destructive ways. Leadership consultant Jeanne Porter writes:

> **'We bring all of ourselves – spirit, soul and body – into our leadership role. And if our spirit, our emotions, our minds, and our bodies are hurting, we will hurt those who follow us… Becoming the leader you were meant to be starts with your innermost self.'**[12] She adds, **'Defensive, over-controlling and insecure people make defensive, over-controlling and insecure leaders – who in turn, create rigid, overly structured, and competitive organizations, businesses, ministries, or agencies. The leader who has not sufficiently worked through her own issues will bring those issues with her into her leadership role.'**[13]

What we lead may be 'out there' but *where* we lead from is largely an internal matter. Therefore, our spiritual, mental, emotional and physical health affects our leadership, for better or worse. If we choose to ignore these aspects of ourselves, the integrity of our leadership suffers as a result.

We cannot do a great deal to change other people's opinions of us, although women, in particular, often waste a great deal of time trying! However, we can work and pray towards transforming our own skewed self-perceptions. Until we do so, we will never truly be free to exercise our God-given leadership, in God-honouring ways.

Defining Women Who Lead

Joyce was visibly struggling with what she had heard, so Sophie said it again, 'You are a leader and you have already been influencing others around you albeit unintentionally. You need to make a decision to become the leader you were intended to be and to impact the lives of others in a way that truly honours God.' Joyce had experienced some profound disappointments with leaders in the past and had determined never to become like them. However, she had spent so many years fearing what she might become that it never occurred to her that she may already have 'chosen' mediocrity for herself. She nodded and smiled as realisation dawned on her…

In spite of a subconscious paralysis, many women exercise clear and decisive leadership and are more than capable of calling forth action from others (the essence of leadership). They regularly exercise leadership gifts in a variety of ways and effectively influence others around them in order to meet specific pre-set goals. Women achieve this by engaging in problem solving and articulating strategic thinking from platforms, as part of committees or simply via the telephone. They manage other people's expectations, ideas, budgets and/or time! Women who lead are highly capable and tend to develop goals, drive a vision, work out a plan, deliver a product or work at creating solutions in their ministry or work life. Some operate with or without a title. Many never think of their activities as the manifestation of a leadership capability but they are leaders nonetheless. Know it or not, wrestle with it or not, even like it or not, as women we cannot escape the indisputable fact or even impact of our leadership!

Female ways?

In my introduction I referred to the unique strengths that women bring to leadership. For example, we are more likely to consult with others, to multitask comfortably and to be collaborative. We are far more focused on empowering others than we are on competing with them in order to get a job done. We even tend to redefine the use of power. Lois Frankel explains, 'Whereas men often define being powerful as getting *someone else* to do what they want or having control over others, women tend to define it as getting to do what *they* want or having control over themselves.'[14] As women we are more likely to judge ourselves against our personal best, rather than wanting to simply be the overall best. We tend toward long range thinking, paying more attention to the big picture than to a need for immediate results. We gravitate toward relationship building and the inclusion of the opinions of others in our final decision-making process.

These strengths are not exhaustive, yet in these and so many other ways, women typify the 'new' leader outlined in my introduction. In this regard, we are remarkably well shaped for the needs of emerging 21st century leadership cultures.

Business consultants Liz Cook and Brian Rothwell emphasise the significance of distinct masculine and feminine leadership traits. However, they are emphatic, 'Difference is not the opposite of equality. Equality means being free to choose the things we want to do and the ways we want to behave as leaders. In contrast, difference means that, as men or as women, we are not naturally inclined to do the same things or behave in the same way when leading others.'[15] However, the unique gifts that women bring are often absent, even when we are seated at the leadership table.

What we have subconsciously come to believe as both men and women is that male ways are superior to female ways, in more than just the realm of leadership. In an interview for *Newsweek* in 2008, Adrian Furnham, professor of psychology at University College London reported, 'Most experts agree there is no real, important overall difference when it comes to gender and intelligence… What I study is *"perceived* intelligence", essentially how smart people *think* they are. I analysed 30 international studies, and found that women, across the world, tend to underplay their intelligence, while men overstate it.'[16] What we believe about ourselves as human beings influences what we do *in* leadership and our approach *to* leadership. Therefore, when we refuse to recognise who and what we are, we tend to lead out of self-imposed limitations that continually sabotage both our purpose and destiny. Until we recognise the validity of the gifts and perspectives that we bring to the practice of leadership we limit our opportunities and possibilities. Therefore, limiting self-perceptions are largely responsible for our narrow, monochrome and one-dimensional views of leadership.

As women and men learn to validate and appreciate both male and female ways of leading, we are then capable of expanding the horizon of leadership and the possibilities of what a leader 'looks' like. This enables us to liberate ourselves and to explore leadership paradigms from diverse cultures and subcultures as well as from different generations! This approach enables women to embrace the idea of leadership because 'leadership' is no longer confined to male categories but is also available in female, cultural and generationally diverse categories. In short, we free ourselves to make our own unique contribution to the ongoing process of leadership. This enables us to recognise that, 'Each sex starts the leadership journey from different places. Neither place is right or wrong. They are just different, and we need to recognise and value this difference.'[17]

Practitioners agree that good leaders learn to appreciate, and recognise, why people are the way they are, they are 'incarnational'; in other words, they learn to walk in the shoes of others and see through their eyes. However, the first step every leader must be prepared to take is toward an understanding of 'self'. Women often fail to see what we could become because we are constantly faced with 'selves' that we struggle to accept.

Women, God's Gift? A Biblical and Church Perspective

The interview had been going quite well until Ann started to explain why she might not be suitable for the job. The irony was that she desperately wanted the post but instead of, how did her husband Roger describe it?... 'selling herself', she found herself apologising for deficiencies that hadn't even been raised by the interviewing panel! Now sitting in her own car preparing to drive home, she felt so frustrated she wanted to cry...

For Christian women, our failure to see ourselves 'correctly' is rooted in an inability to see ourselves from God's perspective. Our beliefs regarding God's intentions for our lives, influence our internal scripts. Many women persist in replaying negative internal records, 'you should have been a boy, you're silly, you're frail, you're stupid, you caused the 'Fall', you should be ashamed'. Subsequently, by adulthood, women have had their inferiority reinforced in countless ways. This pattern makes it nearly impossible for us to experience the freedom 'to be' that scripture promises. Instead, we find ourselves bound by a pattern that we struggle to break free from.

The Christian poet Gordon Bailey wrote a short poem that wonderfully sums up our stubbornly held beliefs regarding men and women. It is entitled, *Chauvinist Creation, 'Dear Earth, here is man, Love God p.s. Here is woman!'.*[18]

The failure to value women

In every culture and people group,[19] women continue to be regarded as inferior. They are frequently dehumanised, marginalised, glamorised, patronised, unrecognised and ostracised! In almost every society a higher value is placed upon having boys than girls. In well over 95% of domestic violence cases the victims are women. Domestic violence is also a leading cause of death among girls and women between the ages of 14 to 44. Human trafficking, a modern form of slavery, affects largely women and girls. Therefore, it is hardly surprising that women still struggle to see themselves correctly, when the general messages from society are still so overwhelmingly negative.[20]

Even the church couches questions regarding the validity of women in a debate focused on their *roles* (the same debate does not exist for men). Although there are relatively fewer men than women who attend UK churches, 43% men to 57% women, women leave UK churches at twice the rate of men.

Interestingly, the level of concern raised over the potential loss of men is regularly expressed through the deployment of 'special measures', notably such measures are seldom, if ever, deployed for women. Perhaps unsurprisingly, there is little or no exploration of the root causes of the exodus of women, which, alarmingly, is on the increase (this is in contrast to resources allocated to addressing the loss of men). In the 1990s, 57% of losses to UK churches were women and this number rose to 65% between 1998 and 2005.[21] Historically, the church has also focused primarily on 'male' questions, issues and models.[22] The underlying assumption, at least, from the church's perspective is that women are far from equal to men. The resulting psychological message is imbibed and embraced by both men and women and further impacts our interactions and self-beliefs.

Are women really an afterthought, a spare rib produced after God had completed the 'real' work of creating Adam? What we believe about ourselves is of fundamental importance, yet it is often far removed from God's declarative statements concerning us. If we're serious about knowing God's intentions for women, it would be utter foolishness to base our conclusions on the sin-filled pattern of the 'Fall', or its effects on the world we live in. However, this is precisely what many men and women who attend churches all over the world continue to do.

Outdated thinking

Much of our thinking regarding male and female is often outdated, culturally bound and unsupported by current research. Yet the Bible encourages us to question our cultural norms, 'Do not conform any longer to the pattern of this world, but be transformed by the renewing of your mind. Then you will be able to test and approve what God's will is – his good, pleasing and perfect will.' (Romans 12:2).

A few years ago, I had a conversation with a young black woman regarding the status of black people in the world. She noted that apart from a few prominent exceptions (e.g. President Obama, Oprah Winfrey), blacks were viewed as relatively powerless and lacking global leverage. Black and African peoples tend to be viewed as debtors, rather than lenders and such nations are subsequently portrayed as needy, with little to contribute to the table of international politics. She further commented that black people are often viewed as second rate and second class wherever they reside in the world. Having reached this conclusion, she disarmed me with the question, 'Does God hate black people?'. It took me a moment or two to realise that she was being completely serious. In fact she was fully convinced that the available data, as she saw it, led to this shattering yet 'inevitable' conclusion. After some discussion, she came to realise that such 'evidence' changes from era to era and is therefore inconclusive. For example, at one time the 'developed world' and all advanced technology existed in the global south, in empires such as Egypt, Nubia and Ashanti (sometimes centuries before Europeans had developed structured and complex societies).

Many people reach the same conclusions regarding women and worse still, women themselves often behave as if God really does hate them. Against all reason (not to mention data), many people still believe there is 'common sense' logic in the idea that women are the 'second sex' in more ways than one. Assumptions regarding the supposed inferiority and unsuitability of women for certain tasks are continually being challenged and revised. This change is occurring as new evidence emerges and as historical records are revisited from the perspective of marginalised groups. 'Common sense', it seems, has a way of adapting! As Rosie Ward notes, '…Women have moved into leadership in many areas of life and are now accepted as competent and capable leaders.'[23]

In the Beginning

Alison, a senior manager in the NHS, was struggling with what she was hearing from the pulpit. Once again, jokes were being made about the general incompetence of women, how they were always in need of the 'guiding hand' of a man (any male was deemed acceptable, related or not!). Everyone seemed to find this amusing but for Alison this was no laughing matter. She wondered if she should raise the subject with the leaders again. However, it seemed pointless and she sensed they were merely humouring her. Initially, she'd wholeheartedly thrown herself into church life but had become increasingly disillusioned by the unhealthy attitude towards women. She chewed her bottom lip. She felt caught between a rock and a hard place…

The fact that women make skilled and gifted leaders should hardly surprise us, as the Biblical record of our beginnings prepares us for such a conclusion. In Genesis 1:26–28 we read, 'Then God said, "Let us make man in our image, in our likeness, and let them rule over the fish of the sea and the birds of the air, over the livestock, over all the earth, and over all the creatures that move along the ground." *So God created man in his own image, in the image of God he created him; male and female he created them.* God blessed them and said to *them*, "Be fruitful and increase in number; fill the earth and subdue it. Rule over the fish of the sea and the birds of the air and over every living creature that moves on the ground."'

In verse 26 God determines to make 'man' (singular) but refers to 'man' as 'them' (plural). The same language is repeated in verse 27, except here the term 'man' refers to *both* male and female, in other words it is a generic term and not specific to any one gender. Indeed, at this stage the *human* (ha'adam quite literally 'earthling') is neither a characteristic male nor a typical human being.

Having resolved to create a 'man', God recognises that his first attempt is unfinished. Until a distinctive expression of both male and female is created, humanity is alive but incomplete. The events of Genesis 2 shed further light and seem to represent a more detailed action replay of the 6th day of creation. As such, it completes what has been left unsaid in Genesis 1 regarding the nature of the human race. God moulds Adam (the human) from the dust of the earth and breathes life into the human form. He then pauses, as he has done after every earlier act of creation, as if to declare once more, 'and it was very good'. However, on this occasion having noted Adam's isolation and incompleteness, God declares for the first time in the whole creation story, 'It is NOT good,' (Genesis 2:16). Subsequently, God identifies the reason for this astonishing announcement and simultaneously devises a solution for it, 'It is NOT good, for the man to be alone. I will make a helper suitable for him.' (My emphasis.)

This does not denote a helper who would become a subordinate, or a servant, or a junior partner or someone in a secondary position. Adam was not in need of a PA! The Hebrew word for helper (ezer) is used overwhelmingly in the Bible to describe the person of God himself in his role as chief helper and deliverer (Deuteronomy 33:7, 29; Exodus 18:24; Psalm 33:20; Psalm 115:9–11). Therefore, what Adam needed is better translated as a *rescuer for this state of affairs!* He needed a true counterpart whose contribution would complete God's image in humanity. This person would be an equal to him in every way, similar and yet unlike any other creature. Rosie Ward elucidates, 'In Genesis 1, the emphasis is on equality: God created human beings in his image, male and female (v 27). In Genesis 2, Adam's response to Eve is that she is like him (v 23). It is commonality rather than complementarity. The creation of Eve was not intended to show a creation order of power, but to reveal unity of flesh and purpose.'[24]

It was not good for the 'man' to be alone, because alone Adam was only half the story and alone, Adam did not conform to the image of God. It transpires that God needed not one but two persons to fully represent his divine image. The text leaves us in no doubt regarding God's intentions for the stewardship of his creation. The 'right' to 'rule' is not determined through the order of creation but by explicit mandate to both parties. The male is given no mandate on the basis of his being created first (neither are the plants or animals!). Likewise, the female is given no mandate on the basis of being the 'grand finale' or pinnacle of God's creative activity! The mandate to steward ('rule') the earth's resources is not announced until both male and female coexist

> Alone Adam was only half the story and alone, Adam did not conform to the image of God

together, 'God blessed *them* and said to *them,* "Be fruitful and increase in number; fill the earth and subdue it. Rule over the fish of the sea and the birds of the air and over every living creature that moves on the ground." (Genesis 1:28).

There is no dispute over the question of whether differences exist between male and female, 'Human beings from all cultures have recognised that there are general differences between men and women, although every culture would not agree on what these differences are.'[25] However, questions need to be raised regarding the significance of such differences, while bearing in mind that social expectations placed upon each sex, in any society, are often far removed and in direct conflict with the Biblical view.

The ancient civilisations for whom the creation stories were initially recorded, generally regarded women as property and of little significance. Women were essentially 'owned' by a father or husband. The inevitable development of this distorted ideology was that men literally 'had' multiple wives who were expected to contribute, preferably, male heirs and very little, if anything else, to the general social order. The emphasis in such societies was upon being male, the son of a son and upon imposing uniformity and conformity on surrounding nations through conquest. Genesis 1 *and* 2 appear to act as reminders, that neither state of affairs was part of God's original design. As we consider the society for whom this Biblical material was initially produced, we begin to understand the importance of the inclusion of the more detailed, expanded creation narrative of Genesis 2 alongside Genesis 1.

For example, a man is commanded to 'leave his father and mother and be united to his wife, and they will become one flesh', (Genesis 2:24). This is almost an exact reversal of the prevailing social order (even today) in which the woman would marry *into* her husband's family and become subject to their demands.

Both texts represent a stark contrast to the widespread order of patriarchy prevalent after the 'Fall'. The fact that such a record survived under such belief systems is a testimony to the trustworthiness of the ancient document and its affirmation of equality, sameness and difference between human beings!

Original thinking

The pattern of the 'Fall' is never presented in the text as God's original plan for humanity, yet it is often the pattern we choose to embrace and articulate. Whatever our perspective on what counts as legitimate masculine and feminine behaviour, our failure to view ourselves in the light of the creation paradigm, lies at the root of much of our leadership malaise.

Describing the impending cataclysmic state of affairs to follow the events of the 'Fall', God pronounces to the female, 'Your desire will be for your husband, and he will rule over you.' Genesis 3:16. In other words, post 'Fall', gender difference will be exploited as a source of inequality.

Consequently, limiting self-perceptions in men may result in a need for significance through status, domination and even independence (in comparison to women). However, in women, limiting self-perceptions may lead to a misplaced quest for significance through intimacy and/or the approval of others. In its extreme form, the latter can be recognised in women's predilection to endure unhealthy co-dependent relationships more willingly than men.

The idea of sin has long been equated with selfishness or self-centredness. Subsequently, many (male!) scholars define sin as the unjustified concern for power and prestige. However, these are traditionally male obsessions. Self-interest can also be expressed through preoccupations that have little to do with either status or supremacy.

Theologian, Jurgen Moltmann, helpfully identifies this distinction, 'To be sure, it is usually said that sin in its original form is man's wanting to be God. But that is only the one side of sin. The other side of such pride is hopelessness, resignation, inertia and melancholy… Temptation then consists not so much in the titanic desire to be as God, but in weakness, timidity, weariness, not wanting to be what God requires of us.'[26]

Although men and women commonly make similar mistakes, they often make them for very different reasons. In other words, while the source of sin may be identical for both, its trajectory may differ.

The great temptation that women often face is to become 'less than' what God intends us to be. Rosie Ward acknowledges the compelling strands of truth evident in the argument of 1960s feminist theologian Valerie Saiving. She suggests that, '…such things as triviality, lack of an organising centre, dependence on others, inability to make decisions for oneself – any negation or underdevelopment of self – may be viewed as sin. In the "sin of hiding", women run from freedom and pour their energy into the lives of others, failing to live as their own person under God.'[27]

> Ultimately, only redemption can free women and men from the expectations imposed by sinful role play

Ultimately, only redemption can free women *and* men from the expectations imposed by sinful role play. In this way both can be empowered to exercise their leadership while simultaneously affirming their unique approaches, thought patterns, attributes and behaviours.

Different and *equal*…

In Genesis 1 and 2, male and female are created different *and* equal by design and each is fashioned in order to bring different strengths to the mandated task of 'ruling' all creation. Unfortunately, in many churches today, people are taught that men alone should rule. In doing so, men and women effectively default to the pattern of the 'Fall' rather than embracing the pattern of Creation. Consequently, the destiny of both male and female is frustrated and the purposes of God remain unfulfilled. Given the clear benefits of male and female partnership in leadership (outlined in my introduction), the absence of women in leadership could prove disastrous in the long term; perhaps it already has...[28]

In Genesis 1:26, we are reminded that God created male and female in his image, with the express intention of co-stewarding his resources. In Genesis 2, it is only *after* the creation of woman that God's image in 'man' is said to be complete. In other words, it is the co-stewardship of male and female that is needed to reflect God's image, understand God's nature and establish God's purposes in his world. The female was therefore created in God's image, equal in every respect to the male, and without woman, God's image in Creation is declared incomplete, 'not good'.

I wish to take this argument still further and suggest that without women leaders, God's image in business, public, charitable and voluntary sectors, yes, even the church, is also incomplete! Therefore, God does not call women because he has no men left to choose from! We are not chosen *in spite* of being women. God calls us *because* we are women and because we have something distinctive and valuable to contribute!

The Creation narrative affirms that difference *and* equality coexist in humanity, a fact that many in church circles failed to grasp throughout the Transatlantic Slave Trade. In addition, the pattern of Creation should be considered superior to all patriarchal paradigms, no matter how benevolent, that emerged as a result of the 'Fall'. The pattern of Creation (and Redemption) alone is worthy of being emulated and modelled.

Perhaps post 'Fall', now more than ever, we need the leadership strengths of both sexes to counteract the weaknesses of both.

The challenge faced by women is to see ourselves as God sees us, to live out of the reality of God's creation mandate and to take our place as co-rulers within God's purposes. As such, women are invited to discover God's intentions for our lives. As we allow him to shape the way we perceive ourselves, and to then live and work from that place of conviction, the quality of our leadership will certainly be transformed.

Breaking the Remould

The deadline for the presentation was 9am the following morning and Suzy had already worked and reworked her material. As usual, she still felt that it wasn't quite up to scratch. She performed another sweep of the internet and glanced through her papers, 'just in case' there was something she might have missed. That's when she found it, a new document dealing with a subject similar to the one she was working on. Her heart sank, the little confidence she'd mustered was rapidly dissolving. Maybe she should ask for the meeting to be postponed? She paused briefly, prayed and reminded herself of all that she'd already accomplished. Suzy then looked up at the note on her wall, it read, 'remember you are good at this, you actually enjoy the challenge and whatever you need to know is already in you, you're not doing this alone, God is with you. Go to bed and get some rest!' Suzy rearranged her papers, put them into her briefcase and moved away from her desk...

Someone who believes in their self-worth will be able to recognise their own expertise and deliver their chosen subject with confidence. Similarly, they are able to walk into a room confident that people want to engage with them. By contrast, someone with low self-worth will feel insecure, imagine the worst and try to avoid the situation all together. A quiet confidence and assured demeanour is vital for a leader who is responsible for inspiring confidence in others.

Originally, human beings were created by God under ideal conditions in a state of 'perfection'. However, the 'Fall' has led to conditions that are far from ideal and to men and women characterised by chronic imperfection. Like a flawed lump of clay on a potter's wheel, we have become profoundly disfigured. As a consequence of our own wrong-doing, we have broken the original mould created by God, and our human attempts at remoulding are far from ideal or easy because the clay in question (i.e. us) literally has a life of its own!

A re-envisioning of God's perception of us is only part of the challenge we face as women in leadership. Any attempt to break away from limiting self-perceptions must also include a radical commitment to honest prayer and a rethink of our significance as women within God's purposes. The following approach enables us to realign our distorted thought processes with God's original intentions.

Inspire yourself

Begin by investigating the lives of women from both *Biblical* and *Church* history. Don't be discouraged by the fact that they are few in number, instead, celebrate the fact that such stories have survived fiercely patriarchal cultures. This is perhaps the greatest miracle of all!

We often forget just how overwhelmingly negative the culture during Jesus' time was toward women and just how radical Jesus' words and actions must have seemed to those who witnessed and experienced them. In a culture that refused to recognise women as teachers or witnesses in court, or as significant contributors, we find four women (apart from Jesus' mother Mary) mentioned within the genealogy of Jesus (Matthew 1:1–16). The first news of the incarnation is given to a woman, Mary. It is not communicated via her father, brother, high priest, male prophet or husband-to-be! (Luke 1:32–35). The first

Samaritan convert was a woman! She also became the first Samaritan evangelist and was ultimately responsible for the conversion of her entire town (John 4:7–42). The first resurrection teaching was given to another woman, Martha, sister of Mary, who like the Apostle Peter, also received a revelation, that Jesus was indeed the Christ. Women were also amongst the first to witness the resurrection and to be commissioned to preach the good news (Matthew 28:9; John 20:16; John 20:18).

In a society that excluded women from the vast majority of public roles, Christianity stood out as being significantly different. Theologian, Walter Wink, observes, 'women received the Holy Spirit at the founding event of the church (Acts 1:14; 2:1) and were coequal with men in receiving prophetic gifts. They headed house churches, opened new fields for evangelism (Philippians 4:2–3), and were Paul's co-workers. They were persecuted and jailed just like the men, were named apostles, disciples, deacons, led churches (Philemon 1–2), and even, in one case, had authority over Paul himself (Romans 16:1–2 "for she [Phoebe] has been a ruler over many, indeed over me")'.[29]

We may not be a Phoebe, Mary, Martha, Woman at the Well or an apostle like Junia but we all have value as women chosen by God. We may not be perfect or faultless, nevertheless, we each have a divine mandate to rule and a responsibility to lay hold of that mandate.

Global history is also replete with influential women ranging from great inventors to gifted writers and passionate activists. There are sufficient women who have made a continuous and powerful contribution to society to inspire us, all we have to do is discover them!

If we wish to develop greater confidence in leadership, we should not only uncover our sources of inspiration, we must also exercise greater vigilance over the beliefs we hold regarding ourselves. Limiting self-perceptions are particularly fuelled by unhealthy patterns of self-talk. In other words, what we say about ourselves remains our greatest challenge. In this area, we very rarely agree with God's assessment of who we are. Yet breaking the remould requires us to re-evaluate what we believe and therefore what we have to say about ourselves.

Adjust your self-talk

Women have a remarkable ability to recognise the potential they perceive in others around them and to offer encouragement. However, when it comes to self-affirmation, the script is often very different.

In order to adjust our self-talk, we first need to become sufficiently aware of its existence. Efforts to identify our self-talk will require us to observe our emotional responses and to ask uncomfortable questions about our reactions. This approach enables us to explore the roots of our self-beliefs and to further question the validity of our convictions. Much of our self-talk is imbided at a young age, this then develops into a standard script that remains relatively unaffected despite our advancing years. Adjusting our self-talk requires us to assess what we *really* know about ourselves.

- **Weigh all the critical 'evidence'**

    Interestingly, self-beliefs and self-talk are very often completely unrelated to reality. We are seldom as 'terrible' or 'useless' as we believe ourselves to be.

    However, when we believe something, we tend to look for supporting evidence, regardless of how tenuous the 'facts' may be. For example, when we hold a low view of ourselves, we become particularly susceptible to what we consider to be the 'negative vibes' others have toward us. Someone's uncharacteristic failure to consult with or inform us prior to a significant decision can serve to reinforce our sense of insignificance. Rather than explore the cause of the oversight with the individual involved, we prefer to entertain falsehoods that are sometimes far from the truth. Only as we pause to ask critical questions of ourselves and others around us do we begin to understand just how absurd much of our 'proof' really is.

Since our beliefs are the most important determinant of our confidence, we need to pay very close attention to them. The following questions may help us to accomplish this:

- **How does what you believe and say help or hinder you?**
- **Is it a limiting belief?**
- **Do you have any evidence that supports the validity of this belief?**
- **Is this belief absurd?**
- **In what way is it absurd?**
- **Why do you believe this?**
- **How are you being helped by holding onto this belief?**
- **What is stopping you relinquishing it?**
- **Does this belief support your self-development and your faithfulness to God?**

- **Speak the truth about yourself, to yourself**
  Much of what we have to say about ourselves is based on faulty beliefs and is actually, usually untrue, especially when we engage in the language of absolutes, e.g. 'I never…, I always…, I'm completely…, I'm definitely not…'

  I noted that the language of one of the leaders we met earlier, Kemi, was frequently characterised by the phrases, 'I can't do… I can't think… I don't know…'. In spite of this, she had experienced a degree of success for many years that frankly belied her own self assessment. However, her self-talk had clearly become a block to further progress. It was only as she revised her language and simultaneously stepped out of her comfort zone that she began to recognise the falsehood of what she had imbibed. She eventually experienced greater success, confidence and more importantly, genuine joy in her work.

The road to recovery begins when we question our self-talk. Proverbs 18:21 is a reminder of how powerfully life-giving or destructive our words can be, 'The tongue has the power of life and death, and those who love it will eat its fruit.' An honest assessment frequently enables us to transform our negative language into the language of affirmation.

Truth is the most powerful antidote that God offers us when we are renewing our minds. The Bible reminds us that only the truth sets us free (John 8:32). However, we must be willing to engage with the truth. Speaking the truth requires us to 'tell it like it *really* is'. For example, it was clear that Kemi was already an accomplished and gifted leader. She had attained and sustained her leadership under relatively unfavourable personal and social conditions. She simply needed to grasp what was immediately obvious to others. Booker T Washington comments: 'Success isn't measured by the position you reach in life, it's measured by the obstacles you overcome.'[30]

> Truth is the most powerful antidote that God offers us when we are renewing our minds

- ## Practice 'I am's'

Beliefs that have been rehearsed over a lifetime, seldom disappear overnight. Our minds seem unable to deal with the absence of a belief, so any disempowering belief we erase must be replaced with an empowering one. This activity serves to re-programme our self-limiting beliefs into transformative beliefs, allowing us to pursue God's intentions for our lives. Suzy, who we met earlier, had already engaged in a process involving re-programming and renewing her mind. She was gradually accepting that perfection (110%) was both unattainable and undesirable, while excellence (80%) was often possible.

We constantly rehearse a whole spectrum of negative 'I am's' that effectively undermine God's truths about us. In an effort to counteract these negative statements we must, firstly, identify which self-perceptions are limiting and in need of revision. For Suzy these included the following conviction 'whatever I produce is never good enough'.

Secondly, we must identify which affirmative beliefs and God-given truths will assist us in moving forward. Some examples might include:

- I am loved
- I am valued by God
- I am entitled to exist
- It is good that I exist
- I am worthy of being valued and taken seriously
- I am entitled to make mistakes
- I'm not perfect but I am blessed
- I am above average (intelligence/hard-working)
- I am unique because… (complete the sentence e.g. no one else has my unique combination of life experiences and knowledge)
- I have done things people in my field haven't done, like… (complete the sentence e.g. I volunteer for animal rights in my spare time)
- I have multiple achievements, such as… (complete the sentence e.g. the certificate I was awarded, the committee I was invited to join)
- I have above-average, hard-to-find skills
- I am significant in God's purposes

Thirdly, make a list of your self-limiting 'I am's' from step one, alongside your new empowering 'I am's' from step two. Having identified the falsehood of your disempowering 'I am's', add at least one reason for your newfound conviction. Suzy had to repeat her new truth,

'I am very good at what I do' alongside the critical evidence as a means of resisting her own temptation to disbelieve all over again, 'I am regularly commended for the quality and value of my work'. In addition, she had to repeat her new truth long before it became a real feeling.

Fourthly, repeat your new script aloud, with passion and conviction and ask yourself if you are ready to leave your limiting self-perceptions behind (don't be afraid to answer back!).

Integrating this new perception into your personality is the final challenge. This can be accomplished by simply imagining the difference the new belief will make. For example, revisit an old disempowering scenario (as we sometimes do) but this time replay it with your renewed mind, allowing the new empowered you to emerge. Meanwhile, note the changes in your imagined outcomes, including the way you have effectively reinforced the new belief. Begin to hold conversations, fully conscious of this new conviction. In addition, ask yourself how this new belief will affect your relationship with your family, friends and colleagues. Over time, this new way of thinking will become habitual until eventually, you will automatically generate empowering and God-honouring beliefs about yourself.

Just do it!

The reality is, we may never 'feel' as confident as we may wish to be, however, we need to step back and imagine ourselves as God sees us. Once we have done this, our greatest challenge is to live in the light of God's creation mandate, as co-rulers within God's creation purposes. In other words, we should discover what we are created to do and '*just do it!*'.

COACHING TIPS

What has God been speaking to you about regarding your leadership development/growth?

What are you dismissing as unimportant or avoiding because it requires too much effort?

In two months' time what would be different about this area of your life (think, feel, see, speak, describe the change)?
How will you rate it on a scale of 1 to 10 (where 1=not great and 10=excellent)?

What empowering belief, image, phrase, scripture can you start to meditate on from today, in order to motivate you to take positive action in this area?

What support (who, when, where, how) might you need to make this happen?

'Find out who you are and do it on purpose.'
DOLLY PARTON[31]

2ND
DEADLY SIN

FAILURE TO DRAW THE LINE

Establish appropriate boundaries

'When you respect your own "NO!"
then others will, too.'

REBBETZIN CHANA RACHEL SCHUSTERMAN[1]

Recognising our Boundaries

Sarah was still deciding whether to turn off her Blackberry when the phone rang again, this time she was actually in the ladies toilet. She craned her neck to check the screen in order to see who was calling. She knew she should ignore the call and deal with the matter later but perhaps she was needed right away. Anyway, she had informed them that she would be fully available to them...

Many leadership, not to mention relationship, challenges that women face in work and ministry are boundary issues. The dictionary defines a boundary as 'Something that indicates a border or limit'. Women are frequently unwilling to establish boundaries for themselves because of fear or a desire to avoid conflict. Ironically, this longing for peace, freedom and liberty in our relationships with others is seriously hampered by our failure to set and manage appropriate boundaries. Ultimately it has the opposite effect and leads to overwhelming feelings of imprisonment.

Geographic and physical boundaries are visible borders and include features such as skin, gates, fences and signs. These barriers act to define and protect territory. They are much easier to identify and to establish than interpersonal boundaries, which are wholly imperceptible to the

> Boundaries inform us where we end and the rest of the world begins

human eye. The latter operate more like invisible lines that surround each individual. Although we cannot see such boundary lines we intuitively know when someone transgresses our boundaries.

Interpersonal boundaries inform us where we end and the rest of the world begins, in other words they identify 'what is me' and 'what is not me'. They define our emotional, psychological and spiritual territory enabling us to determine what counts as our legitimate responsibility and what does not.

Every individual draws their boundaries in different places depending on age, upbringing, culture, ethnicity, gender, personal preferences and emotional health. Whereas newborn babies are virtually boundary-less, the older an individual becomes, the greater the number of healthy and unhealthy boundaries they are likely to erect. The fact that interpersonal boundaries are simultaneously invisible and diverse, suggests that they must be communicated in order to be understood.

God has Boundaries

There are various proverbial sayings, such as, 'Like a city whose walls are broken down is a man who lacks self-control' (Proverbs 25:28). In addition, other texts, including the Parable of the Talents in Matthew 25:14–30, extol the virtues of acknowledging and taking ownership for what lies within our personal remit or sphere of responsibility. These Biblical precedents emphasise the need for us to be 'careful' and productive with whatever lies within our boundaries, whilst allowing others to do the same with whatever lies within theirs.

Genesis 1–3 outlines the story of Creation and 'Fall' and provides a compelling expression of God's concern for appropriate boundaries.

God's speech separates and divides, establishing boundaries between light and darkness, the different kinds of water and between land and sea. Both plants and animals are empowered to reproduce within certain limits or 'after their kind'. A clear distinction is made between humans and the rest of the world. The unambiguous implication is that boundaries are good (see Psalm 74:14–17, 104:9; Job 26:10, 38:8–11 and Ecclesiastes 3:1–8). Clinical psychologist Henry Cloud and psychologist and leadership coach John Townsend demonstrate how the act of creation provides a reflection of the character of God himself, 'The concept of boundaries comes from the very nature of God. God defines himself as a distinct, separate being, and he is responsible for himself. He defines and takes responsibility for his personality by telling us what he thinks, feels, plans, allows, will not allow, likes and dislikes.'[2]

Perhaps the most obvious evidence of God's concern for boundaries is in his attitude toward sin. In announcing the consequences of sin, God provides us with another challenge regarding boundaries, namely, if we want others to know our limits, we must tell them! Although God sets standards, he never imposes limits on people in order to *make* them behave accordingly. How amazing! The one person who has the right to demand that we eliminate all boundaries, respects our boundaries even when they lead to eternal separation from him! God does not violate our boundaries; however, he refuses to allow us to violate his. From the time of Adam and Eve, God provides both freedom of choice and responsibility for exercising that freedom. In other words, God places a limit on what he permits in his own sphere of activity, 'good' is allowed entry but 'evil' is prohibited (in the case of paradise, an angel, complete with a flaming sword, literally bars Adam and Eve from re-entering Eden! Genesis 3:24).

The realisation that God both implements and endorses boundaries has had a revolutionary effect on my own leadership and ministry. It freed me to set limits on my time and energy without feeling guilty for refusing to allow someone's non-emergency to keep me awake at night. At the time I was working 'all hours' in a very demanding and 'needy' urban context. I had imbibed the idea that being perpetually available was 'the Christian thing to do'. I was fortunate enough to have a more experienced Christian leader disabuse me of this idea. Having noted that I often answered the phone at night (I mean after midnight!) she advised me, 'It can wait until morning'. In fact, her exact words were, 'If someone has lived with the problem for 10 years, they can certainly wait another 24 hours for a solution.' It was a liberating experience, I began to take real holidays, say, 'no' to unreasonable requests and draw the line at inappropriate over-familiarity.

Although human beings are given personal responsibility, God sets limits declaring himself out of bounds to those who 'mis-behave'. Cloud and Townsend explain how this principle is applied to the sphere of physical boundaries all the time, 'Trespassing on other people's property carries consequences. "No trespassing" signs usually carry a threat of prosecution if someone steps over the boundaries. The Bible teaches this principle over and over, saying that if we walk another way something else will happen.'[3] In other words, the breaking of a legitimate (or even illegitimate) boundary has tangible and unpleasant consequences.

Women and Boundary Battles

As Suzy closed the office door behind her she walked away hurriedly afraid that someone would see her. She was totally confused by what had just taken place. She had asked to see John, her vicar, because she was keen to make progress in her 'spiritual walk' and to engage her leadership skills around the church. She had great admiration for him. He was dynamic and passionate in his commitment to God, he took an uncompromising stance whenever it mattered, everyone spoke well of him. Suzy was secretly thrilled that he had made time to see her. She had

hoped for guidance, maybe even some spiritual direction. Instead, he had
'made a pass' at her. She was flattered, horrified and didn't quite know
what to do next…

Healthy boundaries are limits or fences that allow us and others to know, 'This is how far I am willing to go.' 'This is what I will or won't do.' 'This is what I am not prepared to tolerate.' They help us to recognise and respect our differences especially when we are challenged in relationships. You may have already noticed that all the above references are framed as 'I' statements. This is because boundary management is essentially about self-leadership, not in the sense of being self-centred or self-obsessed but in the sense that boundaries are concerned with personal responsibility. By default this implies that others also have legitimate responsibilities for which they must take ownership.

Boundaries enable us to control the impact that we have on others and that others have on us. Once again Henry Cloud and John Townsend provide us with the central purpose of setting limits, 'boundaries do not control other people's behavior; they keep other people's behavior from controlling you.'[4]

> Boundary management is essentially about self-leadership

Unfortunately, when women fail to recognise what or where our boundaries are, we also fail to respect the boundaries of others and, indeed, to properly enforce our own. We frequently operate under the misapprehension that the key to establishing great boundaries lies in setting limits for others. In other words, women often waste valuable energy attempting to convince others that they have limits, when our efforts would be best employed in the task of convincing ourselves! Rather than seeking to control the activity of others, our greatest challenge lies in attempting to control our own actions. Karen

Casey, author of *Codependence and the Power of Detachment: How to Set Boundaries and Make Your Life Your Own* captures this well, 'Coming to understand and eventually celebrate our powerlessness over people, places, and things is the key to our freedom – freedom from enmeshment, freedom from fear of rejection, freedom from the fear of failure, freedom from the fear of success.'[5]

Setting healthy personal boundaries can be particularly difficult for women, and drawing the line is seldom as easy as saying 'yes' or 'no'. Women, it seems, are less likely to inform others where our boundaries begin and end and we are less likely to verbalise our discontent once they are breached. Even when others do not know that they are trespassing, women may quietly blame, resent and get angry for how the infringement of our 'territory' makes us feel.

Women may also draw boundary lines in inappropriate ways. For example, boundaries that are self-protective can be so impermeable that they resemble a brick wall! Such barriers arise when women say 'no' when they could be saying 'yes'. In other words, these boundaries have few entry points that allow helpful things in or unhelpful things out. They prevent even healthy interaction or the acknowledgement of personal need. These boundaries leave women stranded, unapproachable and inaccessible, and result in feelings of isolation, loneliness, abandonment, withdrawal and separation. Conversely, when boundaries are highly porous as a result of women's struggle to say 'no', they may allow harmful influences in; meanwhile beneficial influences inevitably leak out. Such boundaries offer inadequate protection and effectively leave women wide open to abuse and exploitation.

These boundary battles are not coincidental, they are fuelled by factors that combine to create a potent and often lethal disposition within women in general, and women in leadership in particular. In other words, unlike many men, women may be more confused and ambivalent about setting limits because of social pressures. For example, women are taught to feel uncomfortable with standing their ground or being angry, unless it is in the service of others, especially their children. They worry about whether they are 'giving enough' and are fearful of being labelled as selfish. Women also do not like to present the impression that they are inadequate, uncooperative or difficult. We often do everything we can to avoid disapproval and overcompensate when we feel responsible for generating displeasure or disappointment in others.

In addition, in most cultures, women are preoccupied with relationships, either with their husbands, their children, parents, families or friends. If they define themselves on the basis of these relationships, they may feel uncertain about their right to exercise control over their lives or they may give that right away to others. While what is defined as an acceptable boundary for women may vary from place to place, there is a pervasive assumption that 'others', apart from the women themselves, should take responsibility for defining those limits. This approach is consciously and unconsciously reinforced by social mores, media, educational systems and even our own fathers and mothers! Indeed, in some contexts, co-dependency (i.e. the act of being excessively preoccupied with the needs of others at our expense) is considered a perfectly acceptable disposition for women. Is it any wonder that women find it so hard to say 'No'?

Wider social indicators also reveal that women and girls are exposed to significantly more boundary violations than men, especially if they are poor. Infringements range from having others touch or stand too close without permission, inappropriate intrusions into a woman's time or space, sex-selective infanticide or neglect, domestic violence, rape, other sexual violence, trafficking, slavery, prostitution and 'honour' killings. All of these offences affect women in far greater numbers than men, some could even be properly referred to as 'women's problems'.[6] There is a certain degree of irony in the fact that girls are expected to actively defend themselves against the abusive advances of others, while they are comprehensively and at times, indiscriminately socialised to be wholly available to meet the emotional and physical needs of others.

Boundaries at Work

Mary was still sitting in front of the screen, it was nearly 2pm. Richard had assured her that he'd send the report through before midday, it was now well into the afternoon and she was still waiting! Mary was seething, she had been kept waiting on almost every occasion only to discover that Richard, her assistant, had completely forgotten or gone out for lunch with colleagues. As usual he'd left it to the very last minute before completing and sending his part of the report. When she'd gently raised the issue with him, he'd laughed, 'I work well under pressure, hope you don't mind?' Well she did but she'd simply smiled back at him…

Although much more could be said regarding the issues of women and boundary management, I want to concentrate on the impact that the failure to set appropriate boundaries may have on our effectiveness as leaders in our work and ministry environments. Leadership experts Claire Shipman and Katty Kay recognise that although wives and mothers, in particular, may be relatively quick to set limits in order to maintain family life, they frequently avoid doing so elsewhere. 'While many of us have done a great job of setting boundaries at home – and especially if there are kids in the house who depend on having boundaries set for them – we've often neglected to transfer the same ability to the workplace.'[7]

Yet boundary problems are at the root of many of the major failings of leadership. They may be responsible for poor time management, work overload, inefficiency and lack of impact, bad communication, low performance, confusion, poor delivery and accountability. If we wish to develop into highly competent leaders we must not only recognise the power of the boundary, we must also learn how and where to draw lines that present us with healthy, effective and God-honouring limits. For those who long to improve the quality of their own leadership and overcome many of their own boundary battles, the following strategies offer critical keys for reflection and action.

Self-identity: where does my responsibility stop and others' start?

The key question that must be posed when faced with a boundary challenge is, *'What is my remit?'* In other words, 'What am I being paid to do?' 'What is expected of me?' 'What is my specific role?' In essence, where does my responsibility stop and the responsibility of others start?

Mary has porous boundaries. Her limits are evident to her but not to her assistant Richard; in fact she has assumed some of his responsibilities and has not established where her obligation stops and Richard's begins. In failing to set proper boundaries Mary has allowed her silence to be interpreted as a 'yes'. It is unclear whether she *believes* she should be saying 'yes' and allowing Richard to inconvenience her or whether she simply fears the consequences of saying 'no'. However, what is patently clear is that she wants to say 'no' but is unaware or unconvinced of its value to her. Mary blames Richard yet fails to take responsibility for her own actions and inaction.

- **Revisiting the 'Fall'**

  Having made us in his own image, God creates us with both physical and interpersonal boundaries. In other words, we are designed to recognise where we stop and where others begin. However, the 'Fall' affects this ability, subsequently Adam blames Eve for the disaster of the 'Fall' and suggests that God is also implicated in his failure. In like

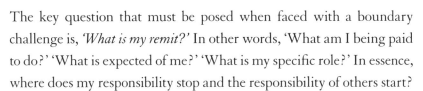

manner, Eve blames the serpent for her deficiency. Interestingly, each one of them, including the serpent, is reminded of the consequence of their personal choice and is expected to take responsibility for it. In spite of their attempts to lay the blame upon others, God does not hold Eve responsible for Adam's actions or vice versa. Whatever the mystery of marriage and the bond of 'one flesh', it precludes any expectations that one could be held accountable for the actions of another, even a spouse's, let alone a work colleague! Adam, Eve and the serpent were each held responsible for their own part in the greatest disaster known to humanity, the 'Fall' (see Genesis 3:8–19 The Message/TM).

Every time a boundary is breached, our physical, emotional, mental and spiritual health is affected. It may even impact the lives of others around us, such as our family, colleagues and friends, as was the outcome for Adam and Eve (affecting all creation in fact!). In order to minimise this effect we must own what is ours and take responsibility for our own leadership. Boundaries teach us that whatever is on my property, in terms of task, problems, feelings, etc belong to me. I am accountable for them, I have to own them and once I own them, I must do something about them. As long as we give control of our 'property' over to others, we will be victims of their irresponsibility. Likewise as long as we take control of their property and what they are ultimately accountable for, we illegitimately enter their territory and the realm of their responsibility. Mary has mistakenly accepted aspects of Richard's responsibility yet has failed to exercise her own responsibility to say 'no', or even better, 'thus far and no further'. By articulating this sentiment

> Every time a boundary is breached, our physical, emotional, mental and spiritual health is affected

Mary would be identifying what is and is not acceptable, as well as where she is establishing her own boundary.

Women often wrestle with questions of, 'When is it my responsibility and when is it not my responsibility?' Rather than behaving like mature adults, we oscillate between two extremes. Either we behave like girls, giving little consideration for *personal* responsibility, or we behave like care-taking mothers, illegitimately adopting the responsibilities of others as if they were our own. When we choose to embrace the girl or mother persona, we render ourselves 'out of bounds' in the workplace and ministry. Swinging between both girl and mother in the same scenario, like Mary, can prove particularly hazardous!

Both the girl and the care-taking mother are two archetypes we should avoid at all cost.

● The girl

The girl either refuses to take enough personal responsibility or she simply isn't expected to. She allows others to regularly cross her boundaries and secretly becomes upset, bitter and angry when others do not understand just how overloaded, tired and overstretched she is. She smiles while accepting yet another task and secretly seethes blaming others for how she feels. She never complains or explains, at least not in the hearing of appropriate others! She is always eager to please and instead she may 'act out' through tantrums, silences and moods. The girl believes that she is powerless, even when *she* decides to abdicate her responsibilities or refuses to engage with others. At the other extreme, the girl may also expect others to pick up after her, manage her mistakes, fill the gaps that she leaves and do the work she is assigned to do. She blames others around her for her own failures and disappointments. The girl gives her responsibility away and then gets mad at God and others for holding her accountable for having done so.

• The care-taking mother

The care-taking mother on the other hand, swings to the other extreme and takes on far too much responsibility. Women (and men!) are quite capable of taking on this role without actually being biological mothers themselves. In a working environment, she is often the one who is totally involved with everybody's life. She assumes inappropriate levels of responsibility for others, effectively crossing and violating the legitimate boundaries of others. She feels responsible for how others feel, wondering if she could do more to make life easier for them. She cannot always distinguish between her own feelings and those of others. She frequently steps in to rescue others from problems they should be solving for themselves. She fails to hold people to account and is overly aware of how challenging their personal circumstances are. So she doesn't like to be 'too tough' on others if they miss assignment deadlines. Others regularly 'dump' unannounced and excessive tasks on her because they know she will 'help them out'. She often does a great job, unfortunately it isn't *always* her job!

> Where does my responsibility end and the responsibility of another begin?

A care-taking mother regularly interrupts the law of sowing and reaping in the lives of others i.e. Galatians 6:7–8, 'People reap what they sow' (Today's New International Version/TNIV). She rescues others from the consequences of their bad behaviour and poor judgement and does for others what they need to do for themselves. You've probably already guessed that the mother is also the one who often complains of feeling overstretched, sick or tired.

Women who make choices that reduce them to girlhood or elevate them to the status of a 'care-taking' mother, forget that God calls us to account for ourselves and our personal responsibilities.

Each leader must ask themselves the question, 'Where does my responsibility end and the responsibility of another begin?' Leaders must learn to set limits for others, while accepting appropriate responsibility for themselves. The Bible is clear that the success of each individual is measured on the basis of what we choose to do with what we have been assigned. This is the essence of what it means to take responsibility for everything within our personal remit. Being more strategic with our 'yes's' and more liberal with our 'no's' may mean that we disappoint, anger and annoy but it may also mean that we are happier, healthier, more straightforward with others and better stewards of our time, energy and efforts.

A close look at the lives of 'successful' men and women provides compelling evidence that they rarely say 'yes' to everything. On the contrary 'successful' individuals, organisations or churches tend to be very strategic about the business or ministry they engage in and ensure that they add clear value to their life's work. They exercise extreme caution and go to great lengths to avoid being distracted or diverted from fulfilling their personal calling, vision or chosen course.

Setting boundaries, announcing them when necessary and maintaining them is hard work. However, this is the only approach that effectively safeguards us from doing the work of others, allowing others to waste our time, rescuing others or ending up overworked, overburdened and burned out. In order to discover our remit we must also value and accept ourselves. Consider saying out loud, 'I am a child of God and frankly, I'm worth it!'

Self-acceptance and self-worth

Yvette had been pushed to the edge once again. She couldn't understand why everyone took her for granted when she did whatever she could to make their lives so much easier. She was virtually doing the work of both her PA and the board of trustees. In fact, she spent almost every evening helping someone to complete a project or task. However, her colleagues failed to reciprocate when she fell behind on her own work, treating her as though she were superwoman and able to manage everything without complaint...

Yvette has difficulty establishing boundaries in leadership because she has a faulty sense of personal value. I began to address this matter when I dealt with the first Deadly Sin of Limiting Self-Perceptions in chapter 1.

There is a relationship between *self-perceptions*, how we see ourselves; *self-confidence*, the sense of stability and certainty we have with regard to something we are engaged in; *self-value*, what we believe about ourselves; and *self-esteem*, how we feel about ourselves.

Each condition is compounded by the other; however, the value we place upon ourselves not only affects the way we treat others it also determines our underlying motives for how we treat ourselves. We frequently fail to set appropriate boundaries because we live our lives for and through others. Our thoughts, feelings, attitude and sense of personal value can be, and often is, dictated by how others think or act. Karen Casey writes, 'There is a difference between letting the reactions of others take over our life and respecting others' opinions while maintaining our own perspective and integrity... Letting someone else decide who we will be, how we will act, and what we will feel implies that we have given up our own life in exchange for whatever the other person wants us to be.'[8]

When challenged by a teacher of the law to expound the greatest commandment, Jesus declared, '"Love the Lord your God with all your heart and with all your soul and with all your mind." This is the first and greatest commandment. And the second is like it: *"Love your neighbour as yourself."*' (Matthew 22:36–39).

The second commandment is usually interpreted as a challenge to avoid selfish and self-serving behaviour. But what we often fail to realise is that this text is also an equaliser. It is a challenge to recognise our own humanity. It requires every human being to more than simply treat others in the way that *they would prefer to be treated* (the essence of the 'golden rule' i.e. 'do to others what you would like to be done to you' see Matthew 7:12). In other words, the second commandment requires more by expecting us to treat *ourselves* with the same level of concern. Author and educator, Parker Palmer writes, 'Self-care is never a selfish act – it is simply good stewardship of the only gift I have, the gift I was put on earth to offer to others. Anytime we can listen to true self and give it the care it requires, we do so not only for ourselves, but for the many others whose lives we touch.'[9] The second commandment presents a challenge to recognise that we have all been created equal and in the image of God. Until we learn to 'love' and value *ourselves*, we may never know what it means to truly 'love' or value *another*.

Our difficulties often emanate from childhood experiences and our family environment. Karen Casey agrees, 'Far too many of us grew up in households that couldn't prepare us to know ourselves as competent, worthy people because our caregivers – sometimes parents, sometimes older siblings – didn't recognise their own worthiness either.'[10] Women, in particular, tend to respect the humanity of others far more than they do their own. This is not to say that we cannot be guilty of devaluing others, but it is to recognise that motivations for such negative behaviour can arise from a sense of low self-esteem rather than a genuine belief in our own superiority. We are also sometimes sorry for the inappropriate rather than the appropriate!

Many years ago, on a return journey I was making on a long-haul flight, I felt too uncomfortable to sleep. I soon realised that this was a direct result of the two men seated on either side of me (neither of whom were known to me). Both were comfortably (for them) spread-eagled across both arm rests making it very difficult for me to turn in either direction. I had somehow unconsciously surrendered the arm rests before the flight had even begun. Later, I was in need of the toilet and having held on until bursting point, I actually apologised for having to disturb them in order to get out of my seat! On the way back, I noticed that most of the women seated next to men in my cabin had also surrendered their arm rests. I began to explore the research and discovered that women invariably apologise when they need to use the bathroom and have to disturb others in the process (e.g. during a flight or on a train), whereas men simply state their need without qualification or reference. This is also the case when women inadvertently bump into others or make minor mistakes at work.

> We can be guilty of subtly controlling others by making ourselves indispensable rather than simply available to them

We generally find it easier to pay attention to the needs of others than to our own needs. We can be guilty of subtly controlling others by making ourselves indispensable rather than simply available to them. We tend to avoid interrupting others, we shy away from making demands, we shun delegating tasks through fear of overloading other people. However, we often feel guilty when we make reasonable requests of others or refuse to allow our work to be interrupted by them. We may also take responsibility for the work or the mistakes of others and allow ourselves to be overloaded and even exploited by them.

Unless we maintain a healthy sense of personal value throughout all our interactions we will fail to honour our God-given time and energy. When we attempt to 'love' others without loving ourselves we contravene the second commandment and allow the concerns of others to supersede the need to recognise our personal limitations.

Karen Casey writes, 'Offering attention to others is not a bad thing. But there is a significant difference between offering loving attention to someone in need and totally giving up attention to one's own needs in the process.'[11] In addition, by failing to establish limits we're in danger of short changing others by refusing to allow them to grow (i.e. we don't really 'love' them at all). Until we learn to love our neighbour *and* ourselves we may hinder our progress as leaders.

On the other hand, the second commandment also requires us to keep our personal value in perspective. We are challenged to recognise that having been created equal, others are just as valuable as we are. This means that we must give proper respect and value to their time, energy, efforts and gifts. Therefore we must take responsibility by addressing any personal challenges that may be rooted in an inflated sense of self-importance. These may include issues such as chronic lateness, missing deadlines, working without reference to others or failing to complete assigned tasks. Galatians 6:2–5 encourages us to carry our own load and to invite others to intervene only when we are incapable of bearing our own burdens. Recognising what constitutes our load is also our responsibility.

We are only able to draw appropriate boundary lines by keeping our sense of personal value and worth in view but we must also be prepared to maintain a perspective that honours our 'neighbour' (colleague, etc). Other questions that enable us to establish healthy limits include:

Self-reflection: what's really going on for me?

Tracy was part of Pastor Lloyd's leadership team at her local church. She couldn't understand why she regularly found herself in conflict with her peers and senior leaders. Although she was constantly performing favours and buying gifts for others, she struggled with many of her personal relationships including her relationship with her husband. She privately believed that the root cause of her problems with others was that they were jealous of her (she and her husband had recently come into a large financial legacy). She shrugged and shook her head and decided that others were definitely the 'real' problem…

Anger, upset and constant complaining about someone or something can be a key indicator that a boundary line has been transgressed and is in need of adjustment. This suggests that the ability to pay proper attention to our emotions may prove beneficial in our approach to setting limits. By default, neglect or suppression of our emotions may actually prove harmful and counterproductive to boundary management. Tracy has little idea that she is regularly transgressing the boundaries of others and that she pays insufficient attention to her own.

In order to recognise where boundaries need to be established we need to cultivate the habit of self-reflection. This is the ability to ask ourselves appropriate questions about our circumstances, the task facing us and our associated feelings. As we engage in this process we should be able to reach some savvy conclusions regarding our spiritual, physical, emotional and mental health, and also understand where our boundaries need to be established.

> We need to cultivate the habit of self-reflection

We cannot afford to ignore the emotional signals that are activated during our working life. Anger and other emotions alert us to our need to explore what we may be struggling with, obsessing over or fearful about. They inform us that hurt, fear and frustration exist within our current circumstances, that internal or external matters may need to be addressed and that 'yes' or 'no' is appropriate. Emotions are not our enemies but rather provide us with useful information about ourselves. Indeed our emotional capacity is a God-given gift. After all, Jesus wept, became angry on more than one occasion and suffered great disappointment.

Women are often accused of being more emotional than men in the work place and stereotypes of emotional, irrational, hormonally-imbalanced women abound. In spite of appearances, there is no such thing as a professional who does not carry emotional baggage to or from work or ministry. Men are just as likely to be emotional in the work context. The difference is that men tend toward more emotionally explosive expressions such as anger, raised voices and dismissive behaviour. Because these meet with the stereotypical expectations of male behaviour in the work place they are accepted as 'the norm'. In contrast, women who cry, become subdued or withdraw in response to emotional challenges in the work place are met with disapproval. Indeed, women are in a double bind because if they exhibit stereotypically 'male' emotional behaviour e.g. through 'ranting and raving' they are considered to be 'unfeminine'.

The process of self-reflection is fraught with many challenges. The prophet Jeremiah reminds us that the human heart has an almost infinite capacity for self-deception and that we all need God's help as we engage in the process of self-reflection. Jeremiah 17:9–10, 'The heart is deceitful above all things and beyond cure. Who can understand it? "I the LORD search the heart and examine the mind, to reward everyone according to their conduct, according to what their deeds deserve."' Once again in Lamentations 3:40 Jeremiah presents the challenge, 'Let us examine our ways and test them, and let us return to the LORD.'

God calls us to be honest with ourselves and such honesty requires a rigorous process of self-examination. Asking pertinent questions is the key to useful self-reflection:

- **Why am I responding in this way?**
- **Why did I apologise?**
- **Why didn't I apologise?**

- **Is this feeling really about the situation or about the argument I had with someone else last night?**
- **Is the problem about this particular person or about a bad experience I had with someone else many years ago?**

There is something to be said about taking the time to talk to ourselves (although it may prove problematic if we then choose to do so in company, especially if we answer ourselves back!). Journaling on a regular basis is also another way of engaging in such self-talk.

Self-reflection allows us to get to know ourselves and to spot patterns of unhealthy behaviours and attitudes toward ourselves and others. It enables us to recognise if we are taking appropriate responsibility or whether we have assumed the responsibilities of others. Typically, it is while we are attempting to lead or when we recall our leadership challenges that we discover the cues informing us of our emotional state. We find them manifesting mostly through our physical body rather than primarily through our thoughts, so we must pay particular attention to such signals. A clenched jaw, a racing heart and a tight chest are very different cues from laughter, banter and relaxation.

I recently pointed out to one leader that she regularly unconsciously clenched her fists, even when she 'thought' she was relaxed. Identifying this involuntary activity enabled her to recognise that she was often in a state of high anxiety. By paying greater attention to such physical indicators she is now learning how to really relax.

Self-reflection recognises that solutions are not forged within a vacuum but within the context of real life circumstances in which feelings and emotions play a very significant role.

Once we have grasped what is really going on for us, we will be ready to take the next step toward boundary management i.e. self-awareness; in other words, do I understand what is really happening?

Self-awareness: do I understand what is happening?

Jocelyn was a highly successful junior partner within a large law firm. Having taken time off following an emotional breakdown she agreed to a few sessions with a counsellor, courtesy of the firm. However, Jocelyn refused to complete the recommended course insisting that she 'felt' better. Since returning to work she hadn't been the most sociable person but she prided herself on being frank and efficient with others. 'People don't mess with me', she thought smugly. What Jocelyn hasn't realised is that she has developed a reputation for being tetchy and brusque. People didn't 'mess' with her simply because they didn't warm to her or enjoy being around her. Ignorant of this, Jocelyn believes that she enjoys a certain degree of notoriety, yet she constantly frets over why she lacks any 'real' friends within the firm...

As we can see, a leader can be their own worst enemy when it comes to self-awareness. Self-awareness is related to self-knowledge and is therefore dependent on how well we know ourselves.

Self-awareness enables us to understand our underlying values, to measure our success and to appreciate our talents and our abilities. When we lack self-awareness, we lack the insight necessary to help us to understand the source of our own motivations and the triggers or invisible forces that influence our actions.

Contrary to promoting self-absorption, the pursuit of self-awareness encourages us to explore how our action and inaction impacts those who live and work around us. It enables us to establish whether we are communicating successfully with our colleagues or whether we are simply 'lost in translation'. Interestingly, self-awareness enables us to become more responsive to the needs of others without becoming enslaved to them. For example, I may decide that an essential meeting would be best held in a particular environment because it would be mutually beneficial to both the supervisor and myself. I may surmise, 'it will work better if I see him in his office, he will be more comfortable and if I make an appointment rather than catch him on the run, he will not be distracted by other demands and I will not feel agitated by what appears to be an apparent lack of consideration.' In fact, the more self-aware we become, the more aware we will be of the needs of others, as well as our own personal needs.

> Without adequate self-awareness we sentence ourselves to a perpetual struggle with issues as basic as time management

Without adequate self-awareness we not only sabotage our leadership we also sentence ourselves to a perpetual struggle with issues as basic as time management. In addition, we are unlikely to effectively engage in appropriate responses to conflict, other people's expectations, the health of our organisations and the focus of our leadership.

Self-awareness requires us to know our own tendencies, so that we are able to helpfully anticipate the likely outcome of any specific course of action. It not only allows us to recognise where we stop and someone else begins, self-awareness also enables us to decide on the appropriate course of action.

Self-management: what am I going to do about all of this?

Janet, a sales representative, had reached her limit. Brian simply refused to meet her deadlines; she had cajoled, berated and complained but nothing had really changed. She was the project manager, so on each occasion when presenting to the board, she had accepted responsibility for failure in all the aspects of the project that relied on submissions

*from Brian. However, Brian would simply sit through the incomplete
presentations as if the problems were not of his making. This left Janet
and her hardworking but frustrated team looking sloppy and incompetent
before the whole board. It was only when she discovered that the board
were considering replacing her with Brian(!) that Janet decided to try
a different approach. She informed Brian that she would no longer be
taking responsibility for his failure to submit work on time and she
put him on notice. Eventually, another deadline was missed. True to
her word, Janet explained to the board meeting that the incomplete
presentation was due to Brian's failure to submit on time. She added
that this was a recurrent problem and that she was considering assigning
Brian to another task. She then commended the efforts of the rest of her
team to the board. Needless to say, Brian, shocked and embarrassed by
the exposure, met every subsequent deadline well ahead of time...*

It is one thing to ask the right questions and to recognise what is going
on for us. It is quite another thing to develop the necessary conviction
and confidence to take appropriate action in order to establish or
reinforce a boundary. In fact, this can be the most painful step of all.

Good leaders are also great managers, not just of others but primarily
of themselves. Ultimately leaders must be prepared to pay the price to
ensure future progress. This means that they must resist the temptation
to allow the behaviour of others to determine their own course of action.
Self-management is essentially about the action we take en route to
fulfilling our task, in order to contain or direct our own responses so
that they are appropriate, considered and measured. Self-management,
elicits an 'I' question and asks, 'What am I going to do about all this?'

Self-management is an essential component of boundary management. It enables us to exercise godly self-control without sinful repression
of the very emotions that alert us to our need for proper boundary
management. The challenge we face is to unpack the emotional 'baggage'

that we carry at work before it interferes with our relationships, keeps us up at night or weighs us down on the job.

Boundary management requires us to manage our emotions before they manage us. For example, the Bible advises that we should, 'Be angry but do not sin' (Ephesians 4:26). Anger turns to sin when it develops into aggression. Women are remarkably good at indirect aggression and regularly express their anger through withdrawal, seething, gossiping, undermining and sabotage. The Bible adds, 'Do not let the sun go down while you are still angry.' In other words, we should never allow others to determine what kind of day we are going to have!

There are a number of healthful ways we may choose to approach the task of managing our emotions. Each requires discipline[12] and the exercise of retraining our responses. For example, we may choose to excuse ourselves from the room, ask for time out to consider the issues, count to 10, breathe deeply, go for a run/walk/swim in order to defuse, so that we can then healthily re-engage. However, there isn't always time for protracted reflection before a response is required. Often, even a brief pause, afforded by repeating the question or summarising the conversation so far, may prove helpful. All of these strategies position us to 'hear' the message of our emotions rather than simply feel the force of them. They ensure that we never simply yield to them or say 'yes' in an effort to avoid conflict or to move matters on. Such attempts at a proverbial 'quick fix' often lead to terrible complications later. Many of us have experienced the short-lived sense of relief at having done something in haste, only to later regret having done the wrong thing.

One Biblically healthful boundary method is, 'speaking the truth in love' (Ephesians 4:15) and it promises to help us to grow up, as we do.

However, the real challenge lies in understanding how we might apply the basic principles encapsulated within this Biblical boundary management model. The following are suggested guidelines:

- **Speak**

  Speaking rules out shouting, raging, exploding, dissolving or with-drawing. Many women struggle to speak up at all because it never 'feels' like the right moment; however, this doesn't mean that there isn't a right moment. We may need to rehearse or engage in role play with a friend or colleague beforehand, in order to develop the clarity and confidence necessary. What we cannot afford to do is to remain silent. Others will never know what we neglect to tell them!

- **The truth**

  This involves engaging in appropriate self-disclosure. Self-disclosure can be as simple as informing others that we have plans, we don't owe anyone the details. In other words, help others to understand where you are coming from without explaining or apologising for your decisions. God calls us to be honest with others as well as ourselves. Would you prefer the truth or a lie? There's nothing worse than hearing someone say, 'but why didn't you tell me all this before?' or 'the solution seems quite simple, why don't we … ?'.

- **In love**

  Truth needs framing, otherwise it can sound like an accusation, an evasion of personal responsibility or a provocation. When we 'briefly' explain where we are coming from it often softens the impact of what may otherwise communicate as brusque and unfeeling.

  Of course there is always a chance that others will be angry, upset, uptight or resentful but *you* will feel better and your conscience will be clear. What others choose to do with the information you lovingly deliver is their responsibility, not yours.

  Remember, love expresses equal consideration and respect toward all parties, you included.

Speak the truth in love: a practice run

Now that you know how you feel, what will help you and the other party and the action you could take, your task will now be to deliver your message without presenting it as a melodrama, a comedy or an epic! 'I' statements provide the perfect means of doing so because they allow us to make pronouncements without blaming others. They enable us to take responsibility for our own actions and feelings seriously. It is less important at this stage to focus on whether how we feel may be helpful or unhelpful, empowering or disempowering. The aim is simply to own and disclose these feelings where appropriate, without blaming them on others and without surrendering our new boundaries in the process. Together with 'yes' and 'no', 'I' statements are effective boundary managers. The following are a few examples.

'I feel badly about this but I will not be able to take on that extra work...'
This sounds so much better than the 'last straw' explosion, 'What is wrong with you, can't you see that I'm drowning here?' or suppressing your feelings and partially surrendering your boundaries, 'Do you realise I'll have to take this extra work home with me? I had quite a busy weekend planned.'

'Look, I feel awkward about saying this, but I am really unhappy with the decision that was taken...' compare this to the 'last straw' explosion, 'You are all deliberately trying to provoke me with this decision...' or the partial surrender, 'You never really explained why you made that decision.'

'I'm not sure how to put this but can we find a mutually acceptable solution?' This is far better than, 'This is all your fault, now I'm going to have to sort the whole mess out...' or 'Your solution is a bit unhelpful...'

'I should have said something earlier but I was worried about how to put this...' rather than, 'Your attitude put me off saying anything earlier...' or 'You didn't really give me a chance to say anything...'

Sometimes even self-identity, self-acceptance, self-reflection and self-awareness do not go far enough. In our attempt to manage our boundaries and grow as leaders we often need the help of others.

Self-development: even if all else doesn't fail, still get help!

While it is important to manage ourselves well, our blind spots mean that there are limits to addressing these aspects of ourselves.

Therefore we often need to look for further support when seeking to set appropriate limits. The area of boundaries is one of the easiest in which to make major mistakes and develop blind spots.

There are two basic mistakes a leader can make and both are boundary breakers. The first type is unavoidable and what I call, *you can't know what you don't know* mistakes! These mistakes are predictable and based on our ignorance of the basic facts that would otherwise enable us to avoid them. The second type are the avoidable mistakes, in other words, mistakes *where you knew better but just failed to do better*. Both kinds of mistake in leadership are inevitable but can be managed and sometimes avoided with the support of others. For example, seeking the support of more experienced individuals immediately increases the knowledge we have access to, thereby reducing the risk of the first kind of mistake. In other words, we can learn from the mistakes of others rather than painfully having to learn from our own.

Leaders who commit themselves to self-development become good leaders, but leaders who

> Leaders who commit themselves to self-development become good leaders, but leaders who recognise that self-development is not a solitary task become great leaders

recognise that self-development is not a solitary task become great leaders. Good leaders never stop growing but there is only so much reading, watching and self-tutoring that any one individual can do. Input without challenge and accountability does not make for effective growth, neither can we reap the kind of reward we need in order to maximise our leadership potential. Others can help us to identify our negative and positive traits, while making us aware of strengths and weaknesses we wouldn't ordinarily become aware of.

There are three types of support I believe we should seek out in the work place and ministry environment. These are based upon a model evident in Moses' network of support described in Exodus 17:8–13 and Exodus 18:13–23.

Moses' 360 Degree Support Structure

Exodus 17:8-13

'The Amalekites came and attacked the Israelites at Rephidim. Moses said to Joshua, "Choose some of our men and go out to fight the Amalekites. Tomorrow I will stand on top of the hill with the staff of God in my hands." So Joshua fought the Amalekites as Moses had ordered, and Moses, Aaron and Hur went to the top of the hill. As long as Moses held up his hands, the Israelites were winning, but whenever he lowered his hands, the Amalekites were winning. When Moses' hands grew tired, they took a stone and put it under him and he sat on it. Aaron and Hur held his hands up – one on one side, one on the other – so that his hands remained steady till sunset. So Joshua overcame the Amalekite army…'

Exodus 18:13-23

'The next day Moses took his seat to serve as judge for the people, and they stood around him from morning till evening. When his father-in-law saw all that Moses was doing for the people, he said, "What is this you are doing for the people? Why do you alone sit as judge, while all these people stand around you from morning till evening?" Moses answered him, "Because the people come to me to seek God's will. Whenever they have a dispute, it is brought to me, and I decide between the parties and inform them of God's decrees and laws." Moses' father-in-law replied, "What you are doing is not good. You and these people who come to you will only wear yourselves out... Listen now to me and I will give you some advice, and may God be with you... select capable men from all the people... and appoint them as officials over thousands, hundreds, fifties and tens... That will make your load lighter, because they will share it with you. If you do this and God so commands, you will be able to stand the strain, and all these people will go home satisfied.'"

Joshua was instructed and mentored by Moses, whereas Aaron and Hur provided peer support to Moses. In the Exodus 18 story Jethro, Moses' father-in-law, supports Moses by advising him in much the same way that a mentor would. As a result of this 360 degree support structure, Moses was able to succeed in his work and ministry.

- **Jethros**

  Jethros are people who have already invented a wheel so that we don't have to reinvent it! These individuals often have a great deal more experience than we do. They are mentors, coaches, pastors, therapists, counsellors and spiritual directors. These relationships exist primarily for accountability and growth. They also give us permission to do things we would never have imagined or attempted without their input.

- **Aarons and Hurs**

  These are fellow leaders, peers who are facing similar challenges to us, they provide us with mutual accountability, they help us to do what we need to do without burning ourselves out. They are cheer-leaders who encourage us to persevere or press through when we least feel like it. They support us and love us no matter what and hold us accountable once we have articulated the work we feel called to do by God. These are sometimes husbands, friends, colleagues or work partners.

- **Joshuas**

   These are people we commit ourselves to mentor. We pass on our accumulated wisdom by spending time with them. We share our insights so that they don't have to reinvent their own wheel but can simply improve on ours. They remind us of our need for consistency and integrity, so that we are leaders who actually do what we teach others.

Although I have not always enjoyed 360 degree support throughout my leadership journey, I have been extraordinarily blessed to have God provide me with key people at critical junctures of my life. Some have been writers or leaders whom I've never personally met; however, each has influenced my life, if only from a distance. Others have been closer at hand and in my life for a relatively brief period. They seem to have been given a specific assignment for a designated time, designed to encourage me through a particularly challenging transition. More recently, I have found myself surrounded by supportive peers, mentees, a great mentor and even a coach. In very different ways, each one enables me to develop my gifts, come to terms with my calling and face my shortcomings. I am profoundly grateful for each one and thank God that I am also able to contribute to their 360 degree support structure in my own distinctive way.

As well as great advice, the 360 degree support structure also provides us with a great opportunity to practise our boundary management, enabling us to avoid the kind of mistakes that lead to leadership disasters.

The challenge of boundary management is greatly reduced when others are involved at key junctures of our leadership journey. They enable us to adjust our boundaries in order to meet the new and greater demands presented by our leadership growth and ever increasing leadership opportunities. Others enable us to remember that the main purpose of setting personal limits is to allow us to reach the full potential of God's purposes for our lives.

In summary, healthy boundaries may be related to a single issue, a specific set of circumstances or a lifestyle decision but each one is based upon a willingness to develop in the following areas:

- *Self-identity*
  A clear sense of where my responsibility stops and that of others begins
- *Self-acceptance and self-worth*
  The knowledge that I am no less valuable than anyone else
- *Self-reflection*
  The practice of self-talk by asking, 'What's really going on for me?'
- *Self-awareness*
  The understanding of what is really happening
- *Self-management*
  A willingness to take appropriate action
- *Self-development*
  By eliciting 360 degree support and input from significant/influential others

As you commit yourself to exploring these various facets of your life and prayerfully invest in establishing a 360 degree support network, you will see more of yourself through God's eyes. In addition, boundary management will become less onerous and far more intuitive, while boundary battles will increasingly become a thing of the past.

COACHING TIPS

On a scale of 1-10 (where 1=not satisfied and 10=very satisfied) how satisfied are you with the health of your boundaries with:

Your team (i.e. those who report to you)?

Your peer group/those you work alongside or personal network (including friends)?

Your mentor/line manager
(i.e. those to whom you are accountable)?

Yourself?

Name one action you could take in each case that would increase your level of satisfaction by two points.

'Appropriate boundaries create integrity.'
REBBETZIN CHANA RACHEL SCHUSTERMAN[13]

3RD
DEADLY SIN

INADEQUATE PERSONAL VISION

Develop and maintain a God-inspired vision

'We are limited, not by our abilities, but by our vision.'

ANON

The Importance of Vision

Janet was a successful pharmacist in a major teaching hospital. Her job was varied and interesting by some people's standards and she was considered highly influential and dedicated by those who knew her. By all appearances she should have been wonderfully content. However, in reality, Janet felt uninspired, lethargic and, she was almost ashamed to admit it, bored. Although she took a wholehearted approach to her work (and to everything else she did), she often wondered whether she was making any significant contribution. Janet simply wanted to do something different, somewhere else. She didn't really know what or where. Every now and then her mind would wander back to her student days and she would recall her dream to work overseas. 'If only,' she thought...

In *The 7 Habits of Highly Effective People: Powerful Lessons in Personal Change*, Stephen Covey writes, 'It's incredibly easy to get caught up in the trap, in the busy-ness of life, to work harder and harder at climbing the ladder of success only to discover it's leaning against the wrong wall.'[1] Covey adds that what men and women frequently define as 'success' is often achieved at the expense of more important personal goals. This can be just as true for the housewife, as it is for the career woman. For example, the former may live a life entirely consumed by the needs of her husband and children, only to discover too late that once the children have left home, she has little self-identity or real purpose. In much the same way, women who 'make it' to the top of their professional ladder, may eventually discover that the climb led them to an undesirable and meaningless destination.

How should women leaders, or indeed anyone, negotiate the challenging terrain of personal vision? Clarity of vision is perhaps the single most important characteristic of a great leader and yet it can be one of the greatest challenges faced by women in leadership. Women are particularly susceptible to inadequate personal vision. Until quite recently, we have never really been expected to have a vision that wasn't entirely eclipsed by romance, children or just plain survival! Yet the overwhelming evidence suggests that women who embrace a healthy personal vision, not only transform their own world but also impact the lives of others in a powerful way.

> Clarity of vision is perhaps the single most important characteristic of a great leader

Consequently, there is no greater tragedy in life than a lack of personal vision or the sense of not knowing who we are, why we were born and what we exist for. People who lack clarity on the issues of identity, purpose and vision, can become consumed by fear, hopelessness, self-doubt, depression and dissatisfaction. Such individuals are capable of destroying the lives of others around them, as well as their own. Without an adequate personal vision, people inevitably succumb to self-imposed limitations. They also become constrained by the limits imposed upon them by others.

Having a Personal Vision

Essentially, personal vision enables us to reach the end of a discrete task or project, a season of life or even our whole life with a deep sense of satisfaction of having accomplished what we set out to do. Above all, personal vision is precisely that, a personal view of our future. This means that our active participation is essential for personal vision to emerge. Indeed, the integrity of our vision depends upon our willingness to manage and navigate our way through the many unexpected and unforeseen obstacles we encounter along the way to its fulfilment. In other words, for a vision to be personal, we must not only be involved and engaged, we must also take responsibility.

In order to imagine what our future might look like in 10 years' time, we need to prayerfully explore every area of our lives in a bid to consider our available options. These spheres might include our professional interests such as work and ministry but it would almost certainly include significant relationships with God, spouse, children and other family members. Our future vision may also involve our general well-being and health (very few of us envision being incapacitated as a preferred future!). Financial and material concerns would arise, since a great deal of an individual's preferred future costs money! This is especially true if we are attempting to 'buy' increasing levels of, what some refer to as, 'security' (e.g. a home, car, children's education).

Our healthiest view of the future will take an inclusive approach to the various aspects of our lives. The vision develops a proper perspective as we seek to envisage the 'whole'. Under these conditions, in theory at least, no single aspect is inadvertently or inappropriately emphasised or eclipsed. In other words, personal vision is the landscape within which the distinct projects, tasks and various aspects of our lives emerge. Personal vision involves more than any specific aim or goal, it encompasses our ethos and values together with our preferred disposition and approach. It is multifaceted and, like a diamond, its consistency, which could be likened to our values, remains fixed in our preferred future. This occurs regardless of which aspect of life we may choose to focus on at any one time. We can extend the imagery of the popular gemstone still further by recognising that, although each 'facet' of our personal vision has its own significance and allure, it is the overall combined effect that provides the distinctive 'wow' factor.

Janet has lost a sense of herself and her personal vision. In order to recapture her direction and focus, she needs to pause and recall her earliest convictions, dreams and hopes. A time of prayerful reflection will enable Janet to re-envision every aspect of her life, to find ways of putting her many gifts to work and ultimately to get back on track.

Benefits of Personal Vision

Proverbs 29:18 declares, 'Where there is no revelation/vision, people cast off restraint.' (Vision is the term used in the King James Bible). In other words, where there is no distinct or identifiable future destination people become negligent and disorganised. Without a clear sense of direction, people who work together become disorderly and uncooperative.

Essentially, a good vision articulates purpose and provides direction, coherence, motivation, enthusiasm, energy and commitment. That is why we need a personal vision that applies to every area of our lives including our families, our relationships, our leadership, our work, our health and anything else we consider to be of personal significance. Personal vision enables us to shape our ministry or organisational vision intentionally. It becomes the umbrella under which every other type of vision we have is subsumed.

When our personal vision is clear, our lives, jobs and projects become characterised by many of the following factors.

Articulation of purpose

Perhaps the most important thing that vision does is to articulate purpose and 'put it to work'. It reminds us that there is meaning, a reason why we exist, that we really were made for something and that we really do matter. Vision raises our awareness that there is something that remains unaccomplished or incomplete without our involvement. Whereas purpose defines why we exist and what we were made for, vision defines the specific God-given assignments that enable us to put our purpose to work.

According to Genesis 1 God has very carefully and deliberately programmed purpose into every animate creature and inanimate object on planet earth. In addition he has a specific vision for each one.

The following is from Genesis 1:11–28, 'Then God said, "Let the land produce vegetation: seed-bearing plants and trees on the land that bear fruit with seed in it, according to their various kinds." And it was so… Then God said, "Let us make human beings in our image, in our likeness, so that they may rule over the fish in the sea and the birds in the sky, over the livestock and all the wild animals, and over all the creatures that move along the ground." So God created human beings in his own image, in the image of God he created them; male and female he created them. God blessed them and said to them, "Be fruitful and increase in number; fill the earth and subdue it. Rule over the fish in the sea and the birds in the sky and over every living creature that moves on the ground."'

> Vision raises our awareness that there is something that remains unaccomplished or incomplete without our involvement

From this passage we gather that on the sixth day, human beings were not only formed but given their purpose and commanded to pursue that purpose. In other words, both men and women have been designed to 'bear fruit' and to 'produce after our own kind', just like the rest of creation. However, unlike the rest of creation we are also called to 'take responsibility' for stewarding the whole world and its resources.

In one sense everyone's purpose is the same, to fill the earth (by reproducing themselves and their gifts in others) and steward it according to God's design. On the other hand, God has ensured that each one of us is totally unique and is neither repeatable nor replaceable. Andy Stanley describes it as follows, 'We serve an intensely creative God. We talk about the fact that no two snowflakes are alike – but God has never made two of anything alike. God's vision for you does not include pressing you into someone else's mould.'[2] This means that in spite of our similarity to one another as human beings and the creation mandate we share in common, our individual and specific purpose may be very different indeed. However, whereas purpose is literally a 'heartfelt' conviction regarding who we are and what we are made for, vision is our unique God-given view of a future we could potentially facilitate into being.

The world offers many options as far as vision is concerned, however, God has tailor-made each one of us with something very specific in mind. 'God has a vision for your life. That is, he has a mental image of what you could and should be as well as what you could and should do.'[3] On a personal level there is a real sense in which we may choose our career, our spouse, our hobbies, and many other parts of our life; however, we do not get to choose our life's purpose or God-inspired vision. Ephesians 2:10 is a reminder, 'For we are God's handiwork, created in Christ Jesus to do good works, which God prepared in advance for us to do.' (TNIV).

God also provides each one of us with a variety of opportunities to discover and implement our unique purpose and vision. We have an assurance that God knows what we 'could and should be as well as what we could and should do'. However, we are also invited to actively pursue and contribute to the process of becoming all that God intends for our lives. We are also expected to move God's purposes forward simultaneously. Purpose and therefore vision have more than merely temporal implications. 'God's visions for your life are the things that will give your life impact beyond this life... God's visions always have an eternal element.'[4]

Direction

The fact that vision provides direction is a perpetual reminder that leadership is a journey complete with a destination. Those who are committed to developing and pursuing a personal vision, commit themselves to reaching the desired destination on purpose. Whereas, those who have little or no personal vision are unlikely to reach the desired destination even by accident!

What occurs in our personal, family, professional and spiritual lives may be deliberate accomplishments or accidental defaults. Vision alone leads us to our preferred outcome. Spectacular leadership failure is often the result of unintentional thought and behaviour that leads to undesirable outcomes.

Personal vision provides us with an end in sight. It is a picture of a desired future or destination that inspires us to undertake the challenging task of designing a strategy i.e. a map or route that enables us to get there.

Personal vision provides us with sufficient focus to help us achieve our goals while also keeping us on track when we are faced with the inevitable distractions. It enables us to make the right decisions about our relationships, time, talent, money, place of service or work, ministry and strategy. Clear vision aids direction by enabling us to set better boundaries. We are able to say 'yes' even when we would rather say 'no', and to say 'no' even when we are desperate to say 'yes'. Vision not only clarifies our priorities, it also enables us to reprioritise what we ultimately count as clarity. It does this by simplifying our decision-making so that 'no go' areas become more obvious and undesirable, while whatever facilitates the vision becomes more attractive.

Every now and again someone approaches me with a wonderful concept or idea that I am conscious God desires to develop and bless. However, it is at times like these that I face the greatest potential diversion from my God-given task and calling. Not so long ago, I was asked to become patron to a wonderful charity working with orphans in Africa. It ticked all the boxes, it was worthwhile and meaningful and could potentially impact the lives of hundreds and eventually thousands of individuals. Unfortunately, before long I was spending so much time developing the microstructure of the charity, that virtually everything else I was engaged in was put on hold. Thankfully, a frank conversation with my mentor revealed that I had simply become swept up in someone else's vision and agenda. It also quickly became apparent that I could not continue to act as patron without being 'unhelpfully' preoccupied. After much soul searching, I simply bowed out. These days, I take regular retreats which enable me to reflect on whether I am attending to my primary calling and vision or simply getting caught up in good ideas. I also work with a coach who helps me to make any necessary corrections to my current course and direction.

It has taken me many years to appreciate that true 'success' is not measured in quantifiable or even qualitative terms but by our faithfulness to the task and process that God outlines for us. Holding fast to this measure of success is necessary if we are to stay on course, particularly if we are supporting the vision of others. Staying on course is also crucial because we seldom understand the nature or the impact of our unique contribution to God's overall universal plan.

Coherence

The dictionary defines coherence as 'the integration of diverse elements, relationships or values'. In other words, personal vision enables what at first appears to be disparate and unrelated to 'fall into place' and to 'come together'. It weaves distinctive strands together to form a beautiful tapestry. It literally 'makes sense' of everything we do, enabling us to see the order in the midst of apparent chaos and to focus in the midst of confusion. Vision reminds us *why* we do *what* we do. It actually generates a kind of efficiency by promoting confidence and the ability to strategise more effectively and with greater clarity.

Motivation

Because vision forms in the hearts of those who are dissatisfied with the status quo, it stimulates us to focus as much attention on the minor details as we do the major events of our lives. It does this by attaching significance to even the most mundane routines we establish. For example, filling envelopes with circulars takes on a very different meaning when we believe that the contents will powerfully impact the lives of everyone who receives them. The task of driving a bus, making 'routine' telephone calls, editing a script, storing and retrieving data all take on a new meaning when we associate them with a higher purpose. However, personal vision also provides the motivation we need to complete a challenging programme, to start a new business, to realign our family, to fulfil a demanding task or to finish a difficult conversation. Personal vision encourages us to see everything we interact and engage with through a different lens.

Vision provides the motivation to keep us going to the very end, even when nothing else will. It enables an idea (i.e. what *could* be done) to be translated into something concrete, that *should* be done by engendering a sense of conviction and compulsion.

Enthusiasm

Enthusiasm is an essential expression of vision. Personal vision is always accompanied by strong positive emotions arising out of a sense of anticipation of what is yet to come. It provides us with a sense of excitement and enjoyment that we identify with passion. It is the gladness that accompanies the prospect of 'success' (however we may choose to define it). We are most alive and most ourselves when we are engaged in God's purpose for our lives and seeking to accomplish our God-inspired visions. Everything else may even feel like a waste of energy, space and time. The stronger the vision, the more pronounced and irrepressible the enthusiasm associated with it.

> Personal vision provides us with a sense of excitement and enjoyment that we identify with passion

Energy

It has been said, *'Vision is what gets us up in the morning and won't let us sleep late at night.'* It powerfully sustains us long after everything else has gone and it enables us to bounce back after rest. Vision not only focuses our human energy, it also gives us access to reservoirs of untapped energy, ordinarily unavailable when we are only mildly interested in what we are doing.

Vision provides us with the necessary momentum to continue working even when there are no immediate rewards. Vision-induced energy propels us over the difficult hurdles and hindrances to its fulfilment and supplies the much needed vitality for the 'final push'. Personal vision even enables us to loan our passion to others who may be flagging or doubtful, as they pursue the vision together with us.

Commitment

Vision keeps us focused and committed to anything that will propel us toward its realisation. It also strengthens us to do whatever it takes to avoid diversions and unnecessary distractions.

The focus and commitment of a clear personal vision keeps us out of the wrong arms, business deal, attitude or habit. It also helps us to get back on track, if we have already taken a diversion. Vision is foundational to the kind of commitment that enables us to persevere against the odds.

Many of the most remarkable leaders I know possess extraordinary levels of commitment to God and/or the cause they are pursuing. I remember the first time I heard the phrase, 'stay focused!'. I had no idea how much it would impact my life and ministry or enable me to stay on track and keep going when I had run out of steam. 'Stay focused', has literally become my signature and even now, I sign much of my correspondence with this phrase with two concerns in mind. The first is the recipient of my correspondence and the second is myself, in which case it acts as a simple reminder of what I should be doing and why I am doing it.

When nothing makes sense and I am unclear about direction, when I have run out of motivation, energy and enthusiasm, it is commitment that has kept me going. However, commitment is just as necessary for the discovery and recovery of vision, as it is for sustaining our visionary focus. This is because every great vision and visionary is contested along the way. Perhaps precisely because personal vision releases us to live the life that God intended, it can be difficult to uncover. The following are key obstacles that get in our way and an outline of strategies to overcome them.

Visionary Diversions

Although true vision awaits each one of us, we tend to follow the path of least resistance. We 'make do' with substitutes rather than pursue the real thing. We are quickly diverted by hindrances and the demands of pressing needs. This is seldom intentional or deliberate but it can prove debilitating. The journey to true vision is strewn with challenges that every woman must face sooner or later.

Imposed vision

Sonique shook herself as she remembered once again just how much her father had wanted her to become a doctor. She would just have to work extra hard as she didn't want to let him down. She was determined to buy in some extra tutoring if necessary and she would just have to avoid all her other distracting pursuits. Failure was not an option in her family. This time she would definitely abandon the animal charity rescue work she did at the weekends. She smiled affectionately as she remembered how she had found the bedraggled dog in the drainage well system and how glad it had been to see her. She thought aloud, 'there is so much we could do to make that work more effective'. She paused and corrected herself, 'they could make it more effective', she sighed…

Imposed vision is based on someone else's agenda for our lives. It is someone else's preferred future for us and is founded on their viewpoint. Imposed vision is what they see us doing, whether it truly articulates our purpose or not.

We may succumb to imposed vision when our need for approval from society, family or friends overtakes us. Women who long to be inoffensive or feel guilty about letting others down, are particularly susceptible.

Imposed vision is what women live out when they focus on trying to be something that someone else wants them to be. Many women feel guilty if they fail to fulfil the demands of others or else they may fear being thought of as selfish or self-indulgent. Women are often entirely oblivious to their own feelings. For example, if disaster struck your family tomorrow (God forbid!), it is highly likely that you would quickly become aware of how other family members such as your husband, children, mother, sisters, brothers and father feel about it. In our haste to manage everyone else's feelings, we often neglect our own. Women are prone to forget that vision is never measured by the number of needs we meet or even by how well we serve others, it is solely based on how well we serve Jesus.

True vision cannot be based on what we think we 'ought' to be doing but what we have been designed and 'fitted' to do by God. Neither can it be rooted in the expectations of others.

During the New Testament era, Jewish people had very strong ideas about who and what the promised Messiah would be. Their views were informed by a mixture of Jewish traditions and contemporary desire. Consequently, they believed that the Messiah would be like King David, a military and political figure who would overthrow their oppressors, rid them of the occupying (Roman) forces and establish God's kingdom through a physical act of war. Jesus did not fulfil these expectations. So we should not be surprised at what we find in New Testament texts such as Matthew 16:21ff. When Jesus began to '…explain to his disciples that he must go to Jerusalem and suffer many things at the hands of the elders, chief priests and teachers of the law and that he must be killed and on the third day be raised to life. Peter took him to one side and began to rebuke him "Never, Lord!" he said. "This shall never happen to you."' Clearly, Jesus' personal 'vision' simply did not measure up to Peter's idea of a triumphant military leadership campaign. As far as Peter was concerned, Jesus was seriously mistaken and had not properly understood *his* Jewish history! Peter had a very clear view of what he wanted Jesus to be and he sought to impose that perspective on Jesus. Subsequently, Peter sought to insist that Jesus conform to Peter's preferred future.

As we continue to read the story, we discover that Jesus was not in the business of allowing others to impose their vision upon him, 'Jesus turned to Peter and said "Get behind me Satan. You are a stumbling block to me; you do not have in mind the things of God but the things of men."' In other words, Jesus had no intention of trying to fit in with the preconceived ideas of others. Throughout his life and ministry Jesus had to struggle against what both his friends and enemies thought he should be, but he stayed true to his calling, purpose and vision.

There are inherent dangers we must face that arise from a refusal to fit in with the expectations of others. For example, Judas became despondent with Jesus' apparent unwillingness to forcefully overthrow the occupying forces. Some scholars believe Judas' betrayal of Jesus was an attempt to provoke him to reveal his true and sovereign identity. If this was indeed the case, Judas' attempts serve as a reminder that sometimes those we are close to may go to remarkable lengths to persuade us to lead our lives according to their agenda.

There are literally thousands of voices telling women what they should do with their lives on a daily basis. These voices come from women's magazines, radio preachers and talk show hosts. Interestingly, men's magazines seldom carry advice from the 'stars'. Horoscopes almost exclusively cater for women. In addition, women are seldom encouraged to form their own opinions. Instead, we are expected to look to others to dress us, affirm us, recognise us and educate us about ourselves. Women who lack long-term dreams and self-confidence are vulnerable to the voices of so-called 'experts', who tell them who they are and what they should do with their lives. After all, we muse, 'What do I know?'

'I stood in mute astonishment, with my mouth open: 'She asked you to do what?' I exclaimed once again. My pitch was a little too high, so I determined to calm down. 'She asked me if I would find you a good husband', my friend said with a smile on his face…' [5]

It is not that I am averse to husbands or, in this case, averse to the idea of having one of my own. What I found alarming was that my mother, who lives in Ghana, had entrusted a courier, someone I had asked to deliver a gift while passing through my homeland, to seek out a 'suitable' man to 'complete' my life. Fortunately this 'courier' happened to be a good friend of mine. The worrying thing is that I'm not sure that my mother knew this and in any case *she* 'didn't know him from Adam', as the saying goes. This particular incident put me in mind of the many other couriers I'd entrusted with bearing a gift to my mother, whom '*I* didn't know from Adam' (or at least I did not know very well). It also got me wondering how many others may have been charged with similar weighty responsibilities in relation to my future happiness.[6]

It is not merely our society or men who may feel inclined to impose false 'vision' on women, our mothers may also share the guilt! Indeed, even our friends can be responsible for imposing unbearable 'peer pressure', as may any of the other women around us.

The following story about Mary and Martha from Luke 10:38–42 provides us with another Biblical example of this very phenomenon.

'As Jesus and his disciples were on their way, he came to a village where a woman named Martha opened her home to him. She had a sister called Mary, who sat at the Lord's feet listening to what he said. But Martha was distracted by all the preparations that had to be made. She came to him and asked, "Lord, don't you care that my sister has left me to do the work by myself? Tell her to help me!" "Martha, Martha," the Lord answered, "you are worried and upset about many things, but few things are needed – or indeed only one. Mary has chosen what is better, and it will not be taken away from her.'"

Here we see Martha busily engaged in what was expected of a woman in her culture. It is also possible that she was genuinely gifted in the area of hospitality and naturally gravitated to this task when Jesus and the disciples arrived. The problem arose when she tried to impose her personal vision on Mary, her sister, insisting that Mary also engage with what was 'expected of her', in other words, with what Martha was doing! Jesus' response is unexpected and intriguing, rather than impose a false notion of what a woman, in this case, Mary should do, Jesus affirmed Mary's choice to sit at his feet and rebuffed Martha's attempts to impose her own vision on Mary.

Women are notorious for imposing their personal vision upon other women. We believe that other women should be married, or career-focused, or stay-at-home mothers, or portfolio workers, just like us. We would do well to remember that Jesus may choose to rebuff us too.

Imposed vision is anything that interferes with the responsibility we have to discover what God would want for our lives.

Borrowed vision

Rheka had always felt short-changed by life. On the other hand, Aeesha seemed to have big plans for her life, her home and her family. The way Aeesha described her husband you'd think he was a regular Prince Charming. She also constantly gushed about how well her children were doing in school, while Rheka tried not to mention her eldest son's two-week suspension. Aeesha always seemed to get the interesting projects too, Rheka thought. The boss liked her, in fact everybody liked her. Rheka despaired, frustrated that Aeesha seemed to have it all. But last week she had made a mistake that had cost the company thousands of pounds and her line manager wasn't too happy. Rheka couldn't stop smiling to herself. At least it wasn't all going Aeesha's way for once, she thought smugly…

You are borrowing vision if you simply long to live someone else's life or dream. Other indicators include, if you envy what someone else has, feel pain at another's success and put successful people down. You may also wish to gain from another's loss, constantly compare yourself to someone who is 'more successful' than you are or attempt to reproduce someone else's experience in your own life. Disappointed and disgruntled with her own life, Rheka was preoccupied with thoughts of what appeared to be Aeesha's 'Bollywood'-shaped dream-life. However, Rheka also deeply resented Aeesha for exhibiting the many signs of 'success' her peers only dreamed of. Until Rheka is prepared to relinquish Aeesha's dream she cannot discover her own.

Some women carry a profound sense of self-doubt often rooted in low self-esteem and a low sense of personal identity. They may be afraid that they are 'not enough', or alternatively they may be entirely consumed with the sense of who they 'ought' to be. Consequently, they may live life preoccupied with a desire for what others have. Such women end up borrowing someone else's personal vision rather than taking the time to discover their own.

Women who borrow vision are consumed with thoughts of how much more fulfilled life would be if they were single, married, had children, had another child, had a child like Sarah's, a husband like Aeesha's, a job like Carol's, a life like Monique's, a body like Rebecca's, a gift like Janet's, a ministry like Brenda's, a family like Sophie's, a house like Ruth's and so it goes on. Of course, women's magazines (even Christian ones) encourage us to borrow too.

Borrowed vision leaves us obsessing about the life we don't have and envying the lives of others to such an extent that we fail to recognise or appreciate our own gifts, accomplishments and blessings. While we are in pursuit of someone else's vision, we not only waste valuable time but we also fail to become ourselves. In short, we fail to begin the journey of self-discovery. We wonder why God broke the mould after the job on 'her' life, since ours was so obviously in need of further help.

Jesus provides us with a good example of how we might resist borrowing a vision. Surrounded, in his day, by many great teachers, rabbis and miracle workers (some of whom were pretty spectacular!), Jesus chose to neither imitate nor follow any particular rabbinical 'school'. Instead, he discovered who he was and worked hard at being himself. Consequently, the persistent New Testament refrain regarding Jesus is that he amazed people precisely because he *neither* taught *nor* behaved like any of the typical teachers but instead 'taught as one who had authority' (Mark 1:21).

It took me many years in ministry before I stopped trying to conform to being a particular kind of Baptist Minister. (This was just as well because for many years I was literally 'one of a kind', a woman, black and single!) Once I'd decided to 'lean' into my own uniqueness, I not only gained a great deal of clarity regarding who I was in Christ, I also began to enjoy myself and my ministry!

It is one thing to, 'Follow my example, as I follow the example of Christ,' as Paul urged in 1 Corinthians 11:1, it is quite another to envy and covet what others have; this is nowhere recommended.

Wishful vision

Pauline couldn't believe that her attempt at baking a cake for her son's 10th birthday party had been such an unmitigated disaster. She coughed, opened a window in an effort to clear the smoke and wept. The moment had been ruined (although she probably shouldn't have left the cake unattended while she attempted to complete her paper work). Paul (her husband) had said she should just buy a cake. 'Tim will appreciate an iced football on top far more than your hand-baked effort,' he'd remonstrated. Pauline had been unconvinced, she wanted to make the cake with her own hands. She wanted everything to be perfect. She always wanted everything to be perfect. In fact, she had placed herself under enormous pressure that week to complete her work and organise the surprise party. It had been quite a strain. The cake had proven to be the tipping point and now she was dangling precariously close to the edge of total panic with only two hours to go before the first guests were due to arrive. She wanted to kick herself, not that it would have done her much good…

Wishful vision simply takes us beyond the realm of God's expectations for us! It is based on what we would like to do, rather than what we are equipped or gifted for. This kind of vision is exactly what it says on the tin! It is all about what we wish were true but it is not based on any of the available facts about us. It is not based on truth but on fantasy.

I attended secondary school in an era when most black girls of my age were encouraged to pursue a future in sports. I was urged to consider long jumping and high jumping in spite of the fact that gravity and I enjoyed a close personal relationship even then! Had this become my preferred future I would have been bitterly disappointed to this day.

Wishful vision isn't really about attempting new things, or taking risks. Unlike borrowed vision which focuses entirely on a desire to live *someone else's* life or dream, wishful vision exists only in the realm of the impossible. In other words, this reality does not exist anywhere because no one, including us, could possibly live up to it! Wishful visionaries attempt the impossible such as becoming domestic angels or career superwomen. This thinking is based on our need to be everything we can never be. We engage in wishful visions when we feel guilty that we cannot do it all or have it all and still stay sane. Our predominant line of thought when we are trapped by wishful vision amounts to, 'I wish I was perfect! I wish I knew everything. I wish I had no responsibilities. I wish I could be all things to all people, all the time.'

We are wishful when we are driven by our needs – the need to be seen to be coping, to have it all together, to be a capable and wonderful mother, wife, daughter, sister, aunty, church member, employee, employer, wonderfully balanced human being and all-round 'super saint'. Wishful vision is what emerges when we buy into the lie that if we push ourselves beyond God-given limits, we'll become great human beings! The problem is that wishful vision is unsustainable.

Jesus had to resist wishful vision, in Matthew 4:5–6 when the devil tempted him to jump off the highest point of the temple. The devil reminded Jesus that should he do so, even the angels would rally to save him. This is a fantastic example of wishful vision, because wishful visions are essentially the temptation to perform the spectacular rather than a desire to fulfil one's true calling.

There are hundreds of demands on our lives as women that threaten to pull us apart. Wishful vision can often be like Jesus' first temptation in the wilderness before the devil tempted him to jump off the temple (see Matthew 4). We are informed that Jesus had been fasting for 40 days when the devil approached him with the first temptation. There he experienced a very real temptation to turn a stone into bread, apart from God's stipulation or sanction. Sometimes we feel tempted to perform what seems to make sense under the circumstances but is far beyond God's desire or intention for us.

I do not intend to discourage those who dream big; after all, the Bible encourages us, 'I can do everything through him who gives me strength!' (Philippians 4:13) However, we often need reminding that there are some things God simply does not require of us. Such dreams should be relinquished before they do us harm.

True vision

Kate was glowing as she shared her story. She could hardly believe it. Three months earlier her life had been in disarray, she hated her job and her marriage had been a disaster area. But since then, she had taken some bold decisions including requesting a reassignment. Against all the odds she had stepped out and ended up being promoted. Her work was now interesting and varied, for the first time she understood what it meant to 'play' to her strengths, gifts and skills. She was also much clearer about who she was and what she had to offer. Kate had truly found her niche! She explained that she no longer felt as if she were 'working', she really enjoyed every aspect of her job. She had also recently learned that she was being head hunted by other departments. She laughed aloud, she was truly happy for the first time in her life...

It should be evident by now that personal vision is discovered rather than created and that true vision seeks to answer the question, 'What was I created to accomplish?' In other words, true vision articulates and gives direction to purpose ('What was I created for?'). True vision is based upon conviction rather than guilt, fear, envy or need.

Periodically, we all experience fear, guilt, anger, neediness and envy but as adults these feelings should never determine what we do with the rest of our lives. As we grow, we all encounter what it means to have vision imposed, as others attempt to influence us 'for the better' (at least in their eyes). We are also prone to borrow vision as we are increasingly exposed to individuals we grow to admire, such as a favourite teacher, icon or significant role model. Some of us even pass through a wishful stage in our development toward adulthood, when we wish we really could leap over walls like Wonder Woman (but perhaps without the over-tight bodice!).

The genus-species name of modern human beings is not Homo sapiens which means 'one who thinks', but rather Homo sapiens sapiens or 'one who thinks about his or her thinking'. In other words, we are only fully human when our thinking is fully aligned with our values and goals. Only when we pause to think about our thinking and adjust ourselves accordingly, do we experience the real integrity necessary to discover true vision.

Imposed, borrowed and wishful visions may all be part of our human development, and may legitimately emerge as we explore the possibilities associated with what we may have been created to do. However, the process that leads us toward a mature understanding of ourselves may stall prematurely. We may fail to graduate to a personal vision (or visions) based on growing conviction and founded upon a God-inspired perspective.

How to 'Discover' Your Personal Vision

Vision emerges as a result of the convergence of two streams. The first is 'revelation'. In other words, vision is a product of intangible, intuitive, God-given insights and moments of clarity we encounter in the course of our everyday lives. The second stream involves significant pieces of 'information' that we glean and 'dig up' along the way. This 'information' is available in various forms, through our likes and dislikes, our fundamental beliefs, the media, books, conferences, seminars and leadership development tools. It is usually extracted through a process of trial, error and deduction. In short, vision is a mixture of common and uncommon sense.

> Vision is a mixture of common and uncommon sense

Developing vision is a process of spiritual insight, self-exploration and clarification. Our vision cannot be substituted, imposed, borrowed or wished, it must be our own, based on our unique makeup, character, temperament, challenges, gifts, passion and so on. When it comes to vision, there is no 'one size that fits all'!

If we wish to discover a true personal vision we must follow the clues that God has woven into our lives and accept that like any 'hidden' or concealed treasure, the process of 'digging it up' can sometimes involve sheer hard work!

Start with God

When we are preoccupied with ourselves we become embroiled in fruitless attempts to manufacture a vision. However, when we focus on what God desires for our lives, true vision can be discovered. If we choose the route of discovery, we commit to our Creator's vision and make a conscious decision to focus on God, rather than ourselves.

Rick Warren explains with regard to purpose, 'The search for the purpose of life has puzzled people for thousands of years. That's because we typically begin at the wrong starting point – ourselves. We ask self-centred questions like, What do I want to be? What should I do with my life? What are my goals, my ambitions, my dreams for my future? But focusing on ourselves will never reveal our life's purpose... You didn't create yourself, so there is no way you can tell yourself what you were created for!'[7] The same could be said of vision.

Although there is a great desire in each of us to make a difference and we are born with great capabilities, most of us will never fulfil our potential or purpose for our lives unless we ask the question, 'Why has God placed me here in the first place and what does God want me to accomplish?' In other words, the questions, 'Why me and what for?' are quite legitimate if we intend to start with God.

Rick Warren reminds us, 'It's only in God that we discover our origin, our identity, our meaning, our purpose, our significance, and our destiny. Every other path leads to a dead end.'[8] Remember vision articulates and gives direction to purpose. A preoccupation with vision enables us to ask the question, 'What could I and should I be doing?'

Not only has the Creator made each one of us with a specific purpose in mind, we are also endowed with a God-inspired personal vision that requires divine support and guidance. In other words, God's vision for your life may be *you*-shaped but it will inevitably be *God*-sized!

I have always found myself simultaneously excited and overwhelmed by the sheer scope of what God asks of me. Whether I am planting a church, starting work on a new project, engaging in conversations with global implications or taking the work of Next Leadership[9] to another level, I find that my prayer life always improves no end!

> God's vision for your life may be *you*-shaped but it will inevitably be *God*-sized!

If we wish to pursue our vision independently, we must start with our Creator God and we must elicit his help in seeking its fulfilment because God has a vision for our lives. Our personal challenge will be to discern and fulfil God's vision for our lives, in every new season of our lives. In order to do this we must develop an expectation that we will hear from God. Believe it or not, God has more invested in you discovering what you are created to accomplish, than you do. However, God is also looking for someone who is paying close attention to what he has to say (Ezekiel 22:30).

Starting with God involves a process of active engagement through the spiritual disciplines of prayer, fasting, Bible reading, reflection and meditation. As we undertake these we are effectively 'positioning' ourselves to 'hear' what the Holy Spirit may be attempting to communicate to us through the normal course of our everyday lives. If we wait patiently enough we will eventually identify God's 'still small voice' amidst the clamour of daily routines and challenges. Guidance will become evident through our circumstances, conversations and Bible verses that seem to 'jump out' at us. We will begin to develop a growing sense of conviction and we may even experience divinely initiated appointments and connections. Even when we struggle to 'hear', God always has a way of making himself heard. As you can see, there is absolutely nothing passive about the Christian view of 'waiting' on God.

Explore the end and the beginning

In Isaiah 46:10 we learn that vision is an essential characteristic of who God is, 'I make known the end from the beginning, from ancient times, what is still to come.'

God makes known the end and he does this from the very beginning. Vision is essentially the ability to see the end *from* the beginning. The person who discovers their vision becomes wholly aware that 'things' are not as they should be. They become conscious of a future seeking to be revealed. The ensuing sense of dissatisfaction leads to an attempt to re-envision things as the individual believes they should be. The Bible states in Romans 8:19–21 even, 'The creation waits in eager expectation for the children of God to be revealed. For the creation was subjected to frustration, not by its own choice, but by the will of the one who subjected it, in hope that the creation itself will be liberated from its bondage to decay and brought into the freedom and glory of the children of God.'

From this we see that even creation yearns to experience things as God would have them, rather than as they presently are. Vision arises out of a deep desire to restore things to God's original intentions. In the first Creation, God's vision produces order out of chaos and leads to reproduction in abundance. In the re-creation, after everything has been messed up by the 'Fall' of humanity (Genesis 3), it is the vision of those who have been remade in the image of God that is capable of once again producing order out of chaos and an abundance.

The ability to 'imagine' a better future and to picture things as they could be and should be for our family, relationships or work is not a ploy to frustrate and annoy us, like a carrot on a stick! Instead, it may be evidence of passion and emerging gifts and abilities, as yet undisclosed.

At its best, vision reveals something of God's purposes and is an attempt to bring a you-shaped piece of God's intentions to whatever arena you are best 'fitted' for. It is there that you will be empowered to envision and accomplish great things. This is just as true for those engaged in the market place, public or voluntary arenas, as it is for church-based ministry.

When you understand the true nature of vision you will be able to better appreciate that you are indeed, *God's gift to the world!* Please bear in mind that this perspective works beautifully as long as you remember that you are not the only one!

In an effort to discover your personal vision, it is essential that you consider the end goal and preferred future from the beginning. What is it that God requires you to accomplish through this task, project, season of life or even your whole life's journey? What are you especially fashioned to do in this season i.e. given your unique present circumstances and personal challenges?

The task of considering the end from the beginning is not quite as straightforward as it sounds, particularly since 'the beginning' can be a difficult source to locate.

Consider the past

In order to see the end from the beginning we may need to contemplate the past.

While some may prefer to sit facing the direction of travel when on a bus or train, others, such as myself, actually enjoy facing the direction they have already come from.

The vast majority of people in the Western world live their lives with their faces to the future, eager to see what is ahead with barely a second glance at the past behind them. In fact, we tend to forget details of the past almost as soon as they are over (unless we are still annoyed, in which case we are quite capable of holding on 'as if there were no tomorrow'!). Consequently, we hardly ever learn from the past or ask ourselves strategic questions in order to improve upon it. Fear of moving on from the past or failure to relinquish it because it was so enjoyable (i.e. the good old days), are simply alternative ways of avoiding applying the lessons of the past to the realities of today.

Hebrew, together with some South American and Pacific languages, views the past as being ahead in full view, while the future (the unseen) lies behind. This perspective, which is rather like sitting on a train with your back to the direction of travel, proves invaluable for those seeking to explore the source of true vision. The process requires us to explore the times in our past when we were clearest about our future. Many women will be surprised to discover that such times may lie as far back as their pre-teenage years.

As girls approach and enter adolescence, especially between the ages of nine to 14, their self-esteem can become more fragile as they become increasingly aware of social expectations and standards, particularly with regard to body image. Consequently girls of this age also tend to lose a sense of themselves as gifted. (The process begins earlier in white than black girls.[10] It is also reported that 'religion and spirituality can have a positive effect on both body image and depression.')[11]

Prior to this, girls tend to be confident, adventurous, secure and certain of their ability to positively contribute to the world. Sadness, anxiety and eating disorders are more prevalent in girls on the brink of becoming teenagers and are frequently evidence of a loss of confidence in their abilities and a lowering of their aspirations. They become more critical of their bodies, less likely to take chances and more reluctant to assert themselves or to take credit for their accomplishments. Girls increasingly refrain from criticising or disagreeing with others or making their likes, wants and needs known. Many also become depressed and lose the sense of adventure and certainty they had freely expressed in their earlier years. Even those who become loud, obnoxious and aggressive are frequently compensating for feelings of uncertainty, insecurity and a longing for popularity and power.

When girls fail to 'recover' from this challenging period of their 'development' they become susceptible to imposed, borrowed and wishful vision not only as teenagers but also as adults. As true vision enables us to see things as they are supposed to be, the past can provide vital clues to our preferred future. We often see the future most clearly during childhood. I remember always wanting to be a writer or poet (my father wanted me to be a doctor!). True vision has a funny way of re-emerging when sincerely sought.

In addition, vision has a tendency to 'leak', particularly as we become increasingly submerged, distracted and even diverted by the demands of our day-to-day activities. Only as we revisit significant points of clarity along our journey are we able to avoid losing sight of our vision.

Considering the past in order to discover the future becomes even more important for adult women who continue to struggle with the challenge of low self-esteem.

Consider the present

Once the past has been considered and our personal vision begins to emerge, there are a number of measures we can employ to move toward its realisation and fulfilment. Committing to a vision is committing yourself to something that has never been done before, at least not by you. It requires constant attention, so we must do what we can to anchor our vision to the present. The following suggestions will enable you to embark on this process.

- **Articulate your personal vision**
  Learn to articulate your vision in a variety of ways in order to aid your

own understanding. You also need to do this for the sake of those who will eventually follow, engage or interact with it. However, having a well articulated vision, written down, pinned over your desk, PC, fireplace or in your Bible is of little value unless its significance is actually expressed through your use of time and energy on a regular basis.

- **Adjust your daily routine**

Make aspects of your preferred future a part of your daily routine. Vision is a day-by-day commitment, so if your use of time, resources and energy does not reflect that commitment then it is not your true vision. Great leaders not only set goals, they also structure each day, their organisations, their resources and energy around the task of fulfilling their vision. In other words, it is no good believing that you were 'fitted' to work with youth or in catering if you never actually engage with young people or have never had a vision to prepare anything more exciting

> Don't adjust your vision, adjust what you are doing!

than a boiled egg! You may not have all the resources available to do everything you've dreamed of right now but those you have can be employed in strategic research and practice. Once you grasp it, your vision will only be realised as you begin to take action to implement it, rather than simply discuss it.

If your daily activity fails to express any aspect of your personal vision, don't adjust your vision, adjust what you are doing!

- **Stop trying to be and do everything**

Trying to please everyone by attempting to meet every presenting need presumes more than God himself!

Many years ago a good friend, aware of my tendency to overwork, challenged me, 'there are no rewards for uncommanded work'. If what you are doing is not aligned with your God-given vision it is time to relinquish it. Ineffectiveness and overload are the inevitable results of over-extending ourselves. Much of what we seek to do is good but not God-given. In fact, you may be expending vital time and energy on something you were never assigned to do. In addition, you may be hindering someone else from exercising their unique gifts and realising their God-given vision.

I am frequently challenged by the story of Jesus at the pool of Bethesda. Jesus was surrounded by many poor, disenfranchised and disabled people yet he met the needs of just one individual, a man who had been crippled for 38 years (John 5:1–14). Jesus spoke about doing only what he saw his Father doing. Jesus was so committed to his Father's vision that he exercised great discipline concerning what he should and should not do under very challenging conditions. Any study of what Jesus actually did during his life on earth is disproportionate to what he eventually accomplished, in and beyond his lifetime.

If you would like this to be true of your own life, you will need to abandon the habit of getting involved where your involvement is literally 'uncalled' for (by God).

● **Be prepared for some tough conversations**
If you take the last point seriously, you will inevitably have to disappoint a few people. Sometimes others around you will have an alternative agenda for your life, so be prepared to have some difficult conversations. This will involve you saying 'no', 'I'm unavailable' or 'it won't be possible for me to get involved', far more often than you or others will feel comfortable with. However, you will get used to it.

● **Be prepared for criticism**
As soon as you are no longer doing what others think you should be doing, you will be criticised. People are unused to women saying

'no' and they will not always understand that your personal vision is not identical to their particular agenda. Your vision will always be challenged by outside forces both spiritual and human. If your vision is similar to something else, it will be criticised, if it has never been done before, it will still be criticised, so be prepared!

- **Practise getting out of your comfort zone**

  Refuse to stay within the confines of your tradition, way of doing things or knowledge. Make a decision to learn new things, try new things and to take some calculated risks. Develop a culture of expectation. When you are open to whatever God may say, you are more likely to discover or recover your vision.

- **Lead and then boldly go…**

  Leaders may not necessarily be responsible for refining the whole vision but they must always embody it, relay it, rehearse it, remind others of it, vision-cast or communicate it and become the primary catalysts for it. If you do this well, others who are similarly inspired will follow, so be bold!

- **Get connected**

  Leaders recognise that vision can never be fulfilled alone. God has created human beings with limitations and with a need to receive 'help' from others.

The strength of a leader lies in our ability to call into being vision that already resonates in the hearts of others in a way that creates ownership. We foster shared beliefs and encourage problem-solving and creative solutions that promote the vision. We create meaning and not just money or numbers. We attract commitment because we understand that people are primarily committed to causes and not just to plans. Many studies show that most people would rather work with someone who has a compelling vision and great values, than with someone who simply pays them a high income.

Finding 'co-labourers' also makes it possible for vision to continue beyond any one individual. In other words it creates a legacy.

- **Recognise the cost involved**

    Every vision is costly and there will be times when you will want to give up (believe me!). However, great leaders will do whatever they can to make their vision work. Many become preoccupied with the rewards of vision rather than the sacrifices involved (understandably). The latter range from long days and late nights and the investment of precious resources, time and energy. For Jesus it meant the cross, 'Let us fix our eyes on Jesus, the author and perfecter of our faith, who for the joy set before him endured the cross, scorning its shame, and sat down at the right hand of the throne of God.' (Hebrews 12:2) Jesus is our ultimate model and exemplifies the cost that may be involved in implementing a vision. Sacrifice is an inevitable part of the equation.

Consider the future

Dale Galloway writes, 'Tell me your vision and I can predict your future.'[12] Since v*ision is the ability to see the end from the beginning*, true vision points to legacy. Vision is not just about the impact of our deeds now but also about how we will affect future generations. Good leaders are constantly picturing possibilities and looking ahead in an effort to make tomorrow better than today. They tend not to focus on what has already been accomplished but on pioneering new thinking and new approaches. Because we are unique, we each have a distinct contribution to make. The Apostle Paul explained that he didn't want to go where others were already at work because he didn't want to reproduce their efforts. Don't just plan, plan ahead!

COACHING TIPS

What area(s) of your life would you like to address (e.g. work, ministry, a specific relationship)?

Where are you now (what does this area look like today)?

Where are you going (what is your end goal)?

What does your future look like (what would you like it to look like in five weeks, five months and five years)?

Are you ready to go (what may be holding you back, apprehensions, concerns, challenges)?

How will you get there (devise a step-by-step strategy)?

What do you need to succeed (do you require any specific resources – material, financial, human)?

'Everyone ends up somewhere in life.
You can end up somewhere on purpose!'
ANDY STANLEY[13]

4TH
DEADLY SIN

TOO LITTLE LIFE IN THE WORK

Establish a healthy work-life rhythm

'Work hard and play hard. But don't confuse the two.'

ANON

Feel the Rhythm

Janice still felt tired, she had been off work now for three months, her arm still throbbed from the pain of her RSI (Repetitive Strain Injury). The doctor had warned her that recovery would be slow but she had not understood just how slow this would be! She got out of bed and checked her answer machine; she groaned as she remembered her lunch date with Mandy and Stacy. She just couldn't face them... In fact she didn't want to see anybody, she was too tired for small talk, she just wanted to feel better about herself and within herself. Her thoughts shifted. What would she do for money now? She only had a few more weeks of paid sick leave and then...? How could she have been so stupid, she was an intelligent woman, why hadn't she seen it coming, all this fatigue? She didn't want to think about it, she didn't want to think about anything...

According to the Biblical account of creation, outlined in Genesis 1, rhythm is the initial evidence of God's order in a non-chaotic universe. It is no exaggeration to assert that rhythm is all pervasive.

Rhythm enables us to measure eternity moment by precious moment. It takes one year or three hundred and sixty-five days for the *earth to go around the sun*. Every twenty four hours the sun rises and sets. We all have sleeping and waking rhythms which often coincide with this motion, times when we are most engaged or least alert. In its broadest sense, rhythm can be defined as the establishment of 'routine characterised by regularly recurring elements, activities, or factors'.[1]

From the simple heartbeat to the motion of the earth around the sun, rhythms keep us alive and provide us with a sense of process and progress. In the Northern and Southern hemispheres we experience the temperate seasons of summer, winter, autumn and spring, while tropical and subtropical climates are characterised by dry and wet seasons. Many of these changes are the result of the larger, often imperceptible, rhythms of the universe.

We speak about the biological clock, harvest moon, tidal flows and sleep without fully realising that we are referring to 'natural' rhythms. In other words, these are regular events which form an intrinsic part of our lives and are a direct result of external forces that we do not fully understand. For example, we all begin life as a baby, develop into childhood, enter adolescence and (thankfully) grow into adulthood! Such events define our life experience from birth until we die. These changes are involuntary and inescapable and are regulated by a combination of internal, often hormonal, and external 'natural' rhythms that are beyond our control.

Although men have mainly imperceptible hormonal rhythms that fluctuate throughout the course of each day, women can appreciate the idea of natural rhythms more readily. Women experience a particularly marked hormonal rhythm, called the menstrual cycle. We even refer to this as our 'period' in recognition of its notable impact upon our lives. Depending on how we view this 'period', we either welcome its monthly arrival or consider it an 'interruption' to the course of our usual activities.

Natural rhythms appear to occur spontaneously as if powered by an intrinsic energy. As such, they differ from the rhythms we attempt to create (or emulate) through music or other means. Such rhythms appear to require very little thought or input from us in order to maintain their momentum. However, this could not be further from the truth (I did say they 'appear')... In fact, although we may not alter their course entirely, we are able to affect these rhythms for better or worse. The effect of decades of prolonged environmental neglect and climate change serves as a potent reminder that the maintenance of natural rhythms actually relies on our commitment to reflect upon and engage with them. In other words, we must become intentional about sustaining natural rhythms and keeping them healthy over the long term. This is important. When our personal and environmental rhythms are working well, we barely notice them. However, as soon as they are interrupted, we notice (immediately, if breathing is involved) because other abilities are quickly affected.

This is no less true in the realm of our leadership and work patterns than it is of our internal and environmental rhythms.

We don't need to be people of faith to recognise the importance of rhythm in our lives. Nothing on earth is designed to run without pause or maintenance for twenty four hours a day, seven days a week! This applies equally to our 'natural' environment, as well as to items we create with our own hands. Everything requires some kind of pause! Birds migrate and bears hibernate. Even our computers, cars, mobile phones and printers all require servicing on a regular basis in order to operate efficiently and effectively.

Often, it seems that human beings alone attempt to live beyond the bounds of natural rhythms designed to assist emotional, spiritual, physical and mental renewal. Nowhere is this tendency more prevalent than in the world of work. Leaders, in particular, experience the worst abuses of work-life rhythm.

Hazards for Women in Work and Leadership

Louise was distracted once again, she hadn't even heard the last comment, she smiled and hoped no one would ask her to clarify her specific role in the project. She would just have to ask about it later. These days she was always distracted, having imaginary conversations in her head with other people. It didn't matter if she was at home or at work, mentally she was always in the wrong place, trying to plan or manage housework, homework, children's clubs, meetings, projects, strategies or presentations. It all seemed never ending and she was beginning to feel the pressure in a way she had never experienced before…

For women in leadership, healthy working rhythms can be extremely difficult to identify or to establish. What follows outlines three main reasons for this state of affairs.

Failure to recognise paid and unpaid work

Global definitions of work tend to be couched in purely economic terms. Therefore, many activities that are primarily undertaken by women are regularly overlooked. This oversight creates significant confusion, particularly for women whose work may or may not take them outside their own home.

Most societies send men and women a consistent message, namely that paid services alone legitimately qualify as work. This further implies that inherent value can be measured by payment. Therefore the more a person is rewarded financially, the more value we may attach to their work. The problem then arises when we consider unpaid occupations. This category of activities barely registers in the human psyche as work, in spite of the significant time, energy and effort we expend on them. Consequently, there are many worthwhile pursuits that women, in particular, engage in, including motherhood and caring for relatives that are often downgraded, or even worse, disregarded.

Therefore, women frequently fail to recognise or value the variety of work-related roles they take on. For example, homemaking requires a significant amount of strategy, people skills and management, not to mention organisational ability. Even unblocking a sink and changing a light bulb requires some technical expertise. However, homemaking doesn't usually register as noteworthy 'work'. Interestingly, making beds and cleaning floors is considered 'work' when it is done by a hotelier or a paid auxiliary but not when it's done by a housewife. Shopping and cooking may be 'work' when performed by a renowned chef but not by a working mum. Looking after children, elderly or sick members of an extended family is considered 'work' when carried out by paid 'professionals' but not when performed by single or married women. With all this and more to consider, women generally fail to recognise the scale or value of their work, even when they feel the pressure of it!

> Women frequently fail to recognise or value the variety of work related roles they take on

Indeed, the levels of domestic work carried out by women far exceed that of their male counterparts, even in the age of Millennium Man! For every hour that men 'work' in the 'developed' world, women perform about two hours (1.7) of labour, this rises to 2.5 hours in the developing world.[2] In the US working fathers typically work 67 hours per week, while working mothers work an average of 71 hours. In developing countries women typically work 60–90 hours per week. Professor of anthropology, Richard Robbins notes, 'The informal slogan of the Decade for Women became "Women do two-thirds of the world's work, receive 10% of the world's income and own 1% of the means of production."'[3]

Although both paid and unpaid work is 'designed' to be a normal part of our everyday experience (more on this later), for women, it too easily encompasses the whole of our lives.

Technological prisons

The confusion regarding what constitutes 'real' work and 'valuable' work is further compounded by an over-reliance on technological gadgets. These were primarily designed to provide both men and women with greater flexibility and freedom from the various demands of work. Secondly, digital technologies including email, mobile, instant messaging, video conferencing, teleconferencing, voice mail and pagers promise to increase efficiency and decrease work load, however such aids usually push us to lead boundary-less lives.

Not only is the office now virtually mobile, it can also be transported almost anywhere in our handbag or briefcase via a laptop, PC or BlackBerry (more appropriately known as the 'CrackBerry', it is so addictive!). These devices make it easier for us to access people anywhere in the world almost instantaneously. Unfortunately, they also make it easier for others to have immediate access to us!

The boundaries we attempt to 'manage' with our modern technology appear to be the very boundaries we eventually undermine! In other words, although technology promises to liberate us, it may actually be responsible for enslaving us. The headline read, 'Why the Blackberry is the new bed partner'. The text reported, 'more than half of business professionals take their Blackberry or mobile phone to bed with them … Widespread use of mobile technology is encouraging longer and longer working days, according to a survey of 15,000 business professionals by Crowne Plaza Hotels and resorts. Three quarters of respondents claimed to work at least three hours overtime a day, and 5 per cent said they regularly worked 14 hour days because new technology made them constantly contactable.'[4]

Our addiction to such technology threatens to rob us of the very rhythms designed to relieve us from the tension and stress our work creates!

To further compound the situation, British men and women, in particular, have overwhelmingly poor work habits. In fact, unhealthy work-life rhythms appear to be a national disease and this introduces a further dimension of disadvantage to women in leadership!

Unhealthy national habits

We cannot overestimate the challenge faced by women in leadership seeking to establish healthy working rhythms. Women tend to wholeheartedly commit themselves to their work, regardless of whether it is performed within or beyond the home. Although overwork is a global phenomenon, British workers, in particular, work longer hours than any other nation in the European Union. Consequently, we suffer from increasing levels of stress, anxiety and depression. Unsurprisingly, we also experience lower levels of relationship satisfaction, a lower sense of purpose, a lower sense of significance and we experience greater levels of pressure in every other area of our lives.[5] In the UK, it is reported, 'eight million people complain that the pressure of work gives them headaches or migraines, 12 million say they get bad tempered and irritable at home, nearly three million need to take time off work and more than two-and-a-half million say they drink too much'.[6] Our national work habits are not only detrimental they also promote unhealthy lifestyles and relationships.

The UK no longer observes a nationally accepted 'pause' in the working week. Consequently, our five or six-day working week has now been transformed beyond all recognition. Since few people continue to recognise Sunday as a 'Sabbath', our nationally recognised work breaks are limited to bank holidays, Easter and Christmas. Increasing usage of modern technology has led to the erosion of weekends, transforming our lives into a single, never-ending working week! After more than 23 years as a pastor, I have become increasingly aware of families who barely spend quality, uninterrupted moments together.

> Women in leadership work nearly 30% longer hours than other women of our age

This matter is exacerbated by the realisation that women in leadership work nearly 30% longer hours than other women of our age. It is also well documented that women are multi-taskers and often move rapidly from one kind of work to another. In other words, we are often preoccupied with concerns other than the matter at hand. Inevitably, women in leadership expend greater degrees of emotional, mental, spiritual and physical energy than those who work for, or report to us.

Taken together, it is hardly surprising that working mothers and female high achievers frequently report feeling over-extended, tired and in need of a break. We are also far more likely to experience stress related conditions and sickness than other women of our age!

A Life Without Pauses

Viv was working late once again. It was nearly morning and much of the work remained incomplete. At least the washing and ironing was 'finished' for yet another week. She would just have to forego her day off tomorrow and work straight through. That would mean cancelling the trip to the zoo with the children. 'John won't mind,' she half-hoped, 'he knows how important this contract is to me.' She remembered John's pained expression the last time she had to go into the office on their Family Fun Day. 'I'll work from home,' she thought, but she knew that neither of them would be happy about it...

While leadership is invigorating, it is also tiring. Like everyone else, leaders are susceptible to feeling drained, depressed and de-motivated. Our lack of clarity regarding our definitions of 'work', means that women in leadership are more likely to sacrifice or simply neglect their physical, mental, emotional and spiritual well-being. We seldom create the 'space' to reflect on whether our relationship with our 'work' is healthy or unhealthy. Neither do we feed our spirit, mind and body in ways that recreate and strengthen us. Women are unused to considering what we really need in order to re-energise and replenish ourselves. We are frequently unable to identify whether some of our 'felt' pressures are self-imposed or are the result of anxiety and an underlying lack of trust in God's ability to meet our needs.

The unique challenges faced by women together with the demands of leadership are further aggravated by the conditions of an already tough 21st century working environment. Women who work in the arena of leadership are therefore particularly susceptible to the ravages of exhaustion. This emerges from a fundamental failure to attend to the natural rhythmic demands for spiritual, emotional, mental and physical replenishment.

A life that is led without pause for rest and refreshment becomes subject to one of the worst natural human disasters of all, namely burnout.

Burnout is the result of a complex combination of false beliefs, wrong motivations and poor physical work patterns. It is also largely self-inflicted and frequently emerges from a life characterised by unhealthy spiritual, emotional, mental and physical rhythms.

I know that I have certainly attempted to push myself beyond my natural limits in the past. I have worked late into the night for many days in a row and have paid the price with outbreaks of flu, other more debilitating 'bugs', a period severely curtailed by carpel tunnel syndrome and two close calls with burnout. However, I have also been among the more fortunate transgressors and recognise that the outcome could have been considerably worse, as we shall see.

Burnout facts and figures

Author Myron Rush writes, 'People experiencing burnout suddenly discover that all of their mental, emotional and physical energies have been consumed. They have exhausted their strength and lost their will to persevere.'[7] In other words, burnout leaves us feeling as if we have nothing left to give. The experience of burnout can be compared to the moment a light bulb fuses, it simply goes out.

Physical exhaustion from overwork alone is not sufficient to produce burnout. People who are seriously at risk from burnout are goal-oriented high-achievers who are 'driven' to overwork. Consequently, leaders are particularly susceptible to burnout and women in leadership, more so. Twenty per cent of high-flyers experience burnout in the first 10 years of their careers. Increasingly, homemakers, single women high achievers and working mothers are also numbered amongst those particularly at risk.

Like most natural disasters there are warning signs that precede burnout. For example, we are particularly susceptible to burnout if:

- We don't have a strong enough sense of who we are
- Our sense of personal value is tied up in what we do
- We are defined by our work/ministry (in other words, we eat, sleep and breathe work/ministry)
- We fail to pace ourselves or pause for re-creation and replenishment
- We constantly feel like a failure
- We have unrealistic expectations of ourselves
- We use work/ministry to feed our soul or make us feel good
- We are addicted to success

- We are constantly trying to meet other people's needs
- We are unconvinced that we are accomplishing anything of real value
- We are in a poor physical, spiritual or emotional condition

Taken separately, these signs do not necessarily point toward burnout but, if there are several, they provide a strong indication that something is seriously wrong and needs to be urgently addressed.

Failure to attend to any of these underlying causes of burnout, inevitably leads to the experience of full-blown burnout, and symptoms may include the following:

- Feelings of chronic fatigue and being physically run down
- Anger at people making demands
- Losing sight of God's work and treating it as if it is our work
- Feeling increasingly apathetic about God
- Feeling unusually irritable and negative about life
- Experiencing recurrent bouts of sleeplessness and depression
- An overwhelming loss of courage
- An acute loss of personal identity and self-worth
- Emotional exhaustion

Tragically, if a leader doesn't take care of herself, no one else will. Unless a leader is blessed with unusually perceptive and caring followers, very few will pick up on signs of fatigue and stress. Worse still, the leader who fails to take care of *herself* will produce followers who replicate the same behaviour and who fail to take care of *themselves*. In other words, the knock-on effects of overwork are highly destructive.

People depend on leaders to produce but we are not super-heroines, running on limitless energy. God loves us too much to allow us to continue with the perpetual self-abuse characterised by the activity and disposition preceding burnout. If we fail to address the initial warning signs of burnout brought about by the loss of healthy spiritual, emotional, mental and physical rhythms, these functions will simply shut down in an attempt to reboot! It appears God has designed us in such a way that even burnout can become an instrument for forcing us to re-evaluate our lives and redirect us from self-destructive tendencies.

> Burnout can become an instrument for forcing us to re-evaluate our lives

Whether we are the kind of person who thanks God it's Friday or who thanks God it's Monday, our ability to develop a healthy perspective toward our working life is essential. If we fail to do so, not only are we in danger of self destruction, the nature and power of a healthy work-life rhythm will also continue to elude us. In order to grasp the significance of this rhythm we must turn to consider the views of our Creator. It makes sense to explore the intentions of the author of all natural rhythm and the one who urges us to embrace 'life in all its fullness'.

God the Author of the Work-Life Rhythm

Joanne hated working, not because of her job, she simply hated the idea of 'life passing her by' while she could be doing something more fulfilling. She had often dreamt of life on a desert island where she could put her feet up and watch the waves break along the soft golden sand. She suddenly laughed to herself as she remembered her first trip to the Caribbean to visit relatives. She had almost been devoured by mosquitoes and the sea air was… well, a bit whiffy (although she had been assured that this was the natural smell of the sea!). She had also been constantly irritated by sand ending up in places she didn't care to mention. 'Maybe not a desert island then,' she smiled…

Work is God's idea

The very first line of the Old Testament in Genesis (the book of beginnings), not only informs us that God exists, 'In the beginning God…' it also informs us that God works! 'In the beginning *God created* the heavens and the earth…' (Genesis 1:1).

Genesis 2:2 describes the act of creation as the work God rested from on the seventh day, 'By the seventh day God had finished the work he had been doing; so on the seventh day he rested from all his *work*.' In other words, the week of creation was a week of work. God's work!

In view of this we should consider work to be good news. Consequently, we should avoid the attitude that work is an enemy or something to be completed, as we wait for our 'real' lives to begin. On the contrary, work is designed to be a very significant part of our lived experience; after all, six of the seven days described in Genesis are dedicated to work. Such a realisation could have saved Joanne a great deal of time spent literally wishing her life away.

In Genesis, God is revealed as *the* Creator, a worker who works not because he has to but simply because he chooses to. In the words of Mark Greene, work is *'part of his plan,* (and) *consistent with his holy nature'.*[8] We also learn that God has designed human beings to work too. Genesis 1:28, 'So God created human beings in his own image, in the image of God he created them; male and female he created them. God blessed them and said to them, "Be fruitful and increase in number; *fill the earth and subdue it. Rule over* the fish in the sea and the birds in the sky and over every living creature that moves on the ground."' This message is then re-emphasised in Genesis 2:15, 'The LORD God took the *Hu*man and put him in the Garden of Eden to *work* it and take care of it.'[9]

According to these passages, both male and female are mandated to exercise a degree of leadership over the rest of creation. Both are also expected to fulfil their purpose through the act of providing for themselves and others.

Work is not only God's idea and practice at the foundation of the world, it is also evident in God's self-expression through Jesus. We learn that apart from his calling as saviour of the world, Jesus worked as a carpenter by trade. Interestingly Paul, the writer of many of the New Testament letters, also worked as a tent maker. For Jesus and Paul, their work may have been a means of supporting their calling, whereas for many others who work in the church and/or market place, they may rightly regard their work as their ministry.

This leads to the inescapable conclusion that we are designed to express a significant aspect of our humanity through our work. Sorry Joanne! Work has intrinsic value and is designed to be a source of joy and yes, even passion!

God enjoys His work

The Bible paints a picture of a creator who not only works voluntarily but who also derives both pleasure and a sense of satisfaction from his work. In fact, God's work is so enjoyable that after completing each phase of his creative activity, we are made aware through the Genesis account that God reflected, 'it was good'. Clearly the work of God's hands was beneficial to all life, however, the refrain also conveys a positive sense of enjoyment that is repeated over and over and over again! In fact, the phrase, 'And God saw that it was good' appears five times before being replaced by its variant 'God saw that the light was good'. A final assertion of enjoyment is then made in Genesis 1:31, 'God saw all that he had made, and it was very good'. God loved what he was doing! In fact, eventually God took a whole 'day' off to enjoy what he had accomplished!

However, it wasn't long before everything went horribly wrong, as evidenced by the 'Fall' of humanity. At this point, work developed a dark side. The repercussions of this are portrayed in Genesis 3:16–19:

> 'To the woman he (God) said, "I will make your pains in childbearing very severe; with pain you will give birth to children. Your desire will be for your husband, and he will rule over you." To Adam he said, "Because you listened to your wife and ate from the tree about which I commanded you, 'You must not eat of it,' Cursed is the ground because of you; through painful toil you will eat of it all the days of your life. It will produce thorns and thistles for you, and you will eat the plants of the field. By the sweat of your brow you will eat your food until you return to the ground, since from it you were taken; for dust you are and to dust you will return."'

This does not imply that food production or childbirth is inherently bad or necessarily lacking in satisfaction or joy. It simply serves as a stark reminder that regardless of how much we love or enjoy our work, it will always include elements of emotional, physical, mental and spiritual stress.

As every leader knows, even the most enjoyable work done well is never quite free from some degree of frustration, boredom or pain. However, our challenge remains to strive for the 'pre-Fall' ideals and God's original intentions, including the attempt to excel in all that we do.

God aims high

Early in Genesis, we discover that God never cuts corners but always produces work of the highest standard. God doesn't simply enjoy his job, he is the very best at what he does! God crafts, he categorises and names, he plans, he arranges and organises his work along a powerful time-line. He also assigns functions and roles to everything in his creation. In addition, for those who appreciate such things, God's branding is literally second to none! It is not only consistent, it is also immediately recognisable, publicising the whole of creation as his handiwork. Psalm 19:1 expresses this sentiment, 'The heavens declare the glory of God and the skies proclaim the work of his hands.'

We also note that God examines his handiwork at every stage, *'And God saw.'* He acknowledges when each job is done well by the use of the phrase, 'it was good'. There is no lack of honesty or expression of false modesty here. Furthermore, God's regard for the work of his own hands is recorded for our benefit. For example, during the process of surveying his own handiwork, God recognises something that is far from ideal or complete. He states, 'It is not good for the man to be alone' (Genesis 2:18). Rather than excusing or ignoring the matter, God remedies the situation and when finished he is able to assert, 'it was very good'!

The following two reflections arise from the indisputable fact that God aims high. God's approach to excellence should be particularly encouraging to women leaders. Firstly:

- **There will always be room for 'it was very good!'**

  Women in leadership are notoriously bad at recognising the value and worth of their own work and regularly 'down play' their achievements and their gifts. Subsequently, we don't always enjoy our work and when we do, we worry about whether we should call it work at all! We are more likely to engage in our work with a certain degree of anxiety and trepidation, 'with our teeth clenched', doubting ourselves and our true capabilities. Perhaps our most troubling attribute is our persistent inability to acknowledge when our own work is 'very good'.

  During one of my early sessions with my coach, I was challenged to keep the equivalent of an 'it was very good' file. I was extremely uncomfortable with the idea, afraid that I was somehow 'blowing my own trumpet'. The Bible (in Romans 12:3) challenges us to 'think of yourselves with sober judgment, in accordance with the measure of faith God has given you'.

It took a while before I realised just how much I struggled to 'think of *myself* with sober judgment' (I could easily see the good in everyone else). I'd always interpreted this scripture to mean, *don't make more of yourself than is actually warranted by the facts*, I hadn't realised that it also meant, don't make less of yourself than God does! In other words aim for an accurate self-appraisal. We all need occasional reality checks as we view our achievements and our failures. For some of us an 'it was very good' file may be exactly what we need!

My file is more than a journal of my journey with God, it also contains a record of events and achievements that, I have come to accept, were really very well done. Some called for great faith, not to mention fresh encounters with Jesus, and were often accomplished in the face of great opposition and against all the odds. These are things I know God smiles at. I have also learned to smile at them too. The file also contains notes, comments, thank you letters, cards and prophecies spoken over my life regarding God's intentions for me. Some of them date back many years. They are points of affirmation and encouragement, reminders of what God has done in and through my life. These items remind me that I am what I am, by God's grace. Therefore, I am learning to embrace that I am indeed, 'fearfully and wonderfully made' (Psalm 139:14). I have no illusions, I know that I would not be who I am without God's intervention, grace and patience but I also know that God is pleased with his handiwork in me.

My 'it was very good' file comes in handy particularly when I am feeling weak, vulnerable, distressed, discouraged or disappointed, it serves to remind me of what God has already said and done. It also enables me to avoid seeking approval and affirmation in all the wrong places.

There is always room for 'it was very good' in all of our lives.

However, women in leadership are also reminded by God's approach to excellence that we are to aim high but not higher than God!

● Don't try to aim higher than God!

All leaders face the challenge of producing quality and consistency. We can fall into the trap of focusing on doing the things we like while settling for mediocrity elsewhere.

Great leaders are distinguished by their willingness to go above and beyond the call of duty and where necessary, to do more than their job description requires. In other words, great leaders aim high but they do so understanding their limitations and their need for healthy rhythms. Having said this, there are legitimate demands that sometimes prevent us from meeting the requirement for natural rhythms when and how we would like. In Mark 3:20 we discover, 'Then Jesus entered a house, and again a crowd gathered, so that he and his disciples were not even able to eat.' Such moments of extreme pressure arise from time to time when we are unable to meet our body's natural demands for food and rest. However, these moments differ significantly from the driven behaviour, so often prevalent in our society, that emerges when our work becomes idolatrous, all-consuming and the focus of our worship.

Jesus also reminded his disciples in Matthew 9:37, 'The harvest is plentiful but the workers are few.' The suggestion here is that although the scope of both work and ministry may seem overwhelming, our calling is simply to apply our very best efforts with the capabilities and gifts God has provided, 'Whatever you do, work at it with all your heart, as working for the Lord, not for human masters' (Colossians 3:23). Our challenge as leaders is to aim high at all times bearing in mind that our focus is not the work but the Lord.

Since there's no such thing as an 'easy' 'post Fall', we are faced with the constant challenge of completing our tasks faithfully with joy. The alternative is to do so half-heartedly with resentment.

The kind of disposition and attention to detail that makes for excellence, usually costs a great deal in extra time and energy. For those concerned with aiming high in leadership, it is a price worth paying as long as we avoid the human tendency to idolise our work.

If we really intend to excel, we must be prepared to strategise and persevere. This means we cannot afford to consider one leadership task or role any more or less important or spiritually valid than another.

Interestingly, the Hebrew word for work is *Avodah*, it is also translated as *'worship'*, with the emphasis on worship as *'service'*. This means that all work is potentially an act of worship (rather than the focus of our worship). Therefore the true value of our work is ultimately determined by the way we approach it. Mark Greene comments, 'How carefully we do our work is often determined by who we think is going to see it… Most of us are atheists when it comes to our work, we don't think that God is looking'.[10] By taking our work seriously we are able to follow God's lead and acknowledge work that is 'not good', while taking appropriate measures to correct it. This means that there can never be any substitute for 'hard' work.

We are not simply challenged to excel in our work, we are commanded to shine. In other words, we are to 'light' up our actions in such a way that God gets noticed! 'In the same way, let your *light* shine before others, that they may see your good deeds and glorify your Father in heaven' (Matthew 5:16).

While it is one thing to aim high and to shine, it is quite another to aim too high through chronic perfectionism. Women, in particular, are prone to self-destructive patterns of perfectionism in their approach to work. Such perfectionism is often caused by living under a shadow of condemnation and experiencing life devoid of significant affirmation, particularly in the early years.

The perfectionist may find it helpful to aim for an 80% satisfaction rate, rather than the ever elusive 100%, as this is likely to be the standard of excellence for everyone else! It is generally recognised that, whilst the initial 80% worth of satisfaction attached to any task requires significant time and energy, the remaining 20% (a relatively small amount) calls for a further investment of four times the original effort. Unless a conscious attempt is made to aim for 80% personal satisfaction, disappointment and failure, not to mention fatigue, awaits the compulsive perfectionist intent on obsessively pursuing the 20% that, in all likelihood, only they will notice.

Perfectionism becomes a compulsion when we regularly aim higher than God. Women, in particular, are driven by many external and internal forces that contribute to this 'dis-ease'. Consequently, they often feel pressured to conform to unrealistic expectations. There are none more unrealistic than superwoman and the domestic angel or, worse, a combination of the two!

Superwoman

Superwoman is driven by ambition and suffers from work addiction. She tends to put work and career before all else. She competes with men on their terms and sometimes feels that she has to be just like 'one of the boys'. She can be aggressive, self-made and unhelpfully competitive. She's often out to prove something to herself and others. She allows her life to be consumed by her work/ministry so that there is little room for healthy relationships with friends or spouse. She always works above and beyond the call of duty and is in 'overdraft' when it comes to her emotional, spiritual and sometimes mental and physical health.

The domestic angel

The domestic angel is only trying to be what she considers 'the perfect woman'. She idolises her family and is often emotionally, spiritually, mentally and physically dependent on her husband and/or children. They provide her with a sense of value. Subsequently, she feels that it is her duty to do everything for them or else she feels neglectful. She works hard at being the ideal hostess, wife, mother and homemaker. She fears being perceived as selfish or self-indulgent, so she never stops. She is uncertain about her gifts and calling because she has never really considered them. In fact, she works all the harder in order to avoid having to think about them altogether!

One friend I know literally lost *all* her hair in her attempts to become both superwoman and the domestic angel. Married and living in inner-city London with a young family, she succeeded in running herself 'into the ground'. She was determined to become the perfect mother, daughter-in-law, supportive wife to her husband (as he struggled to establish his own business) and an excellent teacher in a demanding school. She gave herself little pause for rest, viewing help from others as a sign of failure. She now recounts her story with laughter as she remembers her many ill-fated attempts to avoid exposing her hairless head. Today, her life is very different, both she and her husband run successful and growing businesses, she has few qualms about hiring help and she now has a full head of beautiful thick hair!

Unrealistic expectations work both ways. The demands of others are never wholly responsible for our experience of overload, our personal expectations are also implicated. In other words, reflection may lead us to conclude that we are personally responsible for holding the proverbial 'gun to our head' and that it is our own finger on the trigger!

God designed us to work, therefore we have the capacity to carry a certain amount of pressure. But unlike God, we are finite beings and simply not equipped to bear the kind of pressure we often subject ourselves to. Psalm 103:14 reminds us, 'for he knows how we are formed, he remembers that we are dust'.

Frequently, the attempt to aim higher than God intended is at least

> Unlike God, we are finite beings

partially responsible for our failure to take appropriate breaks for rest and refreshment. The other factor is described by Steve and Mary Farrar, 'Our overwhelming concern for "progress and production" has squeezed out our God-given pause.'[11]

God knows when to stop!

We depart from God's intentions for our lives not only as we fall short (sin) but also as we transgress (i.e. exceed a limit or boundary by going beyond what God intended). Nowhere is this latter tendency more evident than in our work-life rhythms.

Genesis 2:2-3 informs us that, 'By the seventh day God had finished the work he had been doing; so on the seventh day he rested from all his work. Then God blessed the seventh day and made it holy, because on it he rested from all the work of creating that he had done.' In other words, God is not a workaholic! God created the world in six days and then rested on the seventh, not because He was tired but as an example that we should follow. Unlike God, we are created with an inbuilt need to rest and recreate.

We are commanded to work but not in a way that results in the relational and spiritual neglect of those we are called to care for. In the Old Testament the message was very clear and all encompassing, 'Six days you shall labour and do all your work, but the seventh day is a Sabbath to the LORD your God. On it you shall not do any work, neither you, nor your son or daughter, nor your male or female servant, nor your animals, nor any foreigner residing in your towns. For in six days the LORD made the heavens and the earth, the sea, and all that is in them, but he rested on the seventh day. Therefore the LORD blessed the Sabbath day and made it holy' (Exodus 20:9–11).

Women in leadership are notorious for doing the work of others, working without a break, overworking and putting the needs of others before our own. We struggle because we don't want to be perceived as selfish, so we often carry burdens meant for others and continue working when we should stop. We are used to ignoring our greatest and only asset, ourselves! We forget that we will not be given another life to lead, our challenge is to steward the one we already have to the best of our ability and in this we can only reap what we sow.

Work requires physical, emotional, mental and spiritual energy. We cannot expect to keep making withdrawals from these reserves unless we are also prepared to make deposits, otherwise an overdraft or bankruptcy (burnout) becomes a very real danger. When we keep spending this energy without consideration for how we will re-create it, we sentence ourselves to a life of deficit. We must challenge this tendency in ourselves because such an approach to life constantly falls short relationally, emotionally, spiritually, mentally and physically. Mark Greene writes, 'Today we need to set aside the frantic drive to put every day, every minute, to profitable use, to meet our agenda and to slake our thirst for the security we think we can find in constant activity'.[12] We are never encouraged to sacrifice our families on the altar of workaholic addiction.

However, the way we choose to approach the challenge of rest and re-creation, is equally of great importance. The answer to the predicament of overwork and overload does not lie in the popular principle of the work-life balance but instead in the Biblical idea of Sabbath or the development of a work-life rhythm.

The Limits of Work-Life Balance

Five weeks in a row and no proper break. Jackie had worked flat out and she was really looking forward to her week's holiday with the girls in Spain. She silently prayed that she wouldn't go down with another sickness this time. Her last few 'holidays' had been characterised by illness and she had spent most of her days in bed recovering. 'This isn't living,' she thought, and wondered whether she should speak to her doctor or pastor about it. She must be doing something wrong. No one was happy with things as they were, not Steve, the children nor her friends. She was simply never there. Either work seemed to consume all her waking hours or the promise of fantastic holidays was spoilt because she couldn't fully enjoy them…

The achievement of a *perfect* work-life balance is not a Biblical idea. We are never commanded to seek a balance between time spent with God, family, work or leisure in the sense that some leadership experts suggest. Jesus, Paul and all who have ever accomplished anything of worth, actually led spectacularly unbalanced lives! However, this does not mean that we are released from the challenge to pursue a healthy lifestyle punctuated by appropriate pauses.

When we are committed to the principle of achieving balance, we are left with the impression that life is compartmentalised into discrete and separate arenas. If only we can give equal amounts of 'time' to our work, the family, the home, the cat or dog and the church we will have solved our problem. Balance also promotes the false notion that life is about gaining in one area at the expense of another. In other words, it focuses on a need to avoid excess in all areas, which is not always possible or indeed desirable. An emphasis on the discrete compartments of our lives often precludes the notion of intentional overlap. Simply put, balance cannot be our focus. While better time management may be part of the answer to a healthier lifestyle, if we pursue balance rather than rhythm, we will find ourselves constantly frustrated by every new element introduced into our lives. On the other hand, rhythm in the natural world allows for considerable overlap and recognises the necessity of extremes and therefore, some elements of unbalanced living.

Since work is a natural God-given feature, we become far healthier when we attempt to integrate the various components of our lives and accept that a degree of overlap is inevitable and even desirable.

A pursuit of rhythm enables us to prioritise the purposes of God in our lives and accept that we may not always 'have the time' to devote to all that

> A pursuit of rhythm enables us to prioritise the purposes of God in our lives

is worthwhile in our lives. It allows us to challenge our assumptions about career or ministry success. It also enables us to recognise that we cannot fail to benefit if we allow ourselves to be led by the Holy Spirit even when we do not understand his agenda. This pursuit eventually promises us the Shalom peace, harmony and happiness that are part of the abundant life promised by Jesus.

It is the desire for such a life that compels us to explore more fully the benefits of the Sabbath.

Embrace the Gift of the Sabbath: God's Work-Life Rhythm

Liz felt a rush of anticipation as she thought about the steps she had taken. She had recently celebrated her fiftieth birthday with her entire family, a rare and wonderful experience. It was then that she realised just how much she had taken for granted and it was then she had decided to hand in her notice and find a job that would allow her to devote more of her energy to her family and to travelling. In fact, she fully intended, to combine the two together wherever possible! She had been the head of a busy oncology unit in a private hospital for many years and had worked hard for so long that she hadn't noticed the years flying by. She had enjoyed it while it lasted, but wanted to slow down and enjoy God's world and her family before it was too late to do either. She had just submitted her letter of resignation and was now waiting to hear back regarding a job that amazingly paid more but only required three days of her week…

Pause for breath

Life is not designed to be just a job, a ministry or even (I'm very sorry to say) a perpetual holiday! Instead, it is designed to be a delicate rhythm of work, rest and play. Exodus 23:12 is a reminder, 'Six days do your work, but on the seventh day do not work, so that you [all]…may rest and…be refreshed.'

Not only are we commanded to Sabbath, we are also informed of the reason why we are to do so, in order to rest and be refreshed. There is a negative impact associated with a lack of Sabbath rest, such as ill health, absenteeism, depression, stress, conflict.

The Hebrew word *Sabbath* means *'to stop or cease'*. Therefore, we are encouraged to cease from the routine of our usual 'work' activities in order to do something entirely different. We all need a change from cleaning and tidying if this is a part of our normal six-day schedule. However, most women seldom ever stop, even when they are on 'holiday', they simply alter their geography and continue with their work unabated! For this reason, women, in particular, may need to revisit their daily, weekly, monthly, seasonal and even annual activities in an attempt to radically rethink the implications of what it means to Sabbath (cease) in order to rest and re-create. The significance of the Sabbath is clear and the Bible is full of 'sabbatical' moments from week days to feast days and public holidays for everyone. Even the land is to be given a year's break from 'work' every seventh year (Exodus 23:11)!

The Sabbath signals the end of a period or cycle of work. After every six periods, the implication is that we are going to need to take a rest and re-create. Interestingly, the Sabbath is represented by the number 'seven', which in the Bible signals completion. Does this mean we should literally take a break every seventh day? Probably. However, an equally important principle is being established here, namely that we are designed to break regularly for a time of rest and refreshment. The Sabbath gives us an opportunity to check the energy gauge for every area of our lives. In addition, when the gauge indicates that our spiritual, emotional, mental and physical capacities are approaching empty, the Sabbath provides us with the time necessary for refreshment and replenishment. Far from being selfish, such self-preservation is vital to the health of those we lead and keeps us from running on empty.

However, in order to Sabbath effectively, we must learn to discern and understand our own natural rhythms and the cycle of activity that works best for us as leaders, individuals, families and as communities of faith. It is only *after* we Sabbath that we are in a position to return to business as usual all over again!

Jesus made it clear that the Sabbath exists for our benefit. It provides us with a break from the many expectations regularly placed upon us. The Sabbath is not intended to present us with a whole new demand, instead, it signals the cessation of all demands. Therefore, there will be a variety of ways of observing the Sabbath depending on the individual and their unique circumstances. The Sabbath is designed to be a means of blessing. In Jesus' words, 'The Sabbath was made for people, not people for the Sabbath' (Mark 2:27 TNIV).

Trust God

However, breaking the Sabbath is a serious issue. It's more than a sentence to continuous overtime or inevitable burnout. When we fail to Sabbath we are sending a clear message about our beliefs regarding God, life and work. When we observe the Sabbath, we are acknowledging our limitations and our reliance on the One who is greater than us and ultimately in control of all things. We are communicating loudly and

> Sabbath serves as a constant reminder that money isn't everything, work isn't everything and even everything isn't everything!

clearly, *'six days I will labour and then I'll hand it over to God'*. When we ignore the constraints of the Sabbath, we are effectively attempting to take the place of God in our own lives, as well as in the lives of others. The Sabbath serves as a constant reminder that money isn't everything, work isn't everything and even everything isn't everything!

Refreshment Through Rest and Re-Creation

As we pause for breath we are better able to take stock, re-evaluate and if necessary, make course corrections.

The Hebrew word for refresh means 'to breathe'. The presence of the Sabbath is a reminder that we all desperately need to pause for breath and that this breath allows us to rest and re-create ourselves.

Discern and understand your own unique rhythm

Each individual's capacity for work, rest and play (literally re-creation) will depend on many factors, including whether we are 'early birds', 'night owls', contemplatives, activists or whether we work better surrounded by others or when we are left alone. Our capacity for work may also depend on our particular stage in life. The older we get the more pauses to re-create we require. It is no accident that the Bible urges young people to take up the challenge of service to God in their youth (Ecclesiastes 12:1) while they have greater energy and stamina to do so. Our capacity is also affected by the season of work we are experiencing. We all encounter summer schedules when everything is in full bloom, busy but steady, and winters, when surface productivity is low but there is a flurry of background/underground activity. The autumn season is characterised by endings, such as the end of a contract, project, task, plan or job. Spring is perhaps the most demanding work season of all. During this period there is a great deal of new growth and activity, perhaps too much. It may prove particularly difficult to keep up. However demanding the season and regardless of how busy and stretched we may be, the principle of the Sabbath remains unchanged. The Old Testament couches this in terms of the busiest seasons that agriculturalists would have encountered, 'On the seventh day you shall rest; even during the ploughing season and harvest you must rest' (Exodus 34:21).

In order to understand our unique work-life rhythm, we must firstly establish what work, rest and re-creation might look like. Therefore, we must address the following questions:

- **What does work look like for me?**

    Work is whatever we spend the majority of our time doing. It may differ for each one of us and our approach may also differ. Some people appear to manage many hours of intense, focused work each week without burning themselves out; most, however cannot. Some choose to work longer hours because their other responsibilities allow them to do so. In addition, some find aspects of their work intensely energising and refreshing. However, we cannot afford to prolong a working winter without risking what may eventually feel like an ice age. In the same way extending the period of a working summer may lead to a spiritual, emotional, mental and physical drought. A perpetual autumn can become quite depressing as it is characterised by endings. Conversely when spring is extended, there are too many new things happening and work can leave us feeling overstretched and at breaking point. We may not have ultimate control over the emergence of such 'seasons' but we can make God-honouring decisions to re-create ourselves throughout these periods.

Each season we encounter requires a revised approach to the Sabbath, in other words we may require extended breaks of days or weeks, while at other times a few hours will suffice.

- **What does rest look like for me?**

Rest literally involves a pause. It is an opportunity to change gear and slow down. When we rest we intentionally alter the pace of our activity so that it differs from our usual pace. This requires tremendous discipline for some of us.

A wonderfully illustrative story is told of a Westerner travelling in Africa who hired a guide to lead him through the jungle to a remote village. In the mid-afternoon the guide stopped and began to set up camp for the night. The Westerner impatiently asked why they weren't taking advantage of the remaining daylight to make it a bit further towards their destination. 'We have travelled very fast and must allow time for our souls to catch up with our bodies,' replied the guide.

What would it look like for you to allow your soul to catch up with your body?

Rest leads to a restoration of the soul, spirit, mind and body. We discover what rest looks like by exploring our own personalities and engaging fully with our emotions.

- **What does re-creation look like for me?**

Re-creation is usually identified with play and leisure. It conveys the idea of re-creating the emotional, spiritual, mental or physical energy that has been lost through the activity of 'work'. It can be defined as the 'refreshment of one's mind or body through activity that amuses or stimulates'.[13] Whatever feeds and energises a soul, that is, the seat of our emotions, will count as re-creational activity. This may involve a steep ski slope, drinking hot chocolate in a cosy cafe, vitamin D and the simple pleasure of sun, sea and sand or time spent in a busy and bustling environment. Some people may prefer re-creating by having a late or early night, non-stop activity or none. An activist may need activity in order to re-create. For example, someone's idea of re-creation may be running a marathon (please note that I did not say that this is my idea of re-creation!). A relational person may consider re-creating in the company of others, a wonderful break. A contemplative individual will appreciate solitude, such as reading in silence or time alone. The naturalist will seek communion with nature and the 'great outdoors'. A sensate will love sights and sounds such as architecture and music. Some of us may find that we are a combination of these types.[14]

In order to appreciate your unique work-life rhythm we must grasp hold of all that 'makes us tick' and then make it work for us.

Reorganise your life around your unique rhythm

Our time is valuable, therefore, we must make time work for us. We must take advantage of flexible working hours. 'Early birds' should attempt to begin their day earlier while 'night owls' should aim to finish later. Holiday allowances could be rescheduled into shorter more regular breaks e.g. every eight weeks for naturalists and sensates. Activity breaks may suit the activist more than a beach break. A guided group tour may suit the relational person more than the solitude of a retreat (which may leave us feeling even more depleted). Our Sabbath and work-life rhythm is our responsibility, so we must find out what works best for us and work with it!

- **Establish clearer multiple boundaries from your work**

  An example of drawing a mental boundary

  If you are unable to leave your work behind and it dominates your every conversation, develop a strategy. Agree with your family or friends to allow a fixed period of time to 'get things off your chest', discuss to your heart's content and write things down if necessary. Once the time is over, do not revisit the conversation; change gears. This takes a great deal of practice and self-discipline.

  An example of drawing a spiritual boundary

  Pray about the matter, look up relevant scriptures and commit it to God (you may need to do this many times!).

  An example of drawing an emotional boundary

  When an issue makes you feel negative, acknowledge the emotion then use the 'antidote' method to generate the opposite emotion, e.g. If you feel sad, look for the lighter funnier side of the situation. If angry, seek to release the energy through physical activity (e.g. go for a run, walk, swim). If hopeless, inject some inspiration and faith into the matter.

  An example of drawing a physical boundary

  Put some distance between yourself and the issue, e.g. literally turn off all phones/BlackBerry. Leave your phone/Blackberry at home for the day.

  While at work, delegate to those who might benefit from taking on the extra responsibility, this will allow you to focus on the more important aspects of your job.

- **Combine your occupation with your preoccupations (wherever you can)**

  Deal with overlaps with your loved ones (family or friends) creatively and in a way that is capable of meeting a number of needs simultaneously.

Deliberately include your spouse, children and friends in other areas of your life, e.g. discuss aspects of your work with your children, ask for their ideas, advice and let them know what is on your mind. Ensure that this does not become self-indulgent or breaches confidentiality.

Generate support from loved ones for all that you do, in such a way that it leaves you more connected to these significant people in your life.

Find ways to inject play into your work, work into your play and rest all round.

Pray for and then experiment with solutions that have the potential to affect and enhance more than one area of your life simultaneously.

As you take a good long look at your life and make the necessary adjustments, simply marvel and begin to experience yourself relaxing and enjoying life in all its abundance.

COACHING TIPS

What do you specifically want to change?
(Identify an area.)

Does the thought of this motivate you? (Time for honesty.)

How can you measure this achievement?
(What specific changes will be noticeable?)

What might stop you? (Identify specific internal
and external hindrances.)

What resources do you need to make this
change happen and STICK?

What will you do differently
next week? (Identify at least two
specific actions.)

'You will never find time for anything.
If you want time you must make it.'
CHARLES BUXTON[15]

5TH
DEADLY SIN

EVERYBODY'S FRIEND, NOBODY'S LEADER

Defeat the 'disease to please'

'Men kick friendship around like a football and it doesn't seem to crack. Women treat it like glass and it falls to pieces.'

ANNE LINDBERGH[1]

The Power of Relationships

Nicki glanced at her watch again and sighed. She had to attend yet another meeting to reverse the damage that Bee, one of her key team members, had caused over the last few weeks. Naively, Nicki had believed that she had her 'dream team'. Everyone seemed to get on so well, they energised each other and they even generated the creative spark she thrived upon. However, the issue with Bee was turning into a very 'expensive' lesson, not to mention a great personal disappointment. Initially, she had overlooked Bee's behaviour. It had begun with little things, such as turning up late for meetings without apology. This developed into a lack of accountability and a persistent failure to meet agreed goals. Increasingly, Nicki was struggling to manage the overall programme. She eventually realised that Bee was not only taking advantage of her 'friendship', she was also eroding Nicki's authority with the rest of the team. Nicki finally confronted Bee but now the entire team was struggling to come to terms with the breakdown in chemistry. 'If only I had challenged her sooner,' Nicki sighed. This was going to be a long, slow painful repair…

Everything in the universe begins with a relationship. From the first human family, to the preoccupation of quantum physics with subatomic particles, connectedness forms the basis of every type of conceivable relationship. However, it is also the source of every kind of complexity within relationships. Global communication is also net based, as is information technology and the World Wide Web. The emphasis on networks has, perhaps inevitably, contributed to a contemporary view of life that is fundamentally relational.

The central tenet of Christian theology is that God exists in relationship as Father, Son and Holy Spirit. In its opening pages, the Bible also emphasises the importance of relationship. Long before Christians ever entertained the language of the Trinity, God is already identified as a collective. The record reveals that at least up until the sixth day of creation, God had created, ex nihilo (out of nothing), on the basis of His spoken word alone. However, on the sixth day God spoke to the land and commanded *it* to produce both livestock and wild animals. Finally, by the end of the sixth day God created human beings by speaking, it seems, to himself! We 'overhear' this conversation in Genesis 1:26, 'Then God (Elohim, 'the collective') said, "Let *us* make humanity in *our* image, in *our* likeness…"' In other words, God became intimately involved in the act of creating humans and literally moulded the first human beings himself (see Genesis 2). Consequently, we bear the unique distinction of being image bearers of the God who exists in relationship.

God is undeniably relational. He forms creatures that are relational and remains in relationship with them. In Genesis 1, we discover that God *walked* in the Garden of Eden *with* humanity. In Genesis 2 and 3 we encounter God *conversing* with them. Even beyond the environment of the Garden, God's interest in relating to his entire creation, including human beings, continues. On at least three occasions, one human being, Abraham, is described as a 'friend' to the great, almighty, ever-present, all-powerful, all-knowing God (2 Chronicles 20:7; Isaiah 41:8 James 2:23). Interestingly, this designation does not emerge from

Abraham's self-assessment but seems to be a direct consequence of God's own evaluation of their relationship. On another occasion, Moses is described as engaging with God face to face. This experience was apparently so intense that it left a lasting impression that literally radiated from Moses' countenance (Exodus 34:29). Eventually, he had to cover his face simply because the impact of his friendship with God was too much for others to bear (Exodus 34:30–35).

However, it is not enough to claim that human beings are created exclusively for a relationship with God. Social scientists call attention to the very human desire to belong, recognising the negative effects on those who lead an entirely solitary existence. Genesis 2 makes it very clear that we are also intentionally created to enjoy relationships with one another and with the rest of creation.

In the very early years of human development we quickly discover the need to share our lives with others. Social indicators also suggest that men and women thrive on and are most effective within the context of healthy relationships. However, most of us are unaware of the power of our relationships and we very easily take them for granted. Yet, in some fundamental way, healthy relational attachments contribute to our emotional, spiritual, mental and even physical health and stability. In short, relationships represent the substance and fibre of our lives and are a significant source of our self-esteem, affection and encouragement.

> Most of us are unaware of the power of our relationships

The Christian world-view recognises that we only truly come to understand ourselves in relationship with God and one another. In other words, healthy relationships should ideally include a spiritual and human component together with a proper respect for our natural environment.

Throughout the course of our lives we relate to many different people and play a wide variety of roles in these interactions. These range from family member, work colleague, teacher, mentor, student and church member. Some of these roles are prescribed, reflecting our need to be workers, our lack of choice regarding who our parents are or who our children will be. However, other relationships are optional, such as marriage (for some) or friendship and these inject a dimension of affinity, mutual support and shared aims into our lives that enrich them still further.

Whereas today's youth engage in multiple virtual relationships, earlier generations emphasised relationship with one particular group (such as family) over others. Today, men and women intentionally forge a wide range of meaningful relationships and subsequently, potential friendships in their lives. These attempts are important because positive relationships affirm and validate us in intangible, yet highly effective ways. They are capable of enhancing our enjoyment of study, work, parenting and even old age.

Therefore, relationships that develop into friendships characterised by commitment, self-disclosure, trust, honesty and commonality are universally desired and even pursued. Such relationships become a source of intimacy and an important space where we can be known and come to know others.

For many years I was unaware of how blessed I was to have a significant number of close friendships, among them, members of my own family. Some of these individuals I met in the course of my work and ministry, others I met while on holiday in one location or another, still others are friends of friends. Some are Christian believers, others are not. I used to assume that my experience was fairly typical but have since been informed otherwise. However, I am also aware that a few past friendships turned into 'train wrecks'. I have come to realise that great relationships are built on a basis of vulnerability, openness and the very real possibility of betrayal and disappointment. I have seen both during my lifetime and I am grateful to God for a journey that has taught me the value of being open enough to risk being hurt, by doing so I have been rewarded with great joy in my personal relationships.

Our relationships with God, family, friends and colleagues are precisely what make our lives potentially fulfilling and therefore worth living. However, we often relate to each group according to a prescribed set of values and expectations that sometimes prove to be highly dysfunctional. Therefore, as I've already noted, relationships can also be the source of our greatest pain, disappointment, discouragement, fear and loss. As such, they have remarkable power to leave us feeling lost, desperate and heartbroken. Unfortunately, such relationship challenges are a fact of life which we all must face, whether we are at work with our colleagues, at home with our families, out with our friends, in our communities with our neighbours, or at church with our Christian brothers and sisters. In fact, relationships can become so fraught that a Christian might be forgiven for expecting an eternity with some of their 'brothers and sisters' to resemble an extended sentence rather than an eternal celebration! By contrast, when we make a success of our relationships, we experience a level of satisfaction and well-being that leads to true happiness. Similarly, such 'successful' and constructive relationships potentially provide the basis for effective leadership. This is certainly evident in the lives of many successful Biblical leaders.

> 'Successful' and constructive relationships provide the basis for effective leadership

Relational paradigms in Biblical leadership

Relationally speaking, great Bible leaders were invariably well connected. Leaders such as Moses developed close and productive relationships with family members, including his father-in-law, Jethro; his peer leaders,

Aaron and Hur and even his mentee and successor, Joshua. The positive influence of these relationships enabled Moses to impact powerfully the ancient world and assure the emergence of ancient Israel as a nation.

David, who bears the distinction of serving as ancient Israel's greatest king, did not initially receive support for his leadership from his family but from unexpected sources such as his close friend Jonathan, the son of King Saul. It appears that David's father never truly considered him leadership or military material. In addition, his brothers disregarded him and expressed irritation at his concern for Israel's army, when facing Goliath and the Philistines in battle (1 Samuel 17). Yet David later inspired tremendous loyalty and support from others, including, eventually, his own family. Perhaps most famously, he received unstinting support from Jonathan and Michal, the son and daughter of King Saul. He later married Michal.

David eventually succeeded Saul as King but not before Saul had jealously conspired to take David's life on more than one occasion.

David also engendered devotion and legendary greatness from a group of dispossessed malcontents while on the run from Saul and during one of the lowest and most depressing periods of his life (1 Samuel 22).

David's relational support did not emerge from the authority figures in his life but from his peers and those who came to rely on him for inspiration, leadership and encouragement.

Both Deborah and Esther, two of the most compelling women leaders of the Old Testament, understood the value of leveraging their relationships in order to maximise their leadership impact. Both were adept at deploying people according to their strengths and also inspiring whole people-groups to support their God-given visions.

Unfortunately, solitary Old Testament figures, like Samson, were usually walking disasters and were sometimes betrayed by the very people they were trying to help!

In the New Testament, we witness how the Apostle Paul developed an extensive network of friends and co-workers among the people he had brought to faith and the churches he had planted in both Asia Minor and Europe. Even today, we read about Paul's exploits and the kinds of leadership challenges he faced with the men and women he worked alongside. These include John Mark, whom he struggled to 'take seriously', and his co-workers Euodia and Syntyche, whom he encouraged to sort out their differences! Others also supported and enabled Paul to extend his ministry further afield. These include Luke, the doctor, who recorded many of Paul's experiences in the book of Acts, and Barnabus who gave Paul his first real opportunity to preach and who also introduced him to the other apostles. Initially, the apostles received the news of Saul's (Paul's Jewish name) conversion, from persecutor to evangelist, with understandable scepticism. Barnabus changed all that and he made it possible for Saul to be accepted by those he would come to work alongside. Silas, also a co-worker, worked alongside Paul in the early days of his ministry as did Priscilla, Aquilla, Apollos and Junia, his fellow evangelists, teachers and apostles. We are also reminded of Timothy, whom Paul raised as a 'son' in the faith and who was encouraged to embrace the demands and challenges of leadership. Every single one of these remarkable leaders were characterised by a supportive network of relationships that made it possible for them to progress in their respective ministries and to change the world through their leadership.

Jesus had a rich diversity of relationships, not just with God his Father, the Holy Spirit, the crowds and his followers but also with his close disciples. These included the 72 he sent on a training mission in Luke 10; the 12 apostles whom he personally selected and the three Peter, James and John, whom he often took with him into sensitive situations. Finally, there is also the one commonly referred to as, 'the disciple whom Jesus loved' (John 13:23). Jesus also spent time relaxing with his good friends Mary, Martha and Lazarus. Even these relationships provide valuable object lessons for us.

Jesus' ministry was particularly effective *because* of these many relationships and not *in spite* of them. Indeed, the repercussions of the missionary activity of the 12 apostles alone are felt by us even today. Therefore, we should celebrate the fact that Jesus took time to relate with these individuals and that he understood how to deploy and release their unique capabilities.

Jesus also cultivated good family relationships. His relationship with his mother, Mary, is legendary and is closely followed by his relationship with his cousin, John the Baptist. However, these relationships were never permitted to stand in the way of Jesus' higher call. They had *a* very significant place in his heart but not *the* most important place. This was reserved for God alone. Subsequently, Jesus was able to challenge, rebuke, set aside, delay, wait for and even dispense with relationships that interfered with his ultimate purpose. Instead, he chose to obey the Father at all costs and bring salvation to the world through the cross.

Throughout the Bible, we encounter the awesome power of rightly-ordered relationships (i.e. those where God comes first) and the equally destructive power of dysfunctional or wrongly prioritised relationships in the life of a leader.

Leadership is inevitably relational. Indeed, the best leaders are intentionally relational. However, leadership can only be defined as effective when we are prepared to balance the expectations of friendship with the very real constraints of leadership. In other words, good leadership may well be relational but not every relationship makes for good leadership!

Leadership *is* a Multifaceted Relationship

Danielle and Surinder worked well together. People often commented on their remarkable ability to complement one another. However, most people were unaware of the high price they had paid in order to achieve this level of synergy. Not only had they grown to understand and like each other as friends, they had also fought (sometimes with each other!) to get their work 'just right'. They avoided pretence and spoke the truth to each other even when it felt a bit painful. They had also learned to recognise and promote one another's gifts, often deferring to each other in their unique areas of expertise. This was all very evident in their work! Consequently, the standard and quality of their individual and joint projects was noticeably and consistently high…

Great leaders do more than simply inspire, articulate and direct others. Our task is to relate to all parties who have a vested interest, for better or worse, in the 'successful' exercise of our leadership. Therefore, effective leaders must be deliberately and confidently relational. In other words, they must establish their leadership on a strong relational foundation. An approach to leadership that makes relationships the focal point of the leadership process is a departure from many traditional leadership paradigms. Although the best relationships are characterised by trust, loyalty, mutual respect and dependability, these factors are not always evident in leaders. Like any relationship, leadership can be good or bad. It does not merely encompass the benefits but also the potential hazards of relating. Relationships can go well but when trust, loyalty, respect and dependability are undermined, they can prove to be disastrous.

To exercise our leadership effectively we must be aware of who we are to relate to (i.e. the specific individuals involved and not just the organisation or structure) and how we are to engage with them.

Having already established that all relationships must include a spiritual dimension and human interaction, in leadership the most significant relationships are those with God, colleagues and stakeholders. The importance of these relationships is outlined as follows:

Having trust in God

We are not always at liberty to control the conditions attached to our leadership or able to determine who we work alongside. We may either love or dislike what we do. We may commit ourselves wholeheartedly for as little as a few weeks or half-heartedly for what feels like a lifetime! Regardless of our circumstances each leader must recognise that God entrusts us with the 'gifts' of our work, workplace and ministry. Therefore, it makes sense to involve God in both our work and leadership.

Our primary challenge when relating to God, is to trust him, not simply for our concrete and material needs but also for the more intangible and necessary resources of wisdom, insight, direction and strength. In addition, relating to God requires us to ground ourselves in God's Word and in prayer. As we do so, we can reasonably expect to become less vulnerable to bad advice and poor choices. When God fills our vision as leaders, we are able to maintain a clearer perspective, particularly during difficult and trying times. As we increasingly trust God, we come to understand that our problems are a necessary and valuable means of experiencing personal growth and not merely an exercise in clenching our teeth!

However, our relationship with God is also genuinely two-way. In other words, although we are required to trust God, by the same token, God has also undertaken to trust *us*. For example, God trusts us to develop *and* exercise our leadership capabilities, primarily to maximise our contribution to his purposes. Our relationship with God serves as a constant reminder that leadership can never be simply reduced to the demand of the so-called 'bottom line' (i.e. financial reward). Indeed, if we consciously determine to express godly principles and practices through our leadership, we have the potential to change the world (or at least our part of it!).

Taking responsibility with colleagues and peers

Our responsibility towards our colleagues and peers is expressed through a commitment to perform well in our work, while allowing others to do the same. As leaders we are expected to align ourselves to the values and goals of our organisation and to those in senior roles. We must also encourage junior colleagues and peers to follow suit.

We must be prepared to recognise and honour the humanity of our colleagues, as far as it depends upon us. This may be expressed in a number of ways, from enquiring after the well-being of family members to encouraging co-workers to keep reasonable hours. We may even decide to share more of our lives by engaging in social activities beyond our immediate 'work' environment. This may seem somewhat unusual behaviour within certain contexts but it has identifiable and proven benefits. Dr Jan Yager acknowledges, 'Success in many careers is based on relationship building, and nothing builds a trusting relationship faster than the elusive and magical relationship known as friendship.'[2] Wherever this sharing of life is evident, a group's sense of purpose can be significantly elevated. Reggie McNeal describes this dynamic within the context of ministry in the following terms, 'The leader's decision to share his life with his team does not mean that the leader will be everyone's best friend. This is not only impossible; it is undesirable. But the best teams are those who feel a sense of bonding, of sharing life around a shared mission. These teams will charge hell with a water pistol.'[3]

The reality is that people love to follow leaders who care for them. Therefore, workplace relationships that reflect some of the characteristics of friendship often raise the effectiveness of our workplace activities, 'When workplace friendships are positive, it can make the workplace and the work better. Workplace friendships make work more fun; they enhance creativity.'[4] Therefore, when we are able to appreciate the value of engaging with our colleagues, juniors or seniors we may choose to take our workplace relationships a little more seriously.

Being accountable to stakeholders

Essentially, stakeholders present us with a constant reminder that leadership is not an entitlement but is granted through the trust of others. Stakeholders are those for whom we provide a service. This group may include customers, suppliers, clients, church members or service users. Regardless of who they are, we are accountable to them in at least two ways. Firstly, we rely on them because they make it possible for us to do what we (hopefully) love doing. Secondly, they rely on us to invest ourselves wholeheartedly in order to serve them well!

> Models of leadership that overlook relational concerns are impoverished

In Summary

We have established that leadership does not simply include relational components; it is quite literally, a relationship. However, this relationship must be intentionally cultivated, primarily, with regard to God, colleagues, peers and stakeholders. This is undertaken to achieve the best possible results in our working practices. Models of leadership that overlook relational concerns are predictably and inevitably two-dimensional or otherwise impoverished.

Relationships in general and friendships in particular, have been a major preoccupation for women for millennia! Potentially, women should excel in this leadership terrain.

Women and Relational Leadership

Jessica had been doing extremely well at her work for many months now, or was it years? She had lost count of how long she had been employed at one of the country's most prestigious firms. It came as a major surprise to her when her boss recommended her for promotion, making her the youngest director ever. She had also been commended for her leadership style and team development skills. Senior staff had even been asked to observe her approach and to apply its strengths to their own teams. To say that she was thrilled was an understatement, especially since she had felt she wasn't being taken seriously in the past. However, transforming two failing departments into the most productive for three consecutive terms, obviously spoke for itself! She now needed to give some thought to what she had actually been doing right. She was already aware that relationship building was key. She determined to take some reflection time and journal her thoughts...

In the 21st century, relationships are at the forefront of definitions of good leadership. Women, who have always been more attentive to relational matters are, at least theoretically, ideally suited to the current leadership climate. As noted in the chapter entitled, 'Limiting Self-Perceptions', David Gergen's reminder seems particularly pertinent, 'When we describe the new leadership, we employ terms like consensual, relational, web-based, caring, inclusive, open, transparent – all qualities that we associate with the "feminine" style of leadership.'[5]

Men have traditionally and culturally emphasised a need for independence and have historically favoured command and control leadership. Organisations that are very masculine in expression continue to reflect this behaviour. Men often communicate directness and focus on information and competitiveness in their leadership, i.e. 'who is better than...?' However, when these qualities are over-represented in a man's leadership (or indeed a woman's!) they may unintentionally communicate aloofness, a lack of openness, consideration or warmth and an unwillingness to listen closely to others.

On the other hand, women tend to communicate the values of inclusiveness, acceptance, nurture, collaboration and 'friendliness' in their leadership. Subsequently, they prove to be very successful at meeting the need for affirmation in co-workers. This is often because competition is not such an attractive option for them (unless senior roles for women are scarce). This leaves them more available to recognise and promote the accomplishments of others. In addition, women are thought to value the humanity of those around them in ways that lead them to address individual needs, even before the needs of the organisation. Behavioural preferences also mean that women tend toward leadership styles that depend less on command and control and more upon gaining the allegiance and loyalty of others.

The ability of women to establish solidarity (an essential ingredient of leadership), occurs largely through conversation and frequently emerges from the exchange of personal information. Therefore, women regularly use 'talk' as a means of developing intimacy with others and will often tell and retell stories in an attempt to foster relationships. Problems arise when such 'talk' turns into unhealthy complaint or criticism of others. Under these circumstances, women may often disclose more about themselves or others, than is actually conducive to good working relationships. 'Talk' may prove to be entirely counterproductive!

However, it is undeniable that the ability to converse deeply is precisely what enables women to forge and maintain close relationships. Women, it seems, learn primarily through discussion rather than through taking action. Therefore, feminine organisational cultures are highly collaborative and often include a variety of different types of meetings conducted in open, informal and 'friendly' atmospheres.

Liz Cook and Brian Rothwell write, 'The female communicative brain area is larger and more active than its male equivalent. In the region of the cortex related to verbal fluency and short-term memory, the female brain has a 23% greater concentration of cells... [unlike men]. She has listening connections on both sides of the brain and these areas show a 13% greater concentration of cells than a male.'[6] They add that research conducted by British Telecom demonstrates that on average, men spend only three to five minutes on personal calls, whereas, women spend an average of twenty to twenty-five minutes in conversation.

Understanding these differences has been very important for me as a woman in leadership and has enabled me to avoid misconstruing conversations involving male colleagues. Some male leaders I have worked with have been extremely monosyllabic, appear to want to end important conversations 'prematurely' and sometimes have come across as abrupt. It has taken me some time to realise that such behaviour does not necessarily constitute rudeness (although it might suggest a lack of self-awareness) and that my need to 'complete' the conversation may not be a priority for others. I have learned to curtail my natural tendencies under certain circumstances, I forego telling the *whole* story (which I love to do!), get straight to the point and stick to it without digressing too far. At times I have felt as if I am speaking the English language in a whole new dialect. This sometimes proves to be a necessity if we are to be heard by those who take a different approach to communication. I have learned to engage in multiple ways without completely abandoning the style of communication that is most important to me.

Ultimately, women use talking, listening and discussion as a means of engaging others in key activities. They are therefore more likely to consult with others, collaborate and emphasise relationship building, *as well as* fact gathering in their leadership. Consequently, women are typically stereotyped as 'friendly'. Quite literally, people expect women to be 'nice', gentle, less aggressive and less aloof than men.

When women fail to meet these narrow social expectations for 'friendliness', they attract both personal and societal disapproval, thereby exposing the double standard imposed on male and female leaders. Women leaders having to take a hard line, engage in disciplinary action, or challenge a work colleague or church member may encounter this particular dynamic. However, when the fear of such disapproval is combined with a willingness to sacrifice all to preserve relationships, women effectively destabilise their own leadership.

The preoccupation to conform to socially imposed expectations may push female leaders to take inappropriate measures in an effort to maintain relationships. Sometimes this fixation is characterised by a need to be liked and may result in women over-engaging in relationships that ultimately prove detrimental. It is also evident in some attempts at emotional withdrawal characterised by a disregard for the opinion or feelings of others. Either way, the pursuit of idealised relationships can arrest our leadership development and lead to self-absorption, self-defeat and ultimately self-destruction. 'We all have mechanisms that keep us where we are. For men it's about process and linearity. For women it's about not wanting to "rock" relationships, of being unloved if we change something and someone doesn't like it.'[7] Whereas men may use competition to reveal where they stand in relation to each other, women often use relationships and approval. Men, it seems, do not invest the same degree of emotional energy in many of their relationships; this makes this particular temptation a significant dilemma for women.

The 'Disease to Please'

Sharon and Tracy had worked extremely well together for many years. Both were surprised when Sharon was promoted, effectively leaving Tracy under her supervision. Sharon didn't notice the initial subtle changes to the relationship, she was just so pleased about the promotion and the opportunity to try out her ideas. So it took her a while to recognise the signs of aloofness and the slightly cutting comments Tracy made to any of Sharon's suggestions. These days it felt as if Tracy was actively avoiding her, spending as little time as possible in her company. In addition, Tracy always seemed to be in conversation with others when she should be working. It was beginning to affect the entire team who were also becoming increasingly uncooperative. Sharon knew she would have to do something soon or risk an all-out revolt, but Tracy was her friend, they had been through a lot together and she felt awkward about pulling rank at a time when Tracy probably needed her friendship more than ever…

A desire for friendship is good, most of the time! However, when our need for friendship exceeds what a human relationship is designed to deliver, *then* we are in trouble. Men *and* women search for levels of intimacy and security in different ways. However, many still expect someone they know, such as a spouse, family/church member, friend and possibly even a work colleague to deliver levels of affirmation, security and recognition that only God can provide! Conflict inevitably arises whenever relational wires are crossed with leadership wires. This leaves women, who may have made substantial relational investments, particularly susceptible to the downsides of relational leadership. Commenting on women's predilection for building effective relationships, Lois Frankel writes, 'The problem is, we're *so* good at it that we often confuse our leadership responsibilities with a desire to maintain those relationships at all costs.'[8]

It is somewhat ironic that, when taken to an extreme, the very gifts that women bring to leadership become the very characteristics that undermine them. In a desire to be likeable and 'friendly' we can become overly concerned with the need to please others. This condition is more popularly referred to as the 'disease to please'.

When friendship goes awry

Wanting to please other people is both natural and normal. However, the real issue is just how far we are willing to take it. When the need for approval becomes an imperative, it can no longer be equated with a seemingly harmless desire to appear 'friendly' or 'nice'. The habit of putting others first and the compulsive need to please, even at the expense of our own health, can rapidly spiral into a serious psychological syndrome with far reaching physical and emotional consequences. Yet, some women are predisposed to this condition and it lies at the root of many of our stress-related problems.

At first glance, people-pleasing does not appear to be a 'problem'. In fact, many wear it as a badge of honour or even take their ability to please as many as possible, as a compliment. Even the Bible seems to commend the aspiration to please others (see Romans 15:2–3; 1 Corinthians 10:33). However, while it is certainly true that pleasing others and meeting their needs is always highly commended, it is always clearly distinguished from the self-defeating thinking and behavioural habit of striving to be liked by everyone (Galatians 1:10). It is this behaviour that so often betrays the presence of a 'disease to please'.

Almost all of us enjoy gaining the approval of people who are important in our lives. For people pleasers, earning the approval of others and avoiding their disapproval become primary driving forces. Once approval becomes overly important, it places an individual in bondage to the fear of rejection or confrontation.

When people-pleasing has become a compulsive, addictive pattern of behaviour, we begin to respond to the need for approval by accommodating even the most unreasonable expectations. Just because we understand why someone made a mistake, doesn't mean we have to tolerate them making the same mistake over and over again! Attempts to accommodate others, at almost any expense, take on many forms but they are particularly dangerous to those serving in leadership capacities. Not only can we be easily manipulated by opportunistic individuals, we may attempt to prove just how essential we are to others by taking care of every presenting need. Such behaviour when mature, develops into forms of benevolent manipulation, where we foster dependency in others in order to avoid our own feelings of rejection. Similarly, in the name of caring for others, women leaders may also be hesitant to leverage their relationships, believing that they are somehow taking advantage of people when they delegate or ask for 'favours'.

> The 'disease to please' results in leaders who are predisposed to overwork or over-responsibility

The 'disease to please' results in leaders who are predisposed to overwork or over-responsibility and who subsequently spread their already finite resources too thinly. What's more, leaders may also respond to the impulse to please, by over consulting and over collaborating. In doing so, we may effectively undermine our leadership. For example, instead of communicating inclusiveness and acceptance, leaders who are always consulting as many people as possible, can inadvertently communicate indecision and abdication of responsibility. Similarly, an overemphasis on collaboration can communicate an aversion to taking even calculated risks, a very necessary feature of effective leadership.

Women in leadership may even unconsciously undermine their own professionalism by allowing or encouraging an unhealthy over-familiarity from others. This can also result in our being taken for granted. In addition, we may avoid the use of titles or credentials, even in formal settings for fear of emphasising our accomplishments in ways that suggest superiority or inaccessibility. Indeed, high achieving female people pleasers often live with the fear that their accomplishments will backfire when it comes to relationships with others, especially with men. Fear of our own success may lead us to unconsciously sabotage our own careers or personal relationships in an effort to avoid rejection from people who have come to mean a great deal to us. However, such attempts at 'friendliness' in leadership can so easily backfire and communicate our likeability rather than our capability.

One female leader I know confessed that she feared the kind of backlash associated with 'success' and it had deterred her from embracing a more senior role. She was painfully aware that others would cheer her on as long as she was the perpetual 'underdog'. She had seen other women 'elevated' to greater visibility and responsibility only to become targets for those intent on pulling them down 'a peg or two'. I reminded her that her primary responsibility was to God's call on her life and to the exercise of the many great gifts and abilities He had invested in her. Leadership carries a cost, but if we are wise this kind of rejection will not become part of it. The people who matter should never be those who are fickle enough to want to build you up one moment *and* tear you down the next.

Ironically, people pleasing can intensify our fear, cripple our communication and impair our people-skills, particularly as the concern with how other people view us begins to take control. We may be led to assume that people are saying or thinking critical things about us. The truth is they may not be thinking about us at all; on the contrary, they are far more likely to be thinking about themselves! Ultimately, we lose confidence and abandon the path of healthy choices when we become preoccupied with seeking favour and acceptance, particularly from our critics.

Unsurprisingly, people pleasers soon discover that constantly trying to please others is draining, which is why many of us feel anxious, worried, unhappy and tired much of the time. We also tend to feel out of control given the seemingly endless pressures and demands being placed on our lives.

● How it all begins

Many women learn their people-pleasing behaviour in early childhood at a time when girls, in particular, are actively encouraged to be pleasing to others. Girls who rebel against these expectations tend to pay a higher price than boys under similar circumstances. People pleasing can 'spread like a virus' throughout our teenage years, a period when girls are particularly susceptible to the pressure to fit in, conform, or to simply become one of the crowd. However, the initial instinct to please is not necessarily unhealthy. We often express it as a way of gaining the approval of significant adult authority figures in our lives, such as a mother or father. This is because approval from significant others is a powerful source of reward for nearly every human being. Harriet Braiker re-emphasises this fundamental concern, 'From infancy on, our behaviour is highly influenced and shaped by the approval we receive. Our biological and genetic wiring along with our deepest social programming propels us to seek the praise and approval of other people – especially those whom we deem most important by virtue of the rewards they control (e.g., love, social status, school grades, salaries, etc.).'[9] However, a preoccupation with this desire proves to be disastrous particularly if we grow to believe that being pleasing or 'nice' will protect us from unpleasant situations with friends, family and/or colleagues. We may also end up seeking to deploy people pleasing as a kind of psychological armour, designed to protect us from negative emotional experiences with others.

As we exercise both authority and influence, leaders seldom, if ever, make decisions that are likely to please everyone, all the time. The willingness to shoulder this aspect of our leadership responsibility is what, in part, ensures our success. People pleasers addicted to approval and eager to maintain relationships at almost any cost inevitably make poor leaders.

Leaders who commit themselves to the task of overcoming such relational derailments, are those who embrace the necessary constraints that enable them to exercise their leadership responsibly and effectively. A number of these constraints are outlined in the following section.

Leadership Imperatives

Elaine felt a momentary pang of anxiety but thankfully was able to maintain her sense of clarity regarding her earlier decision. As harsh as it seemed, she knew that she would have to serve Lesley her statutory notice period and that she would have to do it soon. It hadn't been an easy decision and Elaine was fully aware of its wider implications. Lesley had two young children and her husband had just started a new job in another part of the country, so this would hit them hard. It had become clear that Lesley had neither the skill nor knowledge to advance further in Elaine's department. However, Lesley had also been unwilling to accept this fact. She had threatened the loss of their personal friendship if Elaine persisted in moving her sideways to another department, 'more suited to Lesley's skills'. The situation had suddenly become critical and Lesley was proving to be a liability. Not only was her work substandard, she had recently attempted to sabotage a major project in protest, and appeared unconcerned at having almost lost a major funding stream. Neither their numerous discussions, nor the referral to a counsellor seemed to have improved the situation…

Establish solidarity

The first thing that every leader must learn to do is to engender a team spirit with their colleagues.

Work or ministry relationships tend to be easier to maintain when they are established between equals. When inequality is introduced into the relational status, so are the potential complications, even when the relationship is regulated by a formal mentoring structure. However, if sufficient openness and willingness exists, such relational challenges are surmountable.

Leaders who are committed to establishing solidarity, create warm working environments. It has already been well documented that people work well in an environment of cooperation and goodwill rather than one of fear and coercion. People work harder when they feel they are part of a family. Consequently, leaders who are aloof and distant tend to create cold work places because their own emotional distance sets the tone for everyone else. The opposite is true for relational leaders. Therefore, the ability to build bridges and cross them is crucially important for effective leadership. We tend to trust people who are honest with us, who are willing to tell us what we may not want to hear and who we are confident have our best interests at heart. Leaders who take time to build relationships, also tend to have greater latitude to say tough things and occasionally even ask for the impossible.

It has already been acknowledged that solidarity is established through being supportive, loyal and showing genuine concern for our colleagues. Such cohesion is only possible when we take the time to build strong relationships with those on whom we depend. However, this bid for friendliness must also be tempered. Great leaders are not primarily guided by a need or desire for solidarity.

- **Things to watch out for**
  In our efforts to be 'friendly', we must refrain from attempts to become all things to all people. We should also resist the temptation to have all our emotional needs met within an environment (e.g. work) where meeting such needs are not the priority. Women who expect 'confessional' style sharing, as normative in their relationships, are particularly prone to disappointment. Leaders have to remember that

followers do not have the same responsibility to support, be loyal to, or show genuine concern for us. Such behaviour on their part is merely a by-product of successfully building trusting relationships, and the primary responsibility for this belongs to the leader.

Every leader should keep in view the task they have been appointed to accomplish. We must remain sufficiently focused to pursue our goals while also encouraging others to do the same. In other words, 'I have a work to do and you have a work to do, and I will do my work and I expect you to do your work.' Jesus who had the highest regard for relationships did not allow himself to be sidetracked by them.

One way of safeguarding against setting ourselves the impossible task of becoming everyone's best friend within our work or ministry environment, is to develop good relationships both *within* and *beyond* our work and ministry circles.

Assess needs and make clear-headed decisions

The leadership task involves an ability to make clear-headed and God-honouring decisions, emerging from our commitment to regular reflection and assessment. Whereas two-thirds of men are less concerned with whether others perceive them as unfriendly and antisocial, two-thirds of women will make their decisions by considering the feelings of others. Furthermore, they will actually put themselves into the shoes of others and will take the time to elicit others' points of view. This approach to leadership has much to commend itself and can result in remarkable levels of clarity and focus for the leader. However, whenever a leader uses collaboration as an excuse to bury their head in the sand and abdicate the task of decision making in the hope that 'problems' will somehow 'go away', leadership is compromised.

We sometimes concede important issues on the basis of our 'friendships' with others. Our ability to 'understand' their personal circumstances can hinder us from making the tough and difficult decisions necessary to progress our tasks, projects or vision.

In order to assess current needs and make clear-headed decisions regarding the future, we must remember a key leadership principle:

- **This is *not* about me**

  In other words, the decision-making process will always involve a bigger picture beyond our own personal need, concern or agenda. At the very least, this view will include our responsibility to honour God and our responsibility to a personal or corporate vision and therefore a desired future. There will also be specific tasks to fulfil or other projects to complete, colleagues to consider, or even a team to build.

  As long as we focus on how particular decisions make *us* 'feel', we limit our usefulness as leaders. In an effort to minimise unhealthy emotional attachment during decision-making moments, the following essential questions will enable us to maintain a necessary degree of critical distance:

  - **What is truly motivating my decision making?**
  - **Why am I 'putting off' the inevitable?**
  - **What is the 'worst' thing that could happen?**
  - **What is the 'best' thing that could happen?**
  - **What are the desired outcomes of this process?**
  - **Am I willing to experience short-term pain, in order to secure long-term results?**
  - **Where is God in the process?**

  Such questions help us to maintain our focus on doing the 'right thing' in any given situation, rather than simply succumbing to the path of least resistance.

Envision what could or should be, and pursue it

Lois Frankel writes, 'The essence of good leadership is the ability to take people to places they need to go, not necessarily where they want to go.'[10] In order to envision and pursue what could or should be, we must be prepared to accept, ironically perhaps in view of the previous point that this is about me.

● **This is about me**

Leaders are often responsible for initiating processes and pursuing vision. Sometimes we must be prepared to do this in a context of specific resistance or against a tidal flow of 'public opinion'. Biblical leaders, Jesus included, inevitably experienced this leadership dynamic as they sought to pursue God's ultimate purposes. Machiavelli (of all people!) noted, 'You will always get resistance from those who may be better off under the old and only lukewarm acceptance from those who may be better off under the new.'[11]

Women sometimes fail to express their expectations clearly or to hold people accountable for the achievement of agreed goals. The reasons for this are often located in a fear of irreparably damaging relationships. However, leaders are ultimately responsible to ensure that goals are achieved. Therefore, we must ask ourselves what we are personally prepared to sacrifice in pursuit of a God-given vision.

When a junior colleague fails to achieve goals, make progress or meet performance expectations, before we challenge *their* shortcomings, we must ask ourselves whether *we* failed to communicate clearly or to check our assumptions as well as their understanding.

The following questions may assist us as we seek to envision and pursue:

- Have I prayed and assessed the current needs?
- Do I know which step I need to take?
- Have I established sufficient solidarity in order to move things forward?
- Have I taken risks that are calculated without being reckless?
- Am I having the tough but necessary conversations with key individuals and groups that will move things forward?

Produce effective results

The task of a leader includes the ability to encourage others to adopt new behaviours that may benefit them, the organisation and other interested parties (colleagues, stakeholders etc).

In order to produce results that represent change and necessary progress, every leader must be prepared to:

- **Take risks**

  In Matthew 14:28 Peter walked on water only after he'd made the following request of Jesus, 'Lord if it's you … tell me to come to you on the water?'

  Women typically like to consider all options before making decisions and they generally want to minimise risk factors before committing themselves to change. As important as this activity may prove to be, taken to an extreme, it becomes procrastination. Such inaction may prolong a process beyond the point of usefulness. Evaluating the wind velocity, position of the boat on the lake, our distance from land, the strength of the storm and the decisions of peers present in the boat with us, may all seem very useful at the time. However, at some point we still need to get out of the boat and step onto the water!

  Interestingly, it was precisely when Peter became preoccupied with the wind and the waves that he started to sink. Women's attention to

> Not every issue needs to be the one we are willing to die for

detailed research and consultation before taking action can backfire when overindulged, unintentionally communicating that they are risk-averse.

However, not every risk is created equal or is as valid as the next one and not every issue needs to be the one we are willing to die for. In other words, we should be very careful about where we choose to make our investments, particularly those that are potentially costly. Taking calculated risks that require us to move beyond our self-imposed comfort zones, enable us to capitalise on our strengths as women committed to sound research, whilst providing us with the necessary impetus for action.

By definition leaders create change and change is risky! If we limit ourselves to the question, 'What's the worst thing that could happen?' we may arrest our development. However, if we are bold enough to ask ourselves 'What will happen if we don't take the risk?' we may free ourselves, and potentially enjoy an amazing stroll on water in the process!

● **Communicate, communicate, communicate…**

One dictionary definition of communication is that it is an 'impartation', in other words, it is a means of 'transmitting a part of oneself in another person'.

Every relationship we have is regulated by communication. When it works well, it becomes the most liberating, energising and productive experience a person can have. However, our verbal and nonverbal messages are often fraught with misconstruction and misinterpretation!

Everyone has a particular communication style that works well for them. Unfortunately, it doesn't always work for us! This can make even straightforward conversations challenging, while our difficult conversations seem almost impossible. We cannot assume that just because we know what we're talking about that someone else will understand us. Neither can we conclude that just because we have the right intentions, others will be able to read our motives.

Women are very good at reading the message within the message. We read body language and pick up subtle changes in moods, even reading 'between the lines'. We are more intuitive and often more discerning than men because we tune into non-verbal messages. However, we are also more likely to misread neutral cues and to interpret them as negative or critical. Good communication is fundamental to good leadership for both men and women. Each must work at discerning the style of others in order to communicate effectively with them and each must consider *what* they are going to say, as well as *how* they are going to say it! However, the ability to read people proves particularly advantageous in circumstances where information needs packaging in a way that works for someone else.

In addition, women tend to be better listeners; firstly because they listen with both sides of their brain! This means they are usually able to listen to more than one conversation at a time! Communication expert, Deborah Tannen explains that women tend to make more listening noises than men and that these noises generally mean, 'I have understood what you are saying, please go on'. She asserts that when men make listening noises, not only are they less frequent, they also signal agreement, as in, 'yes, I agree with what you are saying'. She claims that women commonly conclude something is wrong in a relationship if it is not under regular discussion, unlike men who think there is something wrong when a relationship is under discussion![12] Years of pastoral experience, working with couples in marital difficulty has enabled me to see both the truth and the humour of this irony.

For all our ability to communicate, women's aversion to taking risks with our relationships can interfere with effective interaction, particularly in the arena of leadership. In the process our verbal and non-verbal wires can get well and truly crossed. For example, we can undermine our own efforts simply by smiling or joking when we are dispensing a challenge. Conversely, we may frown when we claim to be happy or look terrified when we are reasonably confident. Tough decisions and tough conversations are an inevitable part of a leader's experience. At some point in our leadership journey, each one of us will be required to have a tough conversation with ourselves and with others.

- **Things to look out for**

The danger for women in leadership is that we are often so aware of the effect that our words may have on others that we concentrate on using them to 'break their fall'. Consequently, there are four traps that women leaders must avoid as they approach the prospect of having a tough conversation:

Put off having the conversation

If we make the mistake of *putting off* a tough conversation, we may end up having it only when we are really angry, in which case we may regret having had it at all!

Have the right conversation but with ourselves in our head!

In this case, we focus on replaying the conversation to ourselves, perfecting its tone and message. We never actually graduate to the task of facing the individual involved. Instead, we visualise the individual while avoiding them in person at all costs, preferring to concentrate on what we 'should' have said or done. We certainly have the conversation; it simply never leaves the realm of fantasy.

Have the right conversation with the wrong parties

This is commonly referred to as 'gossip' and requires no further explanation or excuse.

Have the right conversation with the right party but choose tactfulness over truthfulness!

Leaders who choose this option persistently fail to get to the heart of a matter and are incapable of achieving any semblance of resolution. The gift of leadership is distinguished from every other kind of ability by the simple fact that leaders, even when extremely reluctant, are prepared to make the tough calls and have the tough conversations. Good leaders have the tough conversations but communicate appropriately.

Engage further support if necessary

If you are struggling to break a 'people pleasing' pattern you may find that time spent with a counsellor, mentor, coach or support group is invaluable. The intervention of others who facilitate a reflective process enabling you to 'hear' yourself, others and God, may be exactly what you need in order to break through this destructive cycle of people pleasing.

COACHING TIPS

PRAY
Where am I? (You may as well tell God the 'truth',
He already knows you inside-out.)

JOURNAL
Where am I? (Explore the reality
vs. your perception.)

SHARE
Where am I? (Talk to your support group, counsellor,
coach, mentor and ask for reflections.)

CREATE
Where do I want to be? (Explore this through
different media e.g. collage, paints, artwork.)

ACTIVATE
Where do I want to be? (Explore
further and get 'physical' through
role play. Why not test out different
scenarios and measure your responses
and your progress?)

*'As iron sharpens iron, so one
person sharpens another.'*

PROVERBS 27:17

6TH
DEADLY SIN

COLLUDING AND NOT CONFRONTING

Deal with men (and women!) behaving badly

'Peace I leave with you; my peace I give you. I do not give to you as the world gives.'

JOHN 14:27

The Challenge of Confrontation

Jane was horrified… having invited James to intervene in an effort to resolve the matter, he had effectively undermined both her position and her integrity before all the members of the board. The very thing she had hoped he would do, i.e. confront all parties, including herself, had been side-stepped. Later, when challenged, he admitted his failure to address the key issues but believed that since she had offered an apology for her part, everything else would be fine. Jane had worked closely with the remaining members of the group for some time and she knew that nothing could be further from the truth. Now she was faced with an even greater dilemma…

'Confrontation' is a necessity in a world characterised by conflict. Indeed, a leader's primary task is not to avoid conflict but rather to 'confront' it. This may prove challenging for the leader whose initial instinct is to shun all forms of confrontation. Part of the difficulty lies with the word itself and its associations.

'Confront' is frequently viewed in an extremely negative light. It is also often accompanied by the anticipation of defeat or victory and a preparation to do battle. Therefore, it becomes a stress-filled, anxiety-inducing activity. Despite its negative overtones and its regular association with images of aggression, hostility and discomfort, confrontation has underlying connotations which are far more positive.

The term 'confront' literally means: 'to put face to face; to cause to face or to meet'. In other words, a decision to confront is a decision to 'face up to' a particular person, situation or set of circumstances. This approach to confrontation enables us to deal with even the most unpleasant matters head-on. Therefore, it becomes the only appropriate response to conflict. In the absence of confrontation, disagreement quickly deteriorates into the unholy status of collusion.

> A decision to confront is a decision to 'face up to' a particular person, situation or set of circumstances

In its broadest sense, collusion can be defined as acting in concert with. It is an unholy agreement usually characterised by secrecy or 'behind-the-scenes' activity i.e. conspiring (literally 'breathing together'). Collusion can be unconscious or conscious, premeditated or spontaneous. Situations that are subject to collusion become characterised by negativity, animosity and recrimination.

Without an attempt at confrontation very little can be learned from a situation involving conflict.

Conflict is Inevitable

It was difficult for Li Juan... Had she been a male leader, she would never have been subjected to the same degree of false accusation, lies, opposition and unfair criticism. She had been used as a scapegoat for everything that had gone wrong in the organisation. On a number of occasions Li Juan had attempted to defend herself, to no avail... no one was prepared to listen. Faced with the impossible internal dynamics of the organisation, she recognised that external intervention alone would suffice. Consequently, she invited well-respected male leaders to address the issues and all the relevant parties (she reasoned that this would be the most acceptable solution for all involved). It soon became clear that these leaders lacked the necessary mediation skills. Unfortunately, they only succeeded in making matters considerably worse. Li Juan knew that she was now faced with a difficult decision. Either, she could obsess and become bitter and resentful in the process, or she could entrust the entire miserable scenario into God's hands. This would require her to forgive the wrong inflicted upon her and to summon the courage to move on. She sighed deeply as she considered her options…

Perhaps predictably, human life is full of problems and some of them are people! It is relatively easy to collude in a world where conflict, disagreement and lack of harmony are inevitable facts of life in all human relationships. Many experience conflict, betrayal, personal attack and difficulties with relationships at work, home or in ministry. Depending on our choices, we can become willing or unwilling partners to the problem.

However, conflict is more than a personal or private matter, it is also a communal issue. Increasingly, casualties of war are civilian and the consequences of armed conflict are inclusive, affecting ordinary households as well as trained soldiers. Not only is the human race faced with new and potentially terrifying forms of global terrorism, governments seem virtually incapable of maintaining a world without discord. By all accounts, conflict is globally endemic.

Unresolved conflict frequently wrecks friendships, partnerships, marriages, families, organisations and even churches. However, conflict that is handled successfully can resolve many of the underlying problems that initially brought it to the surface. Surprisingly, conflict can eventually lead to clarity, increased understanding, deeper relationships

> Conflict can lead to clarity, increased understanding, deeper relationships and improved self-awareness

and improved self-awareness.

Regardless of whether conflict is ultimately productive or destructive, it seems both unavoidable and inevitable. Reasons for this are both multiple and varied, simple and complex, as we shall now see...

Circumstances are imperfect

In Christian thought, human beings live in a fallen, imperfect world characterised by brokenness and disorder. In this context nothing is quite as it was intended to be. In other words, our relationship with ourselves, God, the environment and others, have all been adversely affected by our 'fallenness'. Even the most ideal conditions, humanly speaking, are fundamentally flawed.

People are imperfect

It will come as no surprise to most of us that a significant and underlying cause of conflict emerges from the failure of others to measure up to our personal expectations. Interestingly, we are often taken by surprise to discover that we seldom measure up to the expectations of others! Our preoccupation with imperfections inevitably results in disappointment, both theirs and ours! Therefore, we often find ourselves at variance with those we love and who genuinely love us.

Divergence of core values or beliefs

Interpersonal difficulties further arise from actual and perceived differences in the interests or values between individuals and groups. Quite simply, people genuinely and passionately disagree on a whole spectrum of incredibly important issues whether political, social, economic or even theological. Consequently, we must all face the challenge of respectfully disagreeing with others, while holding fast to our personal convictions.

The S-factor

Here 'S' stands for the 'spiritual dimension'. We take for granted many of the visible aspects of our daily lives, such as grass, trees, lakes, animals, people, cities, art and governments. However, behind many visible aspects of the world around us lie the invisible 'spiritual' realities which, frankly, we ignore at our peril. The Apostle Paul alludes to these in 2 Corinthians 4:18, 'So we fix our eyes not on what is seen, but on what is unseen. For what is seen is temporary, but what is unseen is eternal.' Interestingly these 'unseen' realities are attributed great significance by the Apostle.

Our experience of good and particularly evil is unaccounted for by rationalistic, materialistic and secular philosophies and spiritualities. Therefore, we seldom view the world as it really is. Many choose to ignore all but the most cosmic features of the spiritual dimension such as heaven, hell, God and the devil, while others become entranced by idealistic notions of a spiritual realm that is neither good nor evil. For those who have engaged with the spiritual realm, we need no convincing that something evil (as well as good) is out there manifesting itself in the material world.

The 'S' factor is a reminder that discord does not always have its roots in the material and emotional circumstances of the human condition. Not every conflict originates from purely human concerns or divergences, often there are other more malevolent forces at work such as evil spirits. Ephesians 6:12 is a reminder that some conflicts are spiritually derived and therefore energised supernaturally, 'For our struggle is not against flesh and blood, but against the rulers, against the authorities, against the powers of this dark world and against the spiritual forces of evil in the heavenly realms.' Human beings and human activity appear to be the primary targets for such influences and evil spirits seek to exploit the weaknesses in human interactions. Ignorance of the 'S-factor' may ultimately prove to be detrimental to our relational health as well as our spiritual well-being. The Biblical evidence overwhelmingly attests to the fact that the spiritual dimension can seriously complicate existing human interactions!

People are different

Human beings share common experiences regardless of culture, ethnicity, gender, political affiliation, religion, philosophy or theology. Pastor and theologian Emmanuel Lartey frames this principle as follows, 'We are all born helpless, grow from dependence toward relative self-management, we relate to other beings and to a physical environment and ten out of ten die...'[1]

On the other hand, some aspects of our humanity are unique to each one of us. For example, we have different personalities and emerge from distinct historical, cultural and ethnic settings. We experience many different events and relate to unique family circumstances. We may even respond to identical psychological and emotional conditions very differently. Once again Lartey explains, 'Each person has a unique genetic code, voice pattern, fingerprint and dental configuration.'[2]

It is this human diversity (both the physical and ideological) that provides the most potent source of conflict. When such divergence is viewed as an opportunity to learn about others, it can produce positive results. However, when these 'differences' are perceived as a 'clash' of values or interests, they can lead to national and even global conflicts.

Expectations of men and women are different

Human diversity is most evident in the biological and social distinctions between male and female, present in every culture. Such differences have been used to limit and narrow women's self-expression. Consequently, the unique contribution of women is frequently undermined, even if we meet the specific conditions attached to the function of leadership.

Different kinds of women have always worked in a wide variety of informal leadership roles; however, stereotypes have often limited what could be officially designated acceptable 'women's work'. Formal leadership roles have been largely absent from these typecasts. Despite the fact that we live in times of rapid change and witness increasing numbers of women engaging in more formal leadership roles, ideas about leadership are still largely masculine. When people think 'leader', they still tend to think 'male', unless leadership is specifically exercised in acceptably 'feminine' domains, such as education and childcare (including Sunday school). Unfortunately, stereotypical thinking regarding what constitutes acceptable roles for both men and women continue to persist. Therefore, we (society) continue to expect human beings, both male and female, to live up to largely prefabricated cultural and social expectations.

Inevitably, women who do not conform to the prevailing norms and accepted stereotypes are viewed, at best, as exceptions or at worst as 'problems'.

How Women Leaders Can Be Misunderstood

Rachel had been described as 'controlling and aggressive' in her approach to leadership, while Ian had been referred to as 'tough and strong'. Ironically, their leadership styles were remarkably similar. Rachel absentmindedly shrugged her shoulders. She attempted to shake off her growing irritation with the unfair negative associations attached to her leadership, unlike those attributed to 'the guys'. On the bright side, she had been called some unrepeatable names in the past, maybe she should be grateful that things were better than they had been! Naively she had believed herself immune to the constant barrage of patronising and sexist commentary. Rachel now felt quite worn out just thinking about it. Suddenly a smile appeared on her face as she recalled the great results and positive feedback she regularly received from her clients. No one could argue with those. Rachel loved her work but thankfully her job was not 'the be all and end all' of her life. She loved Terry and the children too much for that. However, the demeaning attitude of her organisation towards women in senior positions was eroding her desire to stay. She recalled Terry's persistent suggestion that she should start up on her own. She hadn't given it much thought until now…

Women in leadership are often faced with a series of unique and multiple obstacles. This unfortunate reality results in the routine transfer of unfair emotional baggage into the dynamics of work practices, particularly in relation to women. This 'baggage' frequently has little to do with the actual women themselves. For example, women are often expected to behave in certain prescribed ways and not in others. If they are strong leaders, they may be perceived as 'unfeminine'. If they are perceived as 'feminine' they may be considered 'weak' or unsuitable for leadership. In addition, women frequently pioneer distinctive leadership styles, approaches and paradigms within whichever sector they are part of.

These may initially be unwelcome innovations or viewed as conflicting with already established ways of doing things. Whether women are pioneers in their field or simply 'one of a kind', we are still in the process of defining what women's leadership looks like, how it may differ from men's and what additional benefits it may bring to the leadership table.

In spite of increasing numbers of women in leadership roles, those who engage in 'tough' leadership tactics or disciplinary procedures are still considered 'harsh' and therefore a novelty, strange or exceptional. When a woman takes a 'tough line', double-standards are frequently at play. Women are often expected to be self-sacrificing, helpful, supportive, warm and considerate, even as leaders. Therefore, behaviours that are permissible for men are seldom tolerated coming from women. 'Toughness' is almost always misconstrued in women, as 'control' or 'lack of compassion'. Consequently, many women strive to handle disciplinary procedures and interpersonal conflict in a way that may be overly sensitive to the accusation of being aggressive. Those of us who become ensnared by this mindset are susceptible to the completely opposite vice, that is, we can be so lacking in assertiveness that others are simply tempted to walk all over us!

In our era, the most successful women leaders appear to be both competent and warm, tough and compassionate, assertive yet morally and emotionally responsible, decisive and creative, and are liked as well as respected. Women tend to have greater influence when they blend their leadership style to incorporate these masculine and feminine characteristics. This is a challenging goal for any woman in leadership but one that many women strive to achieve. Until the 'idea' of leadership is both male and female, women's leadership may be prone to greater misunderstanding, resistance, opposition and even greater conflict than their male counterparts.

Men behaving badly!

Women who exercise leadership today are unlikely to be surprised that men of all ages continue to struggle with the notion of women in positions of authority. This may be the case, even if the men in question are fully committed, at least theoretically, to the principle of women in leadership. So called 'progressive' men can be surprisingly non-progressive when exposed to strong female leadership. Old behaviour patterns can re-emerge and may even persist.

Many women in leadership discover quite quickly that changes to equality legislation do not necessarily result in changes to the prevailing social mindset. Similarly, a change in the Biblical understanding regarding the role of women, on the part of men and women in the church, does not necessarily lead to significant changes in their behaviour!

The kind of 'bad behaviour' that women in leadership are likely to encounter from men, may differ depending on the kind of work we are involved in. Some professions wrestle with the notion of women in senior leadership roles, far more than others. These include the church, which still debates the validity of women leaders and the armed forces, which often reduces the argument to the issue of physical strength. The more male oriented the domain, the more the leadership of women is resisted in subtle and not so subtle ways.

There are numerous stereotypes that are regularly projected onto women in leadership by men. For example, women who offer a clear opinion are sometimes described as 'control freaks', while men who speak up are excused as 'passionate'. Women who lead may find their femininity being assaulted through name-calling.

I have personally been called a number of 'choice' and mostly unrepeatable names throughout the course of my leadership and ministry. Namely, by men who were seemingly intimidated, unhappy to see me in leadership or unhappy to be challenged (by anyone) over the treatment of other women around them (namely a mother-in-law, wife or daughter). Some of these men were not well known to me and the vast majority of them were professing Christians and/or supposedly 'progressive' in their views about women. I have also experienced men ignore me or simply 'pretend' I am not physically present. I would have despaired by now were it not for the many positive examples of men (Christians included) I know very well! I recall one particular scenario when I was en route to my church office. I struck up a conversation with a young man who seemed a bit lost, I enquired if he knew where he was going and gave him some directions. I offered to walk part of the way to his destination with him as I was passing by anyway. We walked and chatted amiably for 20 minutes or so, until he understood that I was a pastor and a church leader. At this point he became verbally aggressive as he informed me of his beliefs, that women were not suited to leadership of any kind. I listened politely, suggesting that we could simply agree to disagree on the matter. He refused, insisting that he had a duty to get the truth 'through my thick skull!'. As you can imagine the conversation was short-lived! However, this is an example of one of my less abusive encounters! Having heard stories from other women, I have been struck by the sense of entitlement some men exhibit when expressing both their hostility and disapproval towards women. I have seldom seen such tactics applied to their interactions with other men. I am genuinely amazed at some of the disturbing attitudes I have encountered over the years. It has been a simultaneously painful yet thankfully instructive journey.

Women may also find that their ideas (even good ones) are regularly and openly challenged by men. They may be excluded from key or strategic meetings, given menial assignments outside their job description and designed to 'keep them in their place', such as serving tea and coffee. Men may even openly deride or placate women. In addition, women may find their contribution being ignored and then repeated as original thought by a man in the group (sometimes even during the same meeting!). Such behaviour reinforces the argument that a woman's contribution is frequently overlooked, while a man's input is rarely questioned.

Not all (or even most) men behave badly when exposed to female leaders. However, there are enough men who find ways of undermining and dismissing the validity of female leadership. Therefore, women should be fully prepared to navigate potential resistance and opposition with clarity, tenacity and grace.

Incidentally, women behave badly too!

Some of the greatest challenges that women in leadership face come from other women. In other words, women struggle with the idea of women's leadership and success in domains that have been traditionally male, in much the same way that men do. Far from being empathetic, women can be just as hostile in their disdain for 'successful', influential and powerful women. After all, it is women rather than men who compare their weight, style, appearance, lives, children, gifts, husbands and popularity with women they may never come to know personally or even meet!

In October 2008, a survey carried out among the general public, reported that the top five most loved celebrities were men: Paul McCartney, Lewis Hamilton, Gary Lineker, Simon Cowell and David Beckham. Yet four of the top five most hated celebrities among men *and* women were women: Heather Mills, Amy Winehouse, Victoria Beckham and Kerry Katona. (Interestingly, Simon Cowell was the only celebrity mentioned in both the 'loved' and 'hated' list.)[3]

The roots of such hostility in women may result from feeling threatened, jealous, angry or negative about our own situation or capabilities. Whatever the root cause, it is evident that women learn to mistrust other women, compete for their positions and compare themselves in wholly unhelpful ways. An amusing example of this behaviour occurs when a woman weather reporter, newsreader or preacher is in view. Typically she will be appraised on her appearance long before anything she has to say is taken into consideration. Interestingly, both groups of men and women engage in a similar process of evaluation but for entirely different reasons!

Therefore, women have to deal with the same challenge to renew their minds, as do men.

When conflict places us in the company of the great…

Conflict arises in a variety of contexts for many different reasons. However, it often occurs in the life of a leader simply as a by-product of the very legitimate demands of leadership.

Jesus is defined as sinless, yet attracted extraordinary levels of conflict. Much of this discord was generated by his adversaries and had more to do with their insecurities and jealousy, than it had to do with Jesus himself. The Bible also makes it clear that Jesus ended up nailed to the cross *because* of his unique gifts and claims. In other words, Jesus' extraordinary influence and gift of leadership ultimately led to the many challenges he had to face, including his eventual torture and death. This fact may not provide every leader with the greatest source of assurance or encouragement! However, it is a reminder to us when we find our leadership resisted, opposed and undermined, that our struggles are typical of leaders in general. We may even be standing in the company of the great!

Women in leadership, in particular, attract conflict for reasons other than poor leadership and should take this assurance to heart. However, like men we are also capable of mis-managing conflict and may find help in the pages that follow.

Conflict: the Crucible of Leadership

Joanne couldn't believe what she was hearing. Peter had literally taken her ideas and passed them off as his own. What made matters worse was that the same group who were now smiling and nodding in approval had unceremoniously shot down the very same suggestion she had proposed earlier that month. Joanne sat tight lipped, barely able to suppress her anger and annoyance. However, it took her less time on this occasion to 'catch' herself. She realised that she had reverted to playing 'the girl', she now decided to be proactive and apply the 'antidote' that she and her mentor had devised. Firstly, she prayed and secondly she engaged in a few calming mental exercises. Finally, she did something she had never done before under these circumstances, she opened her mouth and began to address the matter...

A perpetual absence of conflict can signal a lack of personal growth and development. Conflict sometimes reflects the need for change and progress. Therefore, the fact that conflict exists is not necessarily a bad thing. In fact, any attempt to avoid conflict in leadership is virtually doomed to failure because the ability to solve problems is an integral part of our leadership capability. Interestingly, the more a leader successfully deals with the problems she is presented with, the greater the degree of influence God seems to entrust to her.

There is much evidence to suggest that, when permitted, women excel as international peace negotiators. Our preference for collaboration, inclination towards consensus and willingness to compromise prove to be extremely valuable. Although both men and women share 'a commitment to international co-operation', Jessica Tuchman Mathews (president of the Carnegie Endowment for International Peace) demonstrates how differently women behave in their attempts to accomplish such an ideal. Her 2001 study *A Woman's Lens on Global Issues*, revealed that American women are more likely to:

- 'Believe nations need to work together
- Support international programs that meet basic human needs – a "human security" agenda – and empower women
- Emphasize diplomacy over military power'[4]

Marie Wilson, founder of the White House Project, commenting on the 1991–1995 war between Serbia and Croatia, underlines this theme, 'In the words of Haris Silajdzic, former co-prime minister of Bosnia and Herzegovina, "If we'd had women around the table, there would have been no war; women think long and hard before they send their children out to kill other people's children."'[5]

However, while every leader is significantly challenged by the problems of others, it is in the realm of personal conflict that leaders experience their greatest victories and defeats. Leaders are expected to engage regularly with conflict resolution among those who report to them or among their peers. However, leaders also experience their own interpersonal conflicts where they become a willing or unwilling contributor to a conflict they must navigate their way through. Conflict, particularly where it becomes highly personalised, is without doubt, the ultimate crucible of leadership development for both men and women. 'Few things are more powerful than conflict for revealing what we truly believe.'[6]

> It is in the realm of personal conflict that leaders experience their greatest victories and defeats

We may not always play a part in generating a conflict but how we choose to conduct ourselves in the midst of one can be particularly revealing. How we handle attack, criticism and/or 'feedback', are all indicators of our emotional and spiritual maturity. How we manage ourselves, others, circumstances and our relationship with God in the midst of a conflict will determine both our personal and professional growth.

From reactive to responsive

Different people use different strategies to manage their conflicts and the vast majority of approaches are ingrained and instinctive. Consequently, we are largely unaware of how we act and react in different conflict situations. We tend to do what comes 'naturally', based on responses that we learn during childhood. This deep-rooted personal conflict management style often proves to be highly ineffective. Such reactions primarily emerge from childish impulses that remain immature even throughout adulthood. The natural progression referred to by the Apostle Paul, requires us to develop maturity, 'When I was a child, I talked like a child, I thought like a child, I reasoned like a child. When I became a man, I put childish ways behind me.' (1 Corinthians 13:11)

Thankfully because behaviours are learned, we can change them with God's help. We can learn new and more effective ways of managing conflict situations. This is necessary because in many cases, effective conflict resolution skills make the difference between positive or negative outcomes.

Leaders frequently deal with conflict between others and within themselves. Since women leaders may be more likely to attract interpersonal conflict i.e. direct conflict with others, the question of how to effectively handle discord becomes all the more important.

An overwhelming number of women fail to rightly perceive their value; consequently, they respond to conflict through the lens of fear and insecurity. A desire to be liked, combined with a fundamental fear of losing valuable relationships, hard-won collaborative and co-operative working patterns, can paralyse us into inaction. In addition, women who implement disciplinary procedures or engage in conflict resolution are frequently caught between the proverbial 'rock and a hard place' when it comes to confrontation. Due to social expectations attached to the behaviour of women, taking a 'tough line' can be fraught with significant difficulties.

Under such circumstances collusion becomes an extremely attractive alternative to confrontation. It also requires considerably less energy!

What Collusion Looks Like

Collusion in its broadest sense is an attempt to release tension without actually dealing with the real problem. We collude when we establish verbal and non-verbal agreements between ourselves and others that prevent real change in people's attitudes or circumstances. Collusion is conspiratorial. It requires the active or passive support of others in forging unholy agreements that are ultimately destructive.

> We collude when we establish verbal and non-verbal agreements between ourselves and others that prevent real change in people's attitudes or circumstances

Collusion is a reactive stance to conflict and, rather than solving anything, it perpetuates and aggravates the status quo by faking or breaking the peace.

Peace faking

Patterns of collusion include attempts to fake the peace through avoidance and acquiescence.

- **Avoidance (Ostrich)**

  Unless an individual is particularly aggressive, our first inclination when faced with the prospect of conflict is to avoid it. However, when this approach is taken to an extreme, it can become a reactive stance that fakes peace by simply avoiding the real problem.

Avoidance is ostrich-like behaviour. These individuals avoid conflict by withdrawing and 'burying their heads in the sand'. They distance themselves from the people with whom they are in conflict and they stay away from the issues responsible for generating the conflict. In doing so, they sacrifice their personal goals and relationships.

Christians sometimes justify this attempt at avoidance by presenting a facade of super-spirituality and holiness. 'I'll pray about it', can just as easily mean, 'I won't actually do anything about it myself'. Under these circumstances, Martin Luther King Jr's comment becomes both sobering and pertinent, 'We must learn that to expect God to do everything while we do nothing is not faith but superstition.'[7] The idea that, 'Love covers over a multitude of sins', (1 Peter 4:8) has also been abused by Christians to sanction both inaction and passivity in the face of conflict. The true emphasis of this passage lies in its encouragement to Christians to bear with, forgive and forget past offences that have already been addressed.

Avoidance may take a number of forms but a willingness to embrace pretence lies at its roots. Like an ostrich, the avoider ends up living in self-inflicted emotional isolation, pretending that the person or problem no longer exists. Here peace is faked by subtraction. In other words, such people tend to seek peace by wishing or praying the problem away, 'Lord if you take *it* away, then I will have true peace'. The idea that peace can be attained by simply taking away the noisy neighbour, head of department, small group member, work colleague or in-law, is a serious mistake. Just because we cannot 'see' something does not mean we cannot continue to experience its impact. Peace never emerges as a result of simple subtraction. True peace comes from God, and expands in such a way that it overwhelms and alters the dynamic of everything else that it touches. Sevi Regis encapsulates this well and defines peace as, 'the state or condition of restfulness, harmony, balance, equilibrium, longevity, justice, resolution, timelessness, contentment, freedom, and fulfilment, either individually or simultaneously present, in such a way that it overcomes, demolishes, banishes, and/or replaces everything that opposes it.'[8]

The avoider does not experience such peace because they are driven primarily by self-protection. Their overriding concern is to escape and they seek to do this by detaching themselves from real people and real issues.

Many years ago I had a friend whose response to major challenges or interpersonal difficulties was to go to sleep (I mean quite literally). There was no medical condition involved; she simply shut out everything she didn't want to cope with, sometimes for days at a time. Hers was an extreme response to conflict but there are other less overt ways of avoiding matters we should be 'facing up to'.

Women who avoid conflict may either ignore and excuse bad behaviour, or simply abdicate their responsibility at the first obstacle. Those who ignore and excuse may be afraid to confront someone. Some may simply have power *over* others through access to external resources, status and ability or through internal personal power such as charisma and persuasiveness. However, both are overly concerned with not wanting to appear too authoritarian.

On the other hand, women who capitulate often have less power or are in subordinate roles. The presence of conflict under such conditions can result in a fearful aversion to 'rocking the boat'. They justify their avoidance with these thoughts: 'there's no point in bothering; it won't make a difference; it will end up in a nasty mess; he won't listen to me; they will have even more power over me; she'll always hold it against me!'

This approach to conflict fakes peace. Indeed, far from escaping problematic people and issues, it only succeeds in colluding with them. The problems are merely internalised. Subsequently, people who operate on this basis often succumb to illness, aches, pains, mental and physical exhaustion and breakdown.

- **Acquiescence (Chameleon)**

  When a desire to preserve relationships is taken to an extreme, a reactive stance that attempts to fake peace by acquiescing to the problem, may be adopted.

  Acquiescence is chameleon-like behaviour. These individuals want to be accepted and liked by others and will attempt to blend and merge with prevailing opinions in an attempt to secure peace. They are afraid that if the conflict continues, someone will get hurt, and that relationships will be ruined. Subsequently, they give up legitimate goals in order to preserve the relationship at all costs. The underlying premise that drives such behaviour is the belief that people cannot enter into 'heated' discussion or debate without ultimately damaging their relationships. Therefore, a counterfeit 'harmony' is embraced in an attempt to steer clear of discord.

  Women have a propensity to push themselves to their physical and emotional limits in an effort to accommodate the needs of others. Therefore, our awareness of their needs tends to preoccupy much of our time and energy. We may become consumed by what others think of us and how they might be affected by what we say or do. Consequently, we quickly lose sight of our own legitimate aims and goals. Our language becomes characterised by 'if' and 'therefore' and frequently leads us to acquiesce, e.g. 'if he's aggressive…' 'if she's nice…' 'because he's the boss…' 'if she's uncooperative…' 'I know she's going to be difficult…' 'Therefore, I'll give in…'.

  The one who acquiesces struggles, as many women do, with the need to appear pleasing by smiling, looking interested, being calm, supportive, obliging, attentive, uncritical and pleasant. The chameleon often speaks too softly, unsteadily or lacks firmness and clarity in making assertions. We tend to be vague instead of specific. We can become apologetic, passive or blame ourselves in the face of conflict. We usually attempt invisibility because we are anxious about what someone else may think of us. Unfortunately, during a conflict, any silence on our part is often translated as acceptance and this may further be interpreted as permission.

Those who acquiesce and fret about being ignored or dismissed, may unconsciously communicate that we have nothing worthwhile to contribute. If we fail to take ourselves seriously, we shouldn't be surprised if others choose to follow suit!

As long as a desire to escape or to be liked in the midst of conflict is our motivating factor, we will always be peace fakers. Our attempts to establish peace will be reactive and characterised by the collusion of avoidance and acquiescence. In other words, we will mimic ostrich and chameleon-like behaviours.

However, patterns of collusion also include attempts to *break* the peace. This approach to conflict is also reactive rather than responsive.

Peace breaking

Collusion is encouraged whenever a conscious or unconscious decision is made to *break* the peace. This is expressed primarily through 'conspiratorial' acts of aggression and character assassination.

● **Aggression (Bull)**

When the needs of others are of little importance, aggression becomes the primary vehicle for dealing with conflict.

Aggression is bullish behaviour. These individuals release tension through angry outbursts and barely concealed resentment. Their overwhelming tendency is to talk about others behind their backs and blame them for the unsatisfactory state of affairs. They seek to overpower opponents by forcing them to accept their desired solution to a conflict. They are not primarily concerned with the needs of others and they will seek to achieve their goals at all costs. Winning gives them a sense of pride and accomplishment. Losing gives them a sense of weakness, inadequacy and failure. Like the bull, they will try to win by attacking, overpowering, overwhelming and intimidating others.

Ironically, some women are characterised by aggression, particularly when we are anxious and preoccupied with what others may think of us. We may be overly committed to protecting ourselves from others by erecting emotional barriers. This can result in an aloofness and lead to abrupt behaviour toward others. We may also be prone to exercising control by withholding praise or dismissing legitimate concerns without discussion or appeal.

Women who have always had to fend for themselves are particularly prone to aggressive behaviours. Dominating others can become a means of covering our insecurities.

Alternatively, other women attempt to 'survive' workplace and ministry conflicts by 'playing' according to the same aggressive rules as some of the men around them. Women who experience difficulties as they rise in male-dominated environments sometimes forsake the alternative values they started with, in order to survive the new terrain. Such women may indeed succeed at beating men at their own games. However, if the goal of women in leadership is to become just as aggressive, competitive, ruthless and arrogant as some of the men around us, surely we defeat the point of exploring our distinctive contribution as women?

● Character Assassination (Snake)

When concern for others is of little or no consequence, assassination may become the main way of dealing with conflict. Character assassination is perhaps the most recognisable form of collusion and predictably is a major peace-breaker.

Assassination requires the disposition of a killer. Poisonous snakes intentionally paralyse and kill their prey in order to ingest them.

However, the individual who engages in this kind of behaviour does not necessarily intend to maliciously break the peace. The basic problem here is a thorough lack of self-control. The peace-breaker wittingly or unwittingly adopts the role of saboteur through subtle and unsubtle attempts to undermine others. These individuals offer criticism and feedback but always to the wrong person. They 'discuss' others negatively 'behind their backs' and simultaneously disclose their faults in exaggerated ways. They seek to 'paralyse' the reputation or activity of the person who has got in their way.

This particular way of releasing tension is deployed by those who prefer to talk *about* others, rather than directly *to* them. This becomes a substitute for legitimate confrontation. Instead of addressing the correct party, this person conspiratorially seeks to 'recruit' others, to join them in their 'just cause' against the person(s) in question.

Some women are easily tempted to employ their effective verbal skills, as the songwriter said, by killing each other 'softly' with words! The snake that seeks to paralyse its prey has only one goal in mind, its ultimate demise.

I cannot count the number of times I have been subjected to this kind of behaviour. An early recollection involves one leader who took me aside after a meeting because they wanted to discuss 'issues' they had with another pastor. Such people frequently seem to be in everyone else's business (I wish I were exaggerating!). They know things they have no business knowing. Warning bells began sounding immediately, so I asked, 'Have you shared your concerns with the leader in question?' It quickly became clear that not only had no such conversation taken place, no future plans were in place to do so. I reminded the leader of the principle found in Matthew 18:15–16, 'If a brother or sister sins ['against you' is included in some translations], go and point out the fault, *just between the two of you*. If they listen to you, you have won them over. But if they will not listen, take one or two others along, so that every matter may be established by the testimony of two or three witnesses.' I later received a phone call from the same individual, asking if they could share their concerns with me 'for prayer'. My response remained unchanged.

I have not always achieved the right balance. Individuals and groups with a grievance can be highly persuasive and on more than one occasion my discernment has been off balance. Sharing our concerns with a mentor or coach helps to reduce this tendency. However, as a general rule, people who are reluctant to 'face up' to those they accuse, even when offered the support to do so, have only one thing in mind, that is their demise. Those who are happy to discuss others with *you* 'behind their back', will invariably have something equally negative to say to others about you.

Business manuals describe this behaviour as office politics and gossip. The Bible agrees that such people are gossips but it also labels them as divisive and gives some pretty strong advice on how to deal with them (Titus 3:10)! Ignoring such behaviour inevitably leads to a build up of resentment, the development of cliques and the encouragement of a work and church culture where bullying is more likely to occur. There is a difference between collegial concern and malicious conversation.

> We collude whenever we are reactive rather than responsive

We collude whenever we are reactive rather than responsive. When we attempt to fake or break peace through avoidance, acquiescence, aggression and character assassination, we are actively engaged in the destructive practice of collusion.

A willingness to confront ultimately leads us away from ostrich, chameleon, bullish and snake-like behaviours and toward the peace-makers' bridge. This bridge lies between reactive and responsive approaches to conflict. The bridge provides a visual reminder that the peace-maker primarily seeks collaboration. Peace-makers long for win-win solutions that take both their personal goals and the goals of the other party into account. However, 'Shalom' peace-makers, do not seek win-win solutions at any cost. Jesus was clear regarding the nature of peace, 'I do not give to you as the world gives,' (John 14:27). In other words, Jesus' peace and our ideas are not always aligned. The primary intention of shalom peace-makers who desire a Jesus-inspired response, is the peace-full solution that is most acceptable to God. They care primarily about God's perspectives, intentions and designs. However, they also give due attention to the concerns of others and to their personal and professional growth and development. This is a true reflection of the greatest commandment, to love God *first* and *then* our neighbour, (Matthew 22:37).

Avoiding Conflict or Pursuing Peace?

Lorna realised that her attempts to keep the peace were simply not working. Even her best friend informed her that she usually empathised with both parties too much and challenged either side too little. The whole team was in disarray and misinformation and subtle forms of manipulation had been well and truly disseminated. Everyone was now under the misapprehension that Rachel was at fault. Lorna knew that this was not the case but had asked Rachel to maintain her silence anyway. Rather than reducing tension, the team now felt justified in their resentment and were beginning to deploy subtle forms of sabotage against Rachel in her work. Lorna knew that only an external investigation would get things back on track…

The main difficulty with conflict is its tendency to upset our emotional, spiritual and physical equilibrium. Because of the momentary emotional intensity involved, conflict is capable of totally diverting and distracting us. The real danger occurs when we become preoccupied with someone else's behaviour rather than focusing on how we can grow professionally or develop creatively. Both men and women alike, can obsess and over-personalise an issue in such a way that they fail to address the key concerns. Such an attitude to conflict is reactive rather than responsive. By contrast, responsive approaches require great emotional stability, as well as a dedication to self-discipline and self-management.

As we have seen, conflict is inevitable for the leader; consequently, the main task of leadership is the active pursuit of peace, but this is not quite as straightforward as it may seem…

The art of peacemaking!

The Hebrew word for peace, 'Shalom', encompasses far more than the absence of strife. It includes the themes of completeness, wholeness, health, peace, welfare, safety, tranquillity, prosperity, perfectness, fullness, rest, harmony and the absence of agitation and discord.[9] In essence, it is about an approach to wholeness that results in God's will being completed in the life of an individual or group. 'Shalom' peace includes peace with God, others and within ourselves. It does not simply relate to a state of affairs, it also describes the process that guides an individual or group towards that 'ideal' state.

When writing to the Philippian church, the Apostle Paul underlines this point, 'the peace of God, which transcends all understanding, will *guard* your hearts and your minds in Christ Jesus' (Philippians 4:7). The word translated 'to guard' best describes a garrison. This is a military unit responsible for safeguarding a specific locale or area. Since the peace of God is designed to '*garrison* our hearts and minds in Christ Jesus', it is in some way tangible and noticeable. The conflict itself may not be over but when the garrison is in place, the conclusion is no longer in doubt. It is the garrison that makes all the difference between agitation and calm in a person facing conflict. The absence of hostility in any given circumstance is not the primary goal of peace but an absence of stress and an inner confidence and fortitude are symptomatic of those who seek to attain it.

'Shalom' peace seeks to establish Godly characteristics within each situation. This is perfectly illustrated by the statement made by Martin Luther King Jr, 'True peace is not merely the absence of tension: it is the presence of justice.'[10] 'Shalom' peace promises everyone both peace *over* and peace *within* the midst of conflict. However, this peace must be both pursued and practised by advocates of conflict resolution.

Peacemaking becomes the bridge that leads away from reactive approaches to conflict resolution. It is perhaps the most responsive approach. However, it requires an unflinching commitment to engage in confrontation. Such commitment enables leaders to employ Biblical tools, principles and examples that empower us to transition from reactive to responsive pathways in conflict resolution. It also propels us away from a preoccupation with 'survival' in conflict and towards a mindset dedicated to active growth in our personal leadership.

Caring Confrontation

Jenny was hurt, upset and angry. Although the board recognised her gifts and calling, they had still refused to nominate her for the post. The underlying assumption being that the organisation was not quite ready for a woman leader. It seemed as if they would never be ready for a woman leader! When Jenny had finally managed to express her deep concern, she was informed that 'her pain had been noted'. Somewhat frustrated and feeling patronised, she was now wondering whether she had the inclination or the 'energy' to take the matter to the next level…

Ultimately, all confrontation should be caring. When we value goals and relationships appropriately, we can view conflict as a problem to be solved, rather than an individual or party to defeat. It is a commitment to engage in the 'challenging conversations' that are now popularly emphasised by modern management schools of thought.

Whether we face conflict in the home, church or work environment, we must remain committed to the goal of restoration and 'Shalom' peace. As we do so, confronting conflict becomes a way of improving relationships and establishing truth and not simply a means of reducing tension.

Anatomy of a Biblical confrontation

In Genesis 3:1–24 we are introduced to the very first major conflict in human history. In this passage, we witness a variety of responses from the main characters: Adam, Eve, the serpent and God. God is presented simultaneously as the primary challenger and the ultimate peace-maker. In Genesis 3:1–7 a state of discord arises as Adam and Eve defy God's instruction and eat from the tree of good and evil. Caught 'red-handed', they are reactive rather than responsive. They initially attempt to hide from God's presence, betraying their inclination toward ostrich-like avoidance. They then resort to snake-like activity through character assassination by blaming each other, in an effort to shirk personal responsibility. In Genesis 3:8 each party is called to account and challenged to take full responsibility for their part in generating the discord. In order to pursue this course of action, God raises questions about the nature of the conflict, exposing and establishing His truth in the process (see Genesis 3:9–14). Each individual is made liable for their own contribution to the problem and separate consequences are pronounced by God (see Genesis 3:14–20). A strategy is provided by God to ensure future re-engagement. There is a degree of collaboration as each individual has a part to play in establishing the final 'Shalom' peace.

This approach to confrontation is caring, ultimately restorative (for some) but it is *not* pain free. Caring confrontation is a vital skill that every leader should cultivate, particularly if we wish to grow through the challenges we will inevitably face in leadership.

Guidelines for a caring confrontation

Actual confrontation may prove difficult but when fully engaged, it is often accompanied by signs of genuine peace.

Conflicts that arise as a result of our differences are the easiest and quickest ones to resolve. Most conflict stems from misunderstandings that can be easily cleared up through listening to one another. However, conflicts that stem from unresolved bitterness or that require inner healing are the hardest to deal with and require greater attention and care.

- **Pray**

  Philippians 4:7 reminds us of the importance of prayer, 'Do not be anxious about anything, but in everything, by prayer and petition, with thanksgiving, present your requests to God.' In any conflict situation, prayer is vital because it invites God's perspective and not simply God's intervention. Unless we are able to view our conflicts from God's point of view we may miss important lessons. By seeking out the finger-prints of God and not just the boot prints of the enemy (Satan), we may learn to appreciate the benefits of conflict.

  Problems teach us that there is always more to learn and God may use them to expose our fears, pride and prejudice. Conflict may also reveal dangerous weaknesses in our character and work habits that need to be addressed. Often the real issues that separate us from each other are revealed as we pray. The discipline of prayer may further help us to deepen the relationships we value, strengthen our team and yield new ideas that may potentially promote our growth.

When we choose to ignore what God may be doing in and through us, we potentially sentence ourselves to a painful repetition of specific conflict scenarios.

● Explore your own reaction

As women, many of us have an overdeveloped sense of responsibility for others around us. Whether we are dealing with work colleagues or family members, we tend to blame ourselves for any wrong decisions they may choose to take. The most valuable lesson we can learn in life is that we are not responsible for how others choose to react. Thankfully, we are not expected to control anyone's behaviour, only our own.

As we consider the condition of our heart (Luke 12:13–15), there are three questions we should take into account:

Do I have a valid concern?

In other words, is the issue under consideration real or merely perceived? We are faced with many challenges within a work or ministry environment. Those that affect women directly often bear the characteristics of sexism, racism and even ageism. These are undeniably present even within Christian work and ministry contexts. However, we may sometimes hear a putdown where none was intended or wrongly attribute a valid criticism to a sexist, racist or ageist attitude. We must exercise great care and discretion in this matter because it is possible to wrongly interpret the intentions and actions of others.

What we are able to see is very often limited by who we are. We may indeed be wrong and may also need to embrace a particular critique. Mentors are invaluable at times like these allowing us to 'think aloud', not in a bid to assassinate someone else's character but in order to gain clarity about our own! There are some important questions we must ask ourselves if we are to establish the validity of our concerns: 'What is motivating my response? Was I fair? Did I hear right?'

Too often, both men and women associate winning and losing with their inherent value. When our concerns are unfounded we may be tempted to believe that this is a reflection on our self-worth. However, even if our concerns are invalid, we must remember at all times, that we are not!

Does my challenger have a valid concern?

In order to answer this question appropriately, we must attempt to put ourselves into the shoes of the other person. Such an incarnational approach mirrors God's design to redeem humanity by sending Jesus to earth in human likeness. Although we can never *be* the other person, we can at least attempt to understand their unique perspective in order to appreciate their cause. If we reach the conclusion that an individual or group does not have a valid case, we are still able to affirm their humanity. Therefore, the key to effective confrontation lies in our attitude toward others. Our primary goal is to address the problem, not to humiliate the person(s).

Is the issue under consideration the real problem?

This question seeks to establish whether the other party has simply had a negative experience elsewhere that has been triggered by something that you have said or done. It is possible for the 'unfinished' business of others to unintentionally 'spill over' into our area of responsibility. On the other hand, the challenger may simply have a personal agenda, and may be using this situation for their own advantage.

Once you have asked yourself these three questions you may now wish to turn your attention to the issue of goals.

- **Focus on your preferred outcome**

  The goal of conflict resolution is not simply about deciding *what* we may want to accomplish. It is also about choosing *who* (in terms of our character) we want to become. This is important, both throughout and after the process of the conflict scenario. It is no good achieving an acceptable outcome if we become less compassionate, increasingly hardened and resentful individuals as a result of the process.

- **Devise a strategy**

  In order to devise an effective strategy we must reflect on 'how' we intend to approach the confrontation. We may wish to consider the following steps:

  Apply 'the golden rule': treat others as you would like to be treated
  During the course of our leadership, each one of us will be in need of correction, healing or a relationship of accountability. Therefore, we should always give others the benefit of the doubt, however difficult this may prove to be. We should also assume that they are innocent until proven absolutely guilty! When we treat others as we would like to be treated, we affirm God's original design for our humanity.

  Opt for a conciliatory approach
  There is nothing to be gained from polemics. Focusing on common interests, rather than opposing positions, effectively places all parties on the same side of the conflict. This enables each to establish outcomes that are acceptable to everyone. A conversation should begin with the sentiment, 'We all want…'. Meanwhile, we can continue to be tough on the problem.

  When Jesus took on human likeness, it wasn't just any human likeness; it has been said that he took on the likeness of a reconciler. In other words, Jesus opted for a conciliatory approach with humanity. He spent most of his life in a region that included people from a wide variety of cultures, social classes, religions and languages. He managed to bring many of them together. Jesus himself probably spoke three languages: Aramaic, common Greek and Hebrew. In other words, he was able to communicate with those he engaged with in a meaningful way. It is unlikely that this was incidental. During his ministry Jesus preached the inclusivity of the gospel and reached out to people who were not from his own cultural background, whether Samaritans, Romans, or indigenous Canaanites.[11] Women were commonly excluded from active participation in religious schools, yet they travelled with Jesus as part of his entourage.[12] Jesus welcomed sinners and outcasts to join him for dinner. His contemporaries fully understood the profound social implications of table fellowship with those who were ostracised and marginalised. Consequently, Jesus was criticised and vilified for making such choices by the religious elite who had little interest in reconciliation (see Mark 2:15–16). Jesus also, literally, touched those that no one else was prepared to touch, whether they happened to be diseased or 'sinful'. He also reconciled people, one by one, into a relationship with God and with each other. However, there were individuals and groups with whom Jesus could not be reconciled; this is a sobering realisation.

Jesus' behaviour enables us to grasp the significance of some of the prerequisites of a conciliatory approach. Firstly, the ability to acknowledge difference without being phased by it; secondly, ensuring that meaningful communication with diverse parties is possible; thirdly, Jesus also communicates that God is always for the individual (even when their activities are suspect); and finally, Jesus set clear boundaries when it was necessary.

Engage a mediator

A mediator is usually only necessary when direct talks with others have broken down. The presence of a mediator often creates a safe place for both parties to think clearly and speak freely. The task of the mediator is to maintain some critical distance (the ever elusive 'objectivity') and place very clear boundaries between the issues being presented and those they may be dealing with personally. They should thoroughly investigate matters and explore the various points of view with an aim to keep discussions focused and balanced.

Depending on the nature of the issue, the mediator should be someone who is respected by both parties and who knows the strengths and weaknesses of each side. Alternatively, a mediator could be someone without prior knowledge of specific issues and therefore with no vested interest in any individual cause. However, it is vitally important that the potential mediator has some proven mediation skills and is able to listen, investigate and draw conclusions based upon *all* the relevant information. (Unfortunately, I have learned this the hard way!)

- **Outline some personal tactics**
  Personal tactics are the specific methods we choose to employ in our efforts to resolve a conflict. They encourage us to consider 'what' *we*, as individuals, might do in the course of an actual conflict scenario. The following are some basic essentials:

  Take responsibility for your own reactions (Ephesians 4:22-24)
  Ask, 'What may I have done to contribute to this conflict?' Include questions such as, 'Have I colluded in bringing about this problem by behaving like a peace faker or peace breaker?' Check for any falling logs, from your own eye! (Matthew 7:5).

  Take your own thoughts captive! (2 Corinthians 10:5)
  If there are past grudges and injuries involved, refuse to allow negative emotions or speculation to derail the present conversation.

Surrender your ego (Proverbs 16:18)

Ego lies at the root of most of our defensiveness and it becomes a problem when we associate our personal value with the presenting issue. We may then succumb to self-protection, rather than seeking the truth or a just solution to the problem.

Listen carefully (Proverbs 18:13)

Most people, including ourselves, do not confront constructively. We should attempt to listen carefully to what is being said, even when it is poorly communicated. By reflecting back what is said and regularly asking for clarity (even if there is no confusion on your part), we affirm the other party and enable them to reach a point of personal clarity.

Depersonalise the issue as much as possible

Create some distance between your feelings and your attempt to resolve the issue. Feelings are an inevitable part of working life as long as human beings are involved, they should be acknowledged and addressed. If not, they may hinder the process of finding a solution to the conflict. Although the problem may be directed *at* you, it may not be *about* you, so refuse to personalise it. Use protocols and other policies that may be available to you in order to depersonalise the matter as much as possible.

Take yourself seriously (Judges 6:15)

If we fail to take ourselves seriously, why should anyone else? During a critical exchange, how we communicate becomes paramount. However, we must say what needs to be said without trivialising (with laughter or smiling), undermining (by apologising) or negating ourselves (in other words, undoing the good we seek to accomplish by failing to reinforce decisions and/or boundaries).

Set boundaries by clarifying acceptable and unacceptable behaviour

Since every human being is made in the image of God, we have a responsibility to honour that image in others and vice versa. However, we are not obliged to endure aggressive or abusive behaviour from others. Therefore, we should be prepared to identify and articulate what is and is not acceptable behaviour during an attempt to resolve conflict. The establishing of boundaries is Godly behaviour (see chapter two entitled, 'Failure to Draw the Line').

Use appropriate humour when you can – laughter is good medicine for everybody! (see Proverbs 17:22)

As long as we are careful not to undermine our own position by smiling or laughing inappropriately, the use of humour can diffuse a potentially explosive situation.

Role play

Practice doesn't necessarily 'make perfect', however, it certainly makes things permanent! Engaging in role play designed to provide us with a 'live' practice run may prove invaluable. It allows us to test our approach and receive important feedback. Role play works particularly well if play acting is carefully avoided. We are then at liberty to address the difficulty with a trusted friend or mentor. The goal is to attempt to address the challenge so that our meaning is clear, our tone respectful (non-accusatory) and our language appropriate (non-inflammatory).

- **Always take the high-er road**

  If you need to apologise, do so immediately and fully, at the level and to the extent that the offence was committed. 'I'm sorry' should be followed up with specific examples of what you are offering the apology for. Sentences that begin, 'I am sorry for what I *may* have done...' are not apologies but denials!

Avoid: 'if, but and maybe'

Sentences that begin with these words frequently disguise excuses. They frequently permit individual or group abdication from any personal responsibility for what has taken place.

Forgive readily when asked

Forgiveness is sometimes a protracted, life-long event but it needs to be willingly practised if it is to be sincere and authentic. We must also remember that excusing is not forgiving, e.g. 'She's going through a tough time, he'd be devastated if I said anything, we all have our little faults don't we?' Until an issue is confronted, and addressed, at least in our own minds, it remains to be forgiven.

Abandon or resist the desire to get your own back!

This is not as easy as it sounds because in the words of the prophet, 'The heart is deceitful and desperately wicked' (Jeremiah 10:17). The Christian idea of forgiveness involves a commitment to avoid raising the issue again as a weapon to punish, rebuke or exact revenge on the other person at some later stage. Self-awareness and self-management are critical because the unconscious urge to do so, can overwhelm even our best intentions.

Be prepared to live with momentary discomfort

Some conflicts are quickly and easily diffused, while others unfortunately, require us to live with discomfort for much *much* longer! However, 'this too shall pass'. There is always an end, even if it isn't immediately in sight.

Know when to disengage (Matthew 18:15)

Not every great ending concludes with the words, 'and they lived happily ever after'. The Biblical evidence suggests that the appropriate ending for some conflict is temporary or permanent separation.

Women often fail to make the distinction between persistence and useless perseverance. We can be chronic over-stayers and rescuers! However, recognising what we can and can't change is essential for our health and well being! Attempts to persuade, cajole or convince people to do the right thing need to be abandoned. Sometimes an individual refuses to deal with an issue or problem until they hit 'rock bottom'. We are seldom required to follow them there! It is important for us to recognise that we cannot do someone else's growing up for them.

COACHING TIPS

Recall a recent example of a confrontation in which you were involved. What happened?

Who was involved?

When and where did it occur?

Why did it happen?

What is your desired outcome? How would this impact on those who were involved in the confrontation?

How can you move this issue forward?

What will you do to follow up progress?

'Few things are more powerful than conflict for revealing what we truly believe.'

TARA KLENA BARTHEL & JUDY DABLER[13]

7TH
DEADLY SIN

NEGLECT IN FAMILY MATTERS

Be intentional with *your nearest and dearest!*

'To put the world right in order, we must first put the nation in order; to put the nation in order, we must first put the family in order; to put the family in order, we must first cultivate our personal life; we must first set our hearts right.'

CONFUCIUS

Our Nearest are Dearest…

Barbara watched as the tiny figure of her son finally disappeared behind the school gates. She let out a deep sigh as she considered her helter-skelter morning. The twins had complained about having to go to school, reasoning that if they went to work with her instead, they could be a great 'help'. She smiled as she imagined the kind of 'help' they would offer… Ben, her four year old, had also been struggling to master the art of tying his shoelaces, insisting that in spite of constantly tripping up, his way was 'the best!'. She made a mental note to buy him some double velcro fastening shoes. She had left her husband, Eric, still in bed. As she drove away from the school, the all too familiar sensation of guilt settled. She couldn't understand why she felt so bad all the time. She had been told on numerous occasions that she was a great mum and she believed it too (well nearly…). Generally, Eric did his best to help out, although she felt he could afford to do more (then she conceded that she didn't always let him!). She felt guilty if she was at home, when she could be at work and equally guilty when she was at work distracted by thoughts of home. She didn't want to have to choose between work and family but it seemed that she just couldn't win either way…

Striking the right balance between work and family life has long proven to be a major challenge for many women in leadership. We are all too easily plagued by feelings of guilt over neglecting one or the other. We have been led to believe that we must make a choice that excludes one or the other. Research shows that this is particularly true in Western contexts and wherever Western influences and family expectations have been embraced.[1] In other parts of the world, the necessity of having to combine some form of work *together* with family life is generally the accepted norm. Consequently, arguments for or against the presence of women in paid and unpaid work are less prevalent. Unfortunately, this does not mean that the issue of women in leadership within these settings is any less problematic than in Western contexts!

Currently, there are almost as many women as men working in both Europe and America. However, women rather than men continue to be preoccupied with family affairs. In other words, the overwhelming responsibility for housework, children and the care of ageing relatives still rests largely on the shoulders of either married or single women. This is despite the increase in numbers of men who express a desire to engage more fully with 'family life'. Whether such behaviour is determined by our biology or the prevailing social expectations remains the subject of much debate. The fact remains that women continue to demonstrate a greater tendency toward family life than men.

For example, we are largely responsible for arranging family events, organising get-togethers and keeping in touch, even with our in-laws! Indeed, as I have outlined in previous chapters women tend to be more focused on relationships than men. This is particularly evident in the emphasis we place on our family interactions. Consequently, even women in leadership appreciate that family members almost always constitute our 'nearest and dearest' relationships. In other words, family tend to be, quite literally, our most intimate *and* emotionally expensive associations. Family members concern us in ways that appear to differ significantly from men in leadership.[2]

In spite of our greater preoccupation with and involvement in family life, women are seldom aware of the many ways they already exercise leadership within and beyond the home. However, the function and dysfunction of our family life can hinder (or indeed enhance) our effectiveness in leadership for reasons we may be wholly unaware of.

Both family life and leadership beyond the home could potentially benefit us further, if we became more intentional about our family matters. By employing the specific paradigm of self-leadership to our family struggles, plans, goals, hopes and dreams, we could approach many of our challenges with less angst, guilt and self-doubt.

> Our response to life and leadership is often forged in the furnace of our family relationships

It is recognised that women *and* men carry their personal relationships around with them wherever they go. Experiences drawn from our personal family interactions tend to impact every aspect of our lives, regardless of context. This is primarily because our response to life and leadership is often forged in the furnace of our family relationships. The family circle is the place where we learn to become leaders or followers. It is there that we discover who we are and begin to suppress or exercise our gifts. It is also within the family context, that we learn how to express appropriate anger, apologise, accept forgiveness, show generosity, extend hospitality, and express the love and care necessary to experience deep friendships. Ultimately, our family interactions profoundly affect the way we react to pain, disappointment, anger and fear. The family circle is also the place where we learn to love ourselves, as we experience love from other family members and we learn to value ourselves, as we understand what it means to be valued. Eventually, we also experience the inevitability of loss most keenly within the family setting. We hopefully attempt to respond to all these many challenges in healthy God-honouring and life-affirming ways.

The environment of family life can provide the most intensive leadership training experience, especially for women. Not only do we encounter opportunities that allow us to develop our emotional maturity, we are also given the responsibility to exercise a variety of other leadership skills. For example, women tend to engage in the organisation, planning or strategising of family events, outings and meetings. We deliberate, negotiate and referee sticky situations, conflicts, resistance, opposition and negativity. We are sometimes required to challenge family strongholds that have negative spiritual or emotional roots. These may affect our interactions in potentially destructive ways and lead to the breakdown of understanding and communication. Such situations can leave us reluctant to develop family relationships further. Thankfully, we also enjoy family fellowship, successes, developments, breakthroughs, new additions, surprises, support, love, encouragement and protection. These conditions are so desirable that we willingly expend emotional, spiritual and physical resources in an effort to facilitate our family relationships.

While family life potentially draws out the best in us, it can also expose the very worst. The sphere of the family can be the toughest environment in which to lead ourselves and others effectively. Our worst habits tend to emerge within the family arena and it may also be the place where we are taken for granted or indeed, where we take others for granted. In fact, this very setting can often be the context where

> The sphere of the family can be the toughest environment in which to lead ourselves and others effectively

we unintentionally (or even deliberately) forget to apologise or seek forgiveness. It can also be the hardest place to challenge others, 'rock the boat' or make very necessary personal adjustments. Ironically, our innermost family circle can become the final frontier, *within* which we lack the confidence to truly express our leadership gifts and yet this inner circle has the greatest potential for relationally based empowerment.

One church leader I worked with struggled with inconsistency between both family and work life. On my visits I would seek to explore how the whole family were doing. However, I was frequently met with 'assurances' that led me to believe that things were not quite as 'great' as indicated. As I dug a little deeper it became very clear that while church members thought of their leader as a great pastor (adjectives included: 'amazing', 'loving' and 'compassionate'), the family felt very differently. They complained of neglect, verbal abuse and harsh treatment. Further discussion revealed deep-seated issues that required family counselling. The leader in question had effectively eroded his credibility where it mattered most, within his family circle. Eventually, this family dynamic would have 'spilled over' into his work and ministry. Moreover, the 'truth' may have jeopardised his entire future ministry. I have repeatedly witnessed this scenario, particularly in the lives of those engaged in the 'caring professions'. These include doctors, social workers, counsellors and therapists (interestingly it appears to be more of a male problem). The 'Dr Jekyll' facade at work is deeply undermined by the reality of 'Mr Hyde' at home.

> Failure to reflect on our family dynamics can result in the implosion of our leadership

Ironically, much like the fictional character behind the Jekyll and Hyde persona, this particular leader lived in denial about the issue until it was pointed out and backed up with evidence. A failure to reflect on our family dynamics, address self-defeating behaviours and lead ourselves in positive ways can result in the implosion of our leadership.

The power of the 'inner circle'

Leadership experts observe that the people closest to a leader, ultimately determine the leader's potential. These individuals become the most influential group in the leader's life and are capable of affecting both the leader's state of mind and their emotional well-being. They often form the leader's most meaningful relationships and include their most trusted advisors. In leadership jargon, these individuals are referred to as the 'Inner Circle'. John Maxwell defines the nature of their effect on the life of a leader as, 'The Law of the Inner Circle'.[3] He suggests that the inner circle is crucial to every leader's future success. For women in leadership, our inner circle invariably includes members of our own families. When it doesn't, we are generally more concerned about whether it should, unlike the men in our position!

Our feelings toward our family and our interactions with them can be a source of great inspiration, guilt or even consternation. Whether our family is supportive or unsupportive, chaotic or orderly, the overall dynamic is likely to impact how we feel about our leadership and the way in which we express it, both within and beyond the borders of our home lives. Our families can impact us for better or worse, even unintentionally! Given a choice some of us would readily exclude certain members from our inner family circle! Apart from marriage or if we decide to adopt or foster, we inherit the family we are born into. Similarly, we seldom get to choose whom we work alongside, we simply inherit the majority of our colleagues along with our job title! Therefore, when we find ourselves in the enviable position of being able to choose a member of our inner circle (as we do when we are hiring a new employee), we should do so carefully because our interactions with this group may determine the level of our future performance and success!

Given the 'cost' attached to many of our relationships, we tend to opt for family and work interactions that are emotionally, mentally and spiritually inexpensive. We often ask investment-related questions, albeit subconsciously, before we consider taking action. We do so, in the (often mistaken) belief that we may somehow 'save' ourselves a great deal of grief and pain. Our questions tend to adopt the following logic: 'I wonder whether my actions will be 'worth' the resulting aggravation, mood, silent treatment, shouting match, disrespect, pain, fear or indeed verbal and emotional abuse (or worse)?' We struggle with the discipline of 'getting it right' in our relationships, even when failing to do so has painful consequences. As women, we are prone to settle for solutions that lead to self-blame or internalised frustration. Such options appear surprisingly easier unlike the challenge of radically transforming our thinking and behaviour.

We are often desperate to create 'ideal' conditions within our inner circle, especially when this includes family members and friends and may subsequently opt for the 'path of least resistance'. However, we often fail to recognise that were we to apply the very disciplines we exercise as leaders, we could achieve the ideal conditions we long for. Women are sometimes painfully unaware of how lessons learned in one context, can improve our effectiveness in another. For example, women gain skills from running a family and a household that they don't always recognise are transferable to the workplace. Equally, lessons from the workplace, when properly applied, can also help to enhance our family lives. Essentially, our leadership gifts can be applied to more than just the work and ministry context, they can also be deployed to maximise the power of our inner circle.

Your Leadership *is a* Family Matter

Ellie checked her watch one last time, she wasn't going to make it. She was late… again. She prayed silently, decided to double her efforts and began to run. Why did she do this to herself she wondered as she caught her breath? She always hoped to be on time to collect the girls but never made it. In fact, realistically, her schedule made it impossible for her to do so. As head of operations for her department she'd often thought about asking for more flexible working hours so that she could make, what had literally become, her 'school run' but her line manager was uncooperative. Ellie felt disappointed with her life. It just wasn't turning out the way she'd hoped. First the divorce and now her inflexible work regime… Still it paid the bills and she really enjoyed her job (except at times like these!). The problem was, she always felt stressed or in a rush no matter how hard she tried, until she only had sufficient energy to fall into bed exhausted each night. She thought about how grateful she was for her mother's help and the girls seemed happy enough. A moment later, she turned the corner and gave a little wave as she saw all three girls waiting expectantly for her at the school gate…

Like many women in leadership, Ellie's measure of 'success' is not limited to her effectiveness in either the workplace or the home. It is based upon a combination of the two. Achievement in both arenas is frequently cited as a source of major importance to women and not necessarily because we 'want it all'. Recent research noted by the Economic Commission for Europe suggests that encouraging a woman's expression through work and family, is beneficial to family life, society in general and even the national economy! Consequently, in nations where women do not have to 'do it all', in order to 'have it all' and where family and work life is more easily combined, social indicators perform comparatively well.[4]

Unfortunately, when we engage in paid work, we are often made to feel that we have failed to consider properly the needs of our families. This is regardless of whether we are single, married, mothers or childless women. Subsequently, women often conclude that success in the workplace must come at the expense of family life. If we work beyond the home, we invariably feel guilty that we do not give our families enough of our time and energy. If we happen to work within or from the home, we may still feel guilty that the time and energy we give as mothers or carers just isn't good enough. Either way we can end up deeply frustrated and perpetually unhappy with our state of affairs! Women are also prone to feeling bad because we don't see as much of our friends and family members as we would like. On the other hand, we may wrestle with self-reproach for harbouring negative thoughts that we already give far too much time and attention to everyone other than ourselves!

Women in leadership may struggle with the belief that both their family and work life would improve 'if only' an imaginary set of conditions existed. Such circumstances commonly approximate to images seen on the closing credits of a box office hit! Those familiar with Bollywood (Hindi cinema, popular in Asia and the Middle East), Hollywood (USA and Europe), or Nollywood (Nigeria and Africa) may at least recognise that such productions are based primarily on fictional scenarios that exist in the imagination of a script writer. Consequently, 'happy ever after' is what *they* choose to make it. Interestingly, 'happy ever after' can also be whatever we choose to make it but this is only possible when we dispense with fairytales and attend to present realities. In other words, we must abandon the notion that personal contentment can only be found if the people and circumstances *around* us change. On the contrary, we must recognise that happiness emerges only as *we* attempt to think differently about the people and circumstances that surround us. We cannot deny the presence of external factors over which we have little or no control but we should recognise that we

> Happiness emerges only as we attempt to think differently about the people and circumstances that surround us

do, at least, have almost limitless control over ourselves. We can learn to adjust our perceptions and desires with God's help and lead ourselves into a disposition that is more fully aligned with his.

What *we choose* to 'live with', or fail to address can often make or break the conditions of our inner circle. Therefore, principles that focus on self-leadership are particularly important when tackling 'inner circle' challenges. They are a reminder that we can never force change in anyone's behaviour except our own, and even this is far easier said than done!

We have already addressed the issue of self-leadership specifically related to self-awareness and self-management in previous chapters. We have acknowledged that these two characteristics are among the toughest challenges any leader may have to face. However, nothing tests these more than our 'nearest and dearest' family relationships. An intentional approach to self-awareness and self-management within these innermost relationships also presents us with the keys to success.

Self-leadership can be an incredibly powerful tool, particularly when directed toward doing God's will. When we lead ourselves we are capable of impacting our family circle in ways that make a difference both within and beyond the borders of our immediate family. As the opening quote from Confucius reminds us, attention to our personal inner life has the potential to transform the most dysfunctional 'inner circle' into a family that is capable of, well... changing the world!

However, gaining a balanced perspective on the importance and significance of family life is particularly important for us as women.

Families matter to God

The family context is dear to God's heart. This is evident from the frequent displays of God's grace in the context of the family. From the Old Testament and throughout the New Testament, families become a focus for God's activity and his favour. Family members are often blessed by God simply by virtue of belonging to their particular family and not because of any great personal feat or accolade. For example, Noah is described as the only blameless individual on earth prior to the great flood and yet Noah *together* with his entire extended family are saved on the ark (Genesis 6 & 7). Joshua 6:17 clearly identifies Rahab as the individual responsible for hiding the Hebrew spies from discovery in Jericho. However, it is Rahab *together* with her entire family (who do not appear to have played any active part in the rescue) whose lives are delivered and spared after the walls of Jericho fall down. We also learn in Acts 16:22–34 that the Philippian jailer acts as the primary point of contact for Paul and Silas during their imprisonment in Philippi. However, his entire household benefit from his personal encounter and all are eventually saved.

There is clearly something of significance about the family unit that prompts God to both value and promote it. For example, family becomes the vehicle that God uses to fulfil his purpose in bringing salvation to the whole world. It is not incidental that Elizabeth, mother of John the Baptist who prepared the way for Jesus, was related to Mary. Neither is it coincidental that John the Baptist was Jesus' cousin or that James, one of Jesus' younger brothers (see Matthew 13:55–56 and Galatians 1:19) is eventually numbered amongst the chief apostles of the Jerusalem church. Indeed, many of Jesus' extended family became important figures in salvation history.

In addition, some of Jesus' extended family have decidedly 'unusual' credentials. Luke's gospel describes Jesus' family through his mother

Mary, the teenage virgin. Here his genealogy begins with Adam (and Eve) and concludes many generations later with the pronouncement of the Messiah, the 'Son of David'.[5] However, Matthew's genealogy is keen for us to understand that Jesus' family is not unlike our own. This genealogical family is traced through Joseph his adopted (legal) father and includes a number of 'unexpected' female and male relatives. These include the prostitute Rahab; the gentile Ruth and Solomon the son of a murdered man's wife. There is a reminder and encouragement here for those of us who sometimes wonder if our families are just a little too complex and convoluted for God to work with. In fact, we quickly discover that God is committed to working with every kind of family, however 'unorthodox' and he continues to reveal his awesome intentions and plans for us, through them. Therefore, we can never afford to neglect our family life regardless of how complex it becomes, the heart of God is bound to it in profound ways as we shall now discover.

- **Family describes God's character and activity**

  The family plays a significant and central role in God's story of redemption. The language of family is employed to describe characteristics and attributes of the essentially indescribable God. In doing so, God enables us to appreciate some important truths about how he wishes to relate to us.

  God is described as 'The' Father and compared to a mother (Deuteronomy 32:11; Hosea 13:8; Psalm 131:2; Isaiah 66:13; Luke 15:8–10). Jesus taught us to pray to 'Our Father in heaven' in Matthew 6:9. God is said to comfort his people 'as a mother comforts her child', (Isaiah 66:13). Israel is described as son, daughter, people or children throughout the Old Testament. The New Testament book of Revelation 21:7 further underlines this truth through God's promise, 'Those who are victorious will inherit all this, and I will be their God and they will be my children.' In addition, the symbolism of marriage is used to describe the relationship between Christ and the Church in Ephesians 5:21–33. Similarly, Old Testament representations depict God as a husband married to Israel, which is often portrayed as an unfaithful wife (e.g. Hosea).

Both the Old Testament and the New Testament demonstrate a similar regard for families. Jesus' first miracle takes place at a wedding and one of his last actions as he lay dying on the cross was to ensure that his own mother would continue to be supported and cared for as part of someone else's family (John 19:25–27).

Regardless of how dysfunctional or 'unusual' we consider our family to be, it is the place where we all begin and usually where each one of us ends. Therefore, we cannot underestimate the significance of this powerful 'inner circle'. However much family matters to us, we must never forget that it matters a great deal more to God. In Biblical terms, God makes provision for all kinds of families.

A Biblical Perspective on Family Matters

Sade would simply have to rearrange her work schedule in order to care for Jo. They had been friends for over 30 years and since the death of her parents, Jo had become like a mother to Sade. She had also enjoyed the amazing privilege of witnessing Jo 'grow old in style'. Sade smiled as she remembered how they often repeated this phrase in unison. The consultant's report had hit them both very hard. Jo had always been fiercely independent since the death of her husband but now she was simply too frail to care for herself. She would need a great deal of help and support, and Sade was determined to provide it. She knew she would never forgive herself if Jo ended up in a residential care home. Sade also realised that as the company director, she would have to juggle her hours if she was to keep everything 'ticking over'. However, if she prioritised carefully and presented a convincing case to the board, she should be able to work from home more frequently. Without the commute, she could probably even work more effectively. Sade sat on the edge of Jo's bed and stroked the creases out of the frown that had gathered across Jo's forehead. Now came the hardest part. In order to persuade Jo to even consider her solution, she would have to phrase her proposal very carefully indeed…

The Bible does not have a word that directly translates into our modern concept of 'family'. Social units were typically extended families, clans and tribes and took on a variety of shapes and sizes and included the concept of those like Sade and Jo who were not related by blood but who related as mother and daughter. The closest concept to family life in the Old Testament is expressed by the Hebrew term 'bet av' which means, 'household'.

Such households could refer to the nuclear-type family of Joseph which consisted of Joseph, his wife and their two children (Genesis 41:50–52). Extended families such as Noah's included Noah, his wife and three sons, together with their wives (Genesis 7:1). A household might also include relatives such as aunts, uncles and cousins (Genesis 24:38). More complex households incorporated all who lived together and were related by patronage, friendship, business or even ownership and not necessarily by blood. Significantly, even servants and slaves who became part of a family were entitled to an inheritance, (see Genesis 15:3). In other words, households were held together by proximity and land, as well as blood ties.

Biblical families resemble the variety of family units in today's Western society in several significant ways. Many are extended and have grandparents, uncles and aunts sharing space. This is especially true of those who have family ties in the Global South.[6] Some have adult children living at home. Others have just one parent or are widows like the Widow of Zarephath, unmarried (Psalm 68:6), divorced or indeed separated through no fault of their own, like Hagar. Others are childless (Isaiah 54:1), or, like Hannah and Elkanah, Elizabeth and Zechariah, have their children very late in life (1 Samuel 1; Luke 1). Some 'family' members are not directly related by blood but remain fully committed to the family unit nonetheless.

During the course of my work and ministry, I increasingly encounter unmarried women who prefer to live with friends who they 'relate' to as mothers or sisters. This is sometimes a strategic decision for women in leadership positions who appreciate the additional spiritual, psychological and emotional support. In other words, having someone else around can divert us from the sometimes all consuming demands of ministry and work-related leadership and encourage a rhythm of 'normality'.

The main difference between Biblical families and those in today's Western contexts, is that in ancient Israelite society, there were no 'free-floating' individuals. Everyone belonged to someone's household. The family also served other functions. For example, it was the main haven for strangers, the centre for instruction and in the absence of courthouses, schools, churches, hospitals and funeral homes, the family became pretty much all things to all people!

In ancient times, belonging to a family was considered the greatest good. Today, sentiments vary depending on personal experience. However, the impact of the household on individual lives has not altered. Family still matters, most of all to God!

Family ideals are forged in heaven: God's household

The first family or *household* we encounter in scripture is God himself. God as Father, Son, and Holy Spirit is revealed through a variety of means from the earliest pages of scripture. This household demonstrates a clear sense of purpose, vision and commitment to each other and to what they create together. As such, God the Father, Son and Holy

Spirit exemplify the ideal family. Not only are they in perfect relational unity (John 10:30), they also share an unrivalled sense of teamwork and fellowship. From the moment of its first expression in the Bible, the importance of family is underscored over and over again.

The family ideal may have been forged in heaven but human households live on earth! Whatever family perfection we long for, it is always tempered by the fact that we live in a world deeply affected by the presence of sin. Women in leadership need not lament at the lack of perfection within their own families, we are all works in progress, the emphasis being on 'progress'. As long as we have determined to develop ourselves and our family in a specific (God-honouring) direction and take action to do so, we have made a good leadership decision. However, we are not necessarily responsible for all the results.

Family life takes place on earth: Adam, Eve and the rest...

The first human family was created in God's image (Genesis 1:27). Presumably, this means that the human capacity to love, empathise, nurture, encourage and forgive are all directly derived from God's character. God's template for humanity also reveals God's original basis for family life as a union of one man and one woman together for life.

- **The downward spiral**

  However, creation was barely completed before the tranquillity of 'paradise' was interrupted by the sounds of heated dispute between Adam and Eve. The argument focused on who was primarily to blame for the catastrophe of the 'Fall'. Consequently, this very first human family is literally separated from God's presence and prevented from returning to the Garden of Eden by the presence of an angel with a flaming sword (an interesting disciplinary approach!).

Unfortunately, the dynamic of family life continues on a downward trajectory. Adam and Eve initially experience the joy of child birth, only to be exposed to the pain of loss, as one insanely jealous son, Cain, murders his brother, Abel. The family never truly recovers from the devastation and many generations later, Ham so offends his father Noah, that Noah angrily curses not Ham, but his grandson Canaan, (Ham's son, see Genesis 9). This results in a further deterioration of the extended family network and sets the scene for enmity between future generations.

The story of the human family continues as Jacob, having deceived his brother Esau and his father Isaac, barely escapes with his own life (Genesis 27ff). Eventually, he meets his match and is thoroughly deceived by his father-in-law, Laban. A few years later, Jacob adopts favourites within his own family of 12 sons (much like his father Isaac, before him). The boys respond by taking the term 'sibling rivalry' to a whole new level. They promptly 'close ranks', agreeing to sell their brother Joseph into slavery and a life of bitter exile.

In a bid for self-protection, two of the towering figures of the Old Testament, Abraham and Isaac, falsify their wives' identities, declaring them to be no more than their sister. Subsequently, they succeed in compromising the virtue of their wives and bring judgement on their hosts in the process (Genesis 20; 26).

In reality, Biblical families barely resemble what most of us associate with the ideal family. Many of them are surprisingly and almost alarmingly, dysfunctional. Themes of adultery, incest, murder and jealousy punctuate the accounts of many families throughout the Bible. Indeed, we may feel that our family positively glows by comparison!

Ironically, the fact that most families, even Biblical ones, are far from perfect and have areas of dysfunction can be a source of great encouragement to us. It is a reminder that despite imperfection, God demonstrates a commitment and concern for every kind of family imaginable. After all, He remains 'the God of Abraham, the God of Isaac and the God of Jacob', (Exodus 3:6) in spite of Abraham, Isaac and Jacob!

● Putting family life into perspective

The Bible is extremely pro-family and Jesus, in particular, was positively disposed toward family life (he remained unmarried himself). He often instructed those whose lives he'd affected to return and minister to their families (Mark 5.19). We also see that commitment to family was evident among the apostles, most of whom travelled with their wives as they exercised itinerant ministries (1 Corinthians 9:5). On one occasion, Peter even asked Jesus to heal his sick mother-in-law (Matthew 8). Even in the midst of radical discipleship, believers were *never* at liberty to neglect their responsibilities to their families (1 Timothy 5:8). However, while we are never at liberty to neglect our families, neither are we encouraged to idolise the family unit. The family is never presented as an end in itself, and this challenge applies to both men and women.

Jesus did not preach the priority of the family, he preached the priority of the kingdom and discipleship. He was very clear that his demands would sometimes set one family member against another (Luke 12:51–53). On at least one occasion, Jesus' relationship with his own family seemed a little tense. His mother and brothers believing him to be 'out of his mind' arrived to 'take charge of him'. Jesus responded by publicly challenging their right to do so, reminding them and all who listened, that even those closest to him should place the demands of discipleship ahead of everything else (Mark 3:20–34).

On another occasion, Jesus refused to allow women to idolise their role as mothers. One woman called out a well-known chant, "'Blessed is the mother who gave you birth and nursed you." He (Jesus) replied, "Blessed rather are those who hear the word of God and obey it."' (Luke 11:27, 28) Jesus viewed women as more than professional people-producers. Similarly, Jesus rejected the idea that women must prioritise the role of home-making above all else. He reminded his good friend Martha, that although domesticity and being hospitable was important, it just wasn't *the* most important thing in life (Luke 10:41–42).

I have pastored women in leadership, in their early thirties, who have behaved as if their lives are over because they are unmarried. I have challenged married women in leadership who feel ambivalent about having children because it might 'hinder' the career they want to pursue. I have also encouraged married women in leadership who are struggling to have their first or even second child. In some instances, marriage and childbirth have simply taken on a significance God never intended.

Desires for a particular type of family (i.e. I'd like to get married and/or have children) should always be tempered by the demands of discipleship (i.e. how can I best serve God?).

Family relationships are certainly God-given gifts (even when they feel like 'mixed blessings'), therefore, we should cherish them and avoid any tendency to neglect whatever family we have. However, family life should never be worshipped or elevated

> While family is accorded great significance in the Bible, it never competes with discipleship

to a god-like status. While family is accorded great significance in the Bible, it never competes with discipleship.

Whatever the shape or size of our family, it has the potential to contribute something of great value to God's purposes. Although our inner circle can test and challenge our leadership capabilities, they can also enhance them. It is also true that our leadership gifts enable us to empower our family circle, thereby maximising their potential. There are many leadership skills that would serve us well, but none more so than self-leadership.

Develop Your Inner Circle by Leading Yourself

Selina was encouraged by the results. Twenty four hours earlier she had only just managed to avoid her usual tirade. She had found Errol's clothes strewn all over the bedroom floor. This would not usually have been enough to start her off but on this occasion she had just walked past a sink full of dirty dishes. She had also seen a couple of open and unfinished cans of food on the kitchen counter, surrounded by other clutter. Selina had barely been away for three days and the tell-tale signs of chaos were everywhere. There were clothes visible from the open crack in the bedroom doors meaning there was very little discernable floor space remaining in the boys' rooms. Selina was livid but she managed to contain herself and pray. This was a first! She said nothing and simply behaved normally for the rest of the evening. When Errol returned home with the boys, they enjoyed a meal together and on request, she described her conference in great detail. Everyone laughed as she retold some of the funnier jokes and stories. Even work had been better that day and she had been relatively free from the usual obsessing and distracted preoccupation with home life. She didn't raise the matter of the 'mess' with Errol until the following day. She was shocked and genuinely surprised by his response, for the first time Errol apologised, took responsibility and offered to put things right. He also acknowledged that her new approach had been helpful. So while he and the boys made themselves busy, she simply put her feet up…

Stop waiting for others

By definition, a leader is someone who is prepared to take the initiative and go on ahead of others. Unfortunately, like Selina, women are often tempted to wait for others to act. This may even involve waiting for God to take action, when he is waiting for us to do the same! Similarly, we may wait for a colleague or family member to notice us, change their behaviour toward us or give us permission to adjust our own actions. However, central to the gift of leadership, lies the responsibility to take a lead. With regard to our inner circle, this simply means being prepared to change our behaviour without expecting someone else to step up first. Therefore, we don't wait for another person(s) to smile, apologise, seek forgiveness or adjust their attitude, we just do it!

Self-leadership becomes particularly important once we accept the fact that the behaviour of our inner circle is seldom influenced by our relationship to them. Appeals to our role as wife, mother, sister, aunt, niece, colleague, friend or simply neighbour rarely lead to the desired effect and may actually exacerbate matters still further. However, others often unconsciously modify their behaviour in response to adjustments we make.

The ultimate challenge for the leader who is frustrated with the behaviour of inner circle members, lies in taking control of our own behaviour rather than in attempting to control theirs! Women who wait for others to notice that we are tired, hurt, frustrated or angry will find themselves waiting for a very long time indeed! When we change our behaviour and refuse to perpetuate the status quo, others often follow suit.

- **Trust God to help you make the difference**

   The leader who wants to see her inner family circle transformed but fails to appeal to the creator of us all, is embarking on an impossible uphill struggle. The very first human family, Adam and Eve, made only one mistake at the outset of creation, they simply neglected to include God in any of their deliberations. Instead, they chose to rely on hearsay, personal opinions and each other. Having foolishly excluded God's presence and instruction from their decision making, they made a mistake, the repercussions of which we feel to this very day!

A leader's worst enemy can be her desire to make matters right for everyone around her. Consequently, we may take circumstances into our own hands in the mistaken belief that we can rescue, recover and restore the fortunes of our nearest and dearest. However, we are deliberately designed with limitations; therefore, we will always find certain situations beyond us.

We actually need God if we are to live the life he desires for us. The Bible informs us that some things are humanly impossible but 'with God all things are possible' (Matthew 19:26). This should come as no surprise, since only God is capable of influencing hearts, challenging perceptions and addressing attitudes in ways that are truly transformative.

When we put God first, we are acknowledging that only he has the power to bring about the lasting change we seek.

- **Trust God to provide you with the necessary energy**
  We all want to do the best we can for our family, friends, church or job, regardless of whether we are single, married or mothers. Consequently, there are times when we are overwhelmed and drained by the needs of those who rely on us.

  Although we are often blessed and energised by our inner circle, only God can provide us with the spiritual, emotional and physical resources we need to grow in strength, wisdom, and commitment. Our relationship with him through our commitment to prayer, Bible study and reflection can be remarkably energising. In Biblical terms, making room for such interaction, as often as we are able, literally gives us access to the very same power that raised Jesus from the dead (Romans 8:11)! It also promises to provide us with the necessary discernment to structure our time and expend our energies appropriately.

● Focus on God, your highest calling

Women are sometimes encouraged (often unhelpfully), to believe that we exist for no other reason than for marriage and motherhood. This is, indeed, a worthy desire but it makes for an unhealthy goal! According to Jesus the highest calling for both female *and* male is to, 'Love the Lord your God with all your heart and with all your soul and with all your strength and with all your mind'; and, 'Love your neighbour as yourself'. (Luke 10:27 TNIV)

Major difficulties arise when a skewed conviction develops into an unhealthy obsession. Even high powered women leaders feel the pressure if they fail to exhibit the signs of social success that include getting married and raising a family. Women, in particular, are encouraged to extract meaning from family life that not even God has assigned to it! When women (or indeed men) seek to derive their sense of security and personal worth from a role such as a wife and mother (husband and father for men), rather than from their identity as children of God, we can develop a sense of entitlement. This perceived 'right' can come dangerously close to idolatry and the worship of all things 'family'. When the desired role becomes our focus, we sentence ourselves to resentment and perpetual disappointment because family life never delivers what we have always hoped for.

We cross the line from longing to obsession: If as an older single woman we conclude that we have been *cheated* out of a husband; If as a married woman, we behave as if we *have been denied* a *more loving* husband, (like somebody else's); If as a happily married but childless woman, we act as if we have been *cursed* with barrenness; If as a woman with sufficient children we have a sense of entitlement that we should have received *better behaved* children; If as a woman with siblings, we wonder why ours aren't *more understanding*. We have all had the privilege of parents, if not parenting, yet some of us would seriously consider swapping them if others were on offer!

We must all resist the temptation of obsessing over the need to have a 'fairytale' family. Whether we prescribe to the shame culture of the East or the blame culture of the West, putting family ahead of God leaves us vulnerable to the demands of ungodly family 'tradition' and 'reputation'. When family becomes our reason for living, we have crossed over from desire into the dangerous territory of obsession.

A woman's ultimate self-definition is not that of mother, wife, daughter, sister, aunt or niece. These titles are merely roles. Rather, our identity is first and foremost, a child of God, created, redeemed, sustained and empowered by God's grace. It is this identity that enables us to bring purpose, meaning and direction to our family and work.

Focusing on becoming the person God created us to be, allows us to release our family from unrealistic expectations and frees us to enjoy them for who they are. Our family was never designed to become our reason for living but it was always intended to be part of the meaning, joy and challenge of the journey.

- **Resist ungodly social and personal expectations**
  Most of the family disasters recorded in the Old and New Testament emerge when obsession is overtaken by manipulation. The power of social and personal expectations can never be underestimated. Women, in particular, are expected to 'look and play the part' of the perfect wife and mother. When certain cultural assumptions are also involved, the result can be toxic.

  Expecting more from the family than God intended can result in us loving family members conditionally, as long as they 'do things our way' and 'perform' appropriately.

  The parent who gets caught in this trap has little emotional freedom to raise children with their child's welfare in mind. When our sense of affirmation is derived entirely from our family, we may suffer from a need to be popular with our children or indeed the exact opposite.

The latter results in demands for inappropriate obedience that focuses on behaviour that reflects well on *us*. Whereas, the former parenting approach may result in us excusing behaviour in our children that should be challenged. The prophet Eli is a good example of this failure. He zealously enforced God's commands everywhere in Israel but overlooked them in his own home. He tolerated the worst kind of ungodly behaviour from his sons, failed to discipline them and allowed them to run rampant. Consequently, God accused Eli of honouring his sons more than he honoured God. Eli's failure to judge and discipline his sons led to God's intervention. Not only were they judged and disciplined as individuals but Eli's descendants were also disqualified from ever serving in the temple again (1 Samuel 2). Neither approach to parenting demonstrates an appropriate regard for the long-term emotional growth and development of our children.

The wife behaves as if her main purpose in marriage is to fulfil her own desires and the needs of her husband, regardless of how unreasonable either may be. *The single woman* attempts to blackmail and manipulate God into giving her what she believes will help to make her a better believer or human being. *The childless couple* go to any length to 'get' a child in much the same way Abram and Sarai were prepared to go, in an effort to redeem their status in society and to join the ranks of the 'begats' (see Genesis 16).

Women leaders may be particularly susceptible to these temptations. Indeed, the visibility that accompanies leadership can present its own peculiar challenges. Whereas men are seen to be doing something useful if they are following a career path, women are seen to be behaving abnormally. Independent women tend to attract negative associations such as old maid and spinster, while independent men may be identified as bachelors and viewed as brave and heroic.

I have had to face personal, social and cultural pressures of my own. For many black women, marriage and childbirth are seen as rites of passage into adulthood and single people are perceived as immature. A black male friend of mine, who didn't get married until he was well into his forties, was still being referred to as a 'small boy' (although he'd been a pastor for years). Whenever I go home to Ghana to minister I am always asked the question, 'Are you still single?' I am always prayed for, the overwhelming assumption is that my situation is unsatisfactory (I am never asked if *I* am satisfied!). My role as a leader (far from exempting me) provides added incentive for some to attempt to 'solve' what they perceive to be my problem of singleness (and childlessness). On one occasion while I was on a mission trip to Africa, I was introduced to a congregation of nearly 1,000 people with the words, 'please welcome Rev Kate Coleman who is a Baptist minister from London and still single...' You should have heard the ripples that followed and seen the queue of eligible men who felt that it was their duty to rescue me from the perceived affliction of singleness! I didn't know whether to get annoyed or simply enjoy the unexpected attention. I am regularly (even now) faced with similar challenges. It is just as well that I know my own mind and understand God's purposes for my life. Having spoken to married and unmarried women in leadership, I am well aware that such challenges are not unique to me. Women leaders, in particular, can be viewed as public property and they are regularly questioned about when they are going to get married, have a child or even have another child. Such expectations do not affect men in quite the same way.

Stop trying to be like everyone else!

Women today are bombarded with images of what a woman *should* look like in each of her roles. This pressure comes from many sources including the internet, television, radio, magazines and our churches.

Too often our identity is defined by others. Consequently, we may need to reclaim the person God created us to be. Great leaders understand that the best gift we can give to our inner circle, work or ministry is our whole unique selves. However, this requires us to accept our own uniqueness and resist attempts to become like everyone else!

When we try to fit the image of the perfect wife, mother and Christian leader, we sentence ourselves to a perpetual sense of inadequacy and failure. However, if we accept that we have each been created with a unique personality, ability, gifts and strengths we are then further empowered to accept that God has crafted a special combination of roles and opportunities for us, which allow us to exercise the gifts he has given to us.

For some, our opportunities will involve the gift of marriage, children and a home. For others, it will involve another combination of opportunities that may include singleness. No situation is presented by God as being superior or inferior. Each set of circumstances simply represents a unique set of opportunities and a unique set of challenges. Our path will not resemble the next woman's exactly, neither will our inner circle. However, our mission, 'should we choose to accept it', will lead to the greatest possible impact on God's kingdom and the most significant personal fulfilment possible.

Our unique identity makes for a unique calling, which in turn leads to unique challenges. Undeniably, our individual circumstances will affect our opportunities in ministry, work and the home. A married woman with children won't be able to climb the career ladder as speedily or in the same way as a single woman with fewer responsibilities. However, each identity has its own pros and cons.

The opportunities and challenges of the *older single woman* are quite different to those of the *younger single woman*. According to the Apostle Paul, both are 'free to serve the Lord' (1 Corinthians 7:32–35). However, an older single woman is generally responsible for all her household bills, mortgage repayments, road tax, car insurance and the list goes on. Without the rhythm that a husband and children provide, both have to resist the temptation (or demand) of being perpetually available to family, work or ministry.

On the other hand, the *single parent* faces a different dilemma. We do not have the same freedom to chart our own course as a woman without children. We must stay around for the sake of our children. However, we still carry the weight of responsibility for our whole household, with only one monthly income. We can often find ourselves in financial crisis or at the 'mercy' of the extended family to provide support. However, we can also experience levels of love and commitment we may never otherwise experience.

Although the world is slowly changing, the *wife and mother* is still likely to work twice as long, get paid significantly less and contribute twice as many hours to childcare, than her husband. However, we do get to share the financial responsibility and the spiritual and emotional responsibility for our children (at least in theory). Our challenge is to work at intimacy even when interaction is difficult. In this way, 'when one cries, the other tastes salt'. Also we must develop a sense of joint mission together with our partner. We have an amazing opportunity to bless our children, to help them believe in God, have confidence in themselves and to make a positive contribution to the world. Every parent can help to make the world a better place through the inner circle of their family. Therefore, children should never be viewed as a distraction on our way to saving the world, they are entrusted to us as part of that world. We can empower them to respect God, their parents and others. We have a wonderful opportunity to connect to and belong to them. We do not want to miss their significance in our rush to gain success elsewhere. We can challenge them to accept responsibility and prepare them to be a blessing to others. As we do so, we must recognise that not only may our family mission differ from anyone else's, our family may also look and behave differently to everyone else's (for the obvious reason that they are different!).

Each of these roles that women take on may differ, but God calls us to exercise our gift of leadership both within and beyond the borders of our inner circle.

Enjoy the fact that each season is unique

As we consider the roles we currently fill, we do so recognising that they inevitably change as we progress through the various stages of our lives. To allow a single role to define our whole life and identity would prove very foolish indeed.

In order to enjoy the life that God has given us to the fullest, we must embrace each season and situation that he places before us. Paul wrote that he had 'learned the secret of being content in any and every situation' (Philippians 4:12). We find contentment more easily when we recognise that every role involves a degree of sacrifice but also offers special blessings. Depending on our means and calling, some seasons may require us to make our children our full-time ministry. We may also have the privilege of spending much of our time with them. However, the support of friends and our extended family may enable us to continue to work and raise our family simultaneously.

We may discover that in each season, God works to prepare us for the next one. Whether we are supporting a husband or being supported, nurturing an infant, managing a family with growing children, or caring for aging parents, these times may be shaping us for yet another important assignment. We may discover that each experience adds another dimension to our leadership capabilities. Indeed, we may begin to adjust our leadership style and approach according to what we are learning along the way.

In order to fully live within each season requires patience and perseverance. It also requires a discerning heart and reliance on the Holy Spirit.

Get perspective!

Working mothers, particularly those in leadership, often wrestle with feelings of guilt for a variety of reasons. In the words of one report: 'Society puts unrealistic expectations on women to be "perfect" mothers.'[7] This makes it particularly important to get some perspective.

One of the challenges working mothers in leadership wrestle with is not spending sufficient time with their children. However, research reveals that today's mothers provide more childcare than stay-at-home mums did in previous generations.[8] Historically, European mothers were busy with tasks such as baking, cooking, washing and ironing, sewing and tending gardens, and before that possibly spinning and weaving. In the UK, Black and Asian mothers were typically engaged in service that was either indentured or slavery. Even when mothers were available to their children they were usually too busy to engage with them on any personal level.

In the year 2000, employed mothers spent as much time interacting with their children, as stay-at-home mums did in 1975.[9] Today, mothers in full-time employment spend almost as much time with their children as stay-at-home mums. In 2000, the time spent with children by stay-at-home mums amounted to an extra five hours a week more than working mums in full-time employment.

During the 1920s and 1930s good parenting was defined as the ability to provide food, clothing and a safe environment for children to grow up in. In the 21st century this emphasis has shifted significantly. Today, mothers are virtually held responsible for the emotional and psychological well-being of their children. They are also blamed when their children 'go wrong'. In other words, the emotional demands of mothering have increased exponentially and it is now an emotionally intensive activity that frequently leaves mums feeling more critical than pleased with their parenting skills.

Get the help you need!

Women in leadership are good... but we're not that good! We are not designed to be either Wonder Woman or Supermum! Most of us need help to make family life a success. There are some things we will need to ask of others. Thankfully, some gifts are not ours to exercise and some tasks are not assigned to us to engage with alone. Women in positions of leadership sometimes find it difficult to entrust others with important tasks. Either we feel that we alone are 'qualified' to get the job done, or we are hesitant to burden others with what we consider to be our duty and responsibility. The ability to spread the load is much easier to grasp for those who operate in cultures where extended family is the norm. Leadership requires us to establish our priorities, do what we can and get help for the rest. We can also learn from others who have already managed family, work and ministry roles simultaneously. There are many before us, who have the necessary wisdom, insight and experience that we need.

Leadership is already sufficiently stressful and places high demands on our emotional reserves, so we should ensure that we have sufficient emotional support in order to make strong emotional investments.

It is no secret that women in leadership are under more pressure than ever before – this is particularly true if they work full-time and serve in ministry. Today, Christian women are expected to be gifted leaders, faithful and compassionate Christians, competent workers, supportive spouses, nurturing mothers, and efficient homemakers. It's easy to see why many women struggle with balancing the competing demands for their time and attention, while also wrestling with the burden of over responsibility.

We must avoid the temptation to take up the wrong kind of responsibility for our families, whether they are a parent, husband, brother, sister, aunt, uncle or child. We are entrusted to act as stewards, with precious gifts that ultimately belong to God. Consequently, we must strive to make our decisions regarding them, God's decisions.

Be courageous

The decisions we make about key moments in our lives can prove to be particularly challenging, especially if they lead us against the prevailing winds of general opinion or expectation. However, leaders understand that this is simply part of the course. The wise leader will not settle for mediocre, they will take calculated risks and trust God with the results. Doing the right thing in spite of ourselves is not unlike taking the narrow road that Jesus speaks about in Matthew 7:13–14. It may not look particularly promising but I know with certainty that she who dares, definitely wins!

COACHING TIPS

Identify your VIPs (very important people). This will be your inner circle and may include members of your immediate family.

Identify the following for each individual:

STOP
(Something that you do that is self-defeating and definitely not helping.)

START
(Inject a new element into the relationship and find ways in which you can minister to each member of your inner circle.)

CONTINUE
(Something that already works well.)

'Other things may change us, but we start and end with family.'
ANTHONY BRANDT[10]

Afterword 'Going Forward' (quite literally!)

My own leadership journey has taught me that there is always more to us than meets the eye. For many years I tried to be someone I wasn't. I tried to conform to expectations and attempted to 'fit in' with everyone around me.

At the time, I failed to realise that I simply wasn't designed to 'fit in'. There is a very good reason why you and I were created so distinctively.

Choosing to become everything I should and could be has not been an easy option. In fact, it is an ongoing challenge. Whenever I am tempted to choose the path of least resistance over the one that leads me to destiny and calling, I am reminded of an African tale.

There was once a wounded eaglet who was rescued by a kind farmer. The farmer tended the wounds of the eaglet then placed it outside among his many chickens. Unfortunately, the eaglet adopted the behaviour and mannerisms of the chickens. It learned to scratch in the dirt and peck around for food just like a chicken. The eaglet soon came to believe that it was indeed a chicken. One day, one of the farmer's friends came by and asked why the eaglet was behaving in such a strange way. After the farmer explained, his friend responded, *'It's just not right, the Creator made that bird to soar in the heavens, not scavenge in the barnyard!'* So the friend devised a plan to enable the eaglet to remember what it was created to do. Firstly, he placed it on top of a fence; the eaglet simply fell off. Then he tried dropping it from a barnyard roof, but without success. It simply continued to behave like a chicken, pecking at pieces of straw and scratching around in the dirt. Eventually, the farmer's friend took the eaglet to the top of a nearby mountain, pointed the bird toward the light of the setting sun and in full view of the horizon. He then cried out, '*Don't you understand? You weren't made to live like a chicken! Why would you want to stay down here when you were born for the sky?*' He then dropped the bird over a precipice. This time the eagle opened its wings, caught the thermal updraft and soared into the clouds.[1]

Many of us who are called to lead, live our lives as if we are barnyard chickens scratching around in the dirt, entirely unaware of the great potential within us. The persistent negative messages we absorb from our environment and the untruths we have come to believe about ourselves result in a loss of true identity.

This book has essentially been about trading the barnyard for the open sky. However, this is far easier said than done. There is a vast difference between recognition and active engagement. Reading each chapter and reflecting on the various coaching tips will only take us so far. The transformation that we seek requires us to act on our growing convictions. James 1:23–25 is a reminder, 'Those who listen to the word but do not do what it says are like people who look at their faces in a mirror and, after looking at themselves, go away and immediately forget what they look like. But those who look intently into the perfect law that gives freedom and continue in it – not forgetting what they have heard but doing it – *they will be blessed in what they do*.' In other words, the real blessing is reserved for those who wholeheartedly apply the leadership lessons.

During the course of your interactions with this leadership development tool you have gained some valuable insights. These will inform you as you continue on your leadership journey. Perhaps your most important discovery is the realisation of just how valuable you are and how much God has invested in you. However, this does not mark the end of your growth as a leader. As you commit to God's purposes for your life, you will develop your leadership as you continue to:

- Overcome limiting self-perceptions
- Establish healthy boundaries
- Develop and refine a personal vision
- Cultivate a healthy work-life rhythm
- Resist being a people pleaser
- Learn to confront and not collude
- Be intentional with your inner circle

As you rehearse these leadership traits you will soar. Remember, you were made for this!

If you have found this book helpful and challenging, please continue to 'step out in faith'. Although I haven't been able to share this journey with you literally, I am confident that God has been with you throughout. I have an absolute assurance that God longs for you to break through to become everything you are created to be.

You may wish to contact me through our website with your comments or personal stories. If you would like to hear more about the '7 Deadly Sins of Women in Leadership', engage with any of our programmes or network with other like-minded women, please go to **www.nextleadership.org** or **www.the7deadlysins.org**.

Whatever you choose to do, my prayer is that you will approach your leadership with renewed hope, vigour and with the conviction that God has called you and is equipping you for the task.

Kate Coleman

Endnotes

Introduction

[1] Liz Cook and Brian Rothwell, *The X and Y of Leadership: How Men and Women Make a Difference at Work*, The Industrial Society, London 2000, p.4.

[2] Jeanne Porter, *Leading Ladies: Transformative Biblical Images for Women's Leadership,* Innisfree Press, Inc., Philadelphia, PA 2000, p.31.

[3] Although it is generally agreed that human development is influenced by both hereditary and environment, researchers remain undecided regarding the overall extent of each influence. The question of whether human beings are primarily products of genetic information passed on to them via their parental ancestry or whether they are essentially forged in the unique environmental conditions of their earliest and most formative years remains a topic of heated debate.

[4] This is the spiritual component of the almost tangible sensation of oppression and malevolence that is rooted in demonic activity and 'mischief' that is unleashed against those who would seek to do God's will.

[5] Steven Croft, 'A Theology of Christian Leadership' in Steven Croft, *Focus on Leadership: A Theology of Church Leadership,* Church Leadership Foundation, London 2005, p.13.

[6] Reggie McNeal, *Practicing Greatness: 7 Disciplines of Extraordinary Spiritual Leaders,* Jossey-Bass, San Francisco 2006, p.6.

[7] Rosie Ward, *Growing Women Leaders: Nurturing Women's Leadership in the Church*, The Bible Reading Fellowship 2008, p.111.

[8] Lois Frankel, *See Jane Lead: 99 Ways for Women to Take Charge at Work*, Warner Business Books, New York 2007, p.xviii.

[9] David Gergen in Linda Coughlin, Ellen Wingard and Keith Hollihan, *Enlightened Power: How Women are Transforming the Practice of Leadership*, Jossey-Bass, San Francisco 2005, p.xix.

[10] Ibid, p.xxi.

[11] S. Carter and E. Shaw, *Women's Business Ownership: Recent Research and Policy Developments*, Small Business Service, London 2006.

[12] National Women's Business Council (advisors to the President, Congress and SBA), 'Women Business Owners and their Enterprises', Fact Sheet, July 2007.

[13] See more on these encouraging signs from Spain in Dr Ruth Sealy, Professor Susan Vinnicombe OBE and Elana Doldor, *The Female FTSE Board and Report 2009*, Cranfield University School of Management, p.7. In addition, the number of FTSE 100 companies with multiple female directors has more than tripled in the last 10 years (from 12 to 37) and the number of women on executive committees had increased in 2007 by 40% See in Sarah Hanson, 'Why Women Leave', June 2007, *Director Magazine*. See also *Female FTSE Report*, Cranfield International School of Management, International Centre for Women Leaders, 2007, p.6–10. There was another substantial increase between 2008 and 2009 consequently the number of women on executive committees is now approaching 20% in total, '77 companies (up from 71 last year) have a total of 175 (substantially up from 139) women (executive directors and/or listed senior executives) in their top executive teams'. See *The Female FTSE Board and Report 2009*, p.25. In the US, the number of women in managerial-administrative (except farm) roles, had risen from 13.8% in 1950 to 26.1% in 1980, while the slightly revised category of management, professional and related occupations approached 45.2% in 1990. By 2008, the figure was closer to 50.6%. See Current Population Survey, Bureau of Labor Statistics, 'Table 11: Employed persons by detailed occupation, sex, race, and Hispanic or Latino ethnicity,' *Annual Averages 2008* (2009). www.bls.gov/cps/cpsaat11.pdf Research undertaken by Catalyst based on the 500 largest and most productive companies in the US (i.e. the Fortune 500), puts the number of women corporate officers at 15.7% in 2008, up from 8.7% in 1995. See Catalyst, Women in US management, February 25 2009 **www.catalyst. org/publication/207/women-in-management** (Catalyst provides the only numerical count of women corporate officers in the US) See also comparable figures cited in Amy Joyce *Washington Post* 6 August 2006. However, this progress was relatively slow compared to Norway, 'in 2004 83% of ASA companies (now regulated) in Norway had women on their boards. This has now moved to 100%'.

[14] See the foreword to the *Female FTSE Report*, Cranfield International School of Management, International Centre for Women Leaders 2007, p.1.

[15] Peter Brierley, *Pulling Out of the Nosedive A Contemporary Picture of Churchgoing: What the 2005 English Church Census Reveals,* Christian Research, London 2006, p.165.

[16] Rosie Ward, *Growing Women Leaders: Nurturing Women's Leadership in the Church*, The Bible Reading Fellowship 2008, p.187.

[17] Ibid, p.187. Rosie Ward writes 'In the Church of England the number of women clergy in 2002 was 2539, 20 per cent of the total; by 2006, it was around 3000. The percentage of women being ordained each year is increasing. In 1995 there were 44 women and 314 men priested. In 2006, it was 244 women and 234 men: parity was reached'. *The Church Times* carried a similar article. However, what it failed to clarify was that the majority of women were ordained to non-stipendiary posts and that only 95 women compared to 128 men were ordained to full-time stipendiary ministry and that women were still seriously under-represented in senior posts. However the figures still represent a remarkable achievement for a denomination that has been ordaining women from only 1994 (the historic vote took place in 1992!).

[18] This paradigm reveals a perspective that focuses on the idea that leadership effectiveness has to do with the ability of a leader to promote connectedness and positive relationships within an organisation through humility, listening, collaboration, community and cooperation. See especially, Linda Coughlin, Ellen Wingard and Keith Hollihan, *Enlightened Power: How Women are Transforming the Practice of Leadership*, Jossey-Bass, San Francisco 2005; J. M. Kouzes and B.Z. Posner, *The Leadership Challenge (4th Edition)* Jossey-Bass, San Francisco 2007, p.22–23.

[19] See Sally Morgenthaler's essay, 'Leadership in Flattened World: Grassroots Culture and the Demise of the CEO model' at **www.worshipteamtraining.com/ShowNotes/Leadership_Flattened_World_Morgenthaler.pdf** checked 5 June 2010, p.179–180.

[20] Bob Jackson, *The Road to Growth: Towards a Thriving Church,* Church Publishing House 2005, p.41.

[21] These include female Prime Ministers of the major South Asian regions of Sri Lanka, India, Pakistan and Bangladesh. Sirimavo Ratwatte Dias Bandaranaike, prime minister of Sri Lanka between 1960–1965; 1970–1977; 1994–2000; Begum Khaleda Zia, prime minister of Bangladesh from 1991–1996; 2001–2006; Indira Gandhi of India (1966–1977; 1980–1984) and Benazir Bhutto of Pakistan (1988–1990; 1993–1996).

[22] Sirimavo Ratwatte Dias Bandaranaike, prime minister of Sri Lanka between 1960–1965; 1970–1977; 1994–2000.

[23] *Real Business*, 'Britain's 100 Most Entrepreneurial Women' in Association with Bank of Scotland Corporate, **www.bankofscotland.co.uk/corporate/day-to-day-banking/hbos-women/top-100-women/index.html**, checked 16 April 2010.

[24] Liz Cook and Brian Rothwell, *The X and Y of Leadership*; Anna Dickson, *Women at Work: Strategies for Survival and Success*, Kogan Page, London, Dover 2000.

[25] Linda Coughlin in Linda Coughlin, Ellen Wingard and Keith Hollihan, *Enlightened Power: How Women are Transforming the Practice of Leadership*, p.xix. Summarising the global scene she adds, 'thriving wealth-producing organizations and societies are ones that promote the full and equal partnership of men and women leaders'. p.3.

[26] Ibid, p.7. See also Anne Marie Valerio, *Developing Women Leaders: A Guide for Men and Women in Organisations,* Wiley-Blackwell, West Sussex, United Kingdom 2009, p.20.

[27] Riane Eisler in Linda Coughlin Ellen Wingard and Keith Hollihan, *Enlightened Power: How Women are Transforming the Practice of Leadership*, 'The Economics of the Enlightened use of Power', p.28.

[28] Marie Wilson, *Closing the Leadership Gap: Add women, Change Everything*, Penguin Books, New York 2007, p.12.

[29] Claudia Dreifus, 'A conversation with Scott E. Page In Professor's Model, Diversity = Productivity', 8 January 2008, *New York Times* **www.nytimes.com** (7 March 2010).

[30] Peter Brierley, *Pulling Out of the Nosedive A Contemporary Picture of Churchgoing*, p.186.

[31] Bob Jackson, *The Road to Growth: Towards a Thriving Church,* Church House Publishing, London 2005, p.41.

[32] See Aida Besançon Spencer, 'Does God Have Gender?' in Priscilla Papers Volume 24, Number 2, Spring 2010, p.11. Christians for Biblical Equality, pp.5–12.

[33] Marie Wilson, *Closing the Leadership Gap*, p.xiii.

[34] Augusto Lopez-Claros and Saadi Zahidi, *Women's empowerment: Measuring the global gender gap*, World Economic Forum, Switzerland 2005.

[35] Ibid, p.2.

[36] For statistics on women in international politics, see Women in National Governments, the Inter-Parliamentary Union at **www.ipu.org** as of 30 April 2009.

[37] Liz Cook and Brian Rothwell, *The X and Y of Leadership,* p.4.

[38] There are various versions of this quote but the original is attributed to Robert Thaves the creator of the comic strip Frank and Ernest. In 1982 Thaves wrote about Fred Astaire 'Sure he was great, but don't forget that Ginger Rogers did everything he did, backwards…and in high heels'.

[39] Sarah Hanson, 'Why Women Leave', June 2007, *Director Magazine*.

[40] Big businesses are clearly haemorrhaging highly gifted women. This is not entirely due to family demands but is also because they opt to establish companies where they are at liberty to determine a work ethic and value base in which they do not 'feel' out of place. It is also a well known phenomenon that church women with leadership skills are more likely to be engaged in overseas or mission contexts engaging in what would be otherwise prohibited to them at 'home'.

1st Deadly Sin

[1] See at **www.quotes.net/quote/10252**.

[2] Lois P. Frankel, *See Jane Lead: 99 Ways for Women to Take Charge at Work*, Warner Business Books, New York, Boston 2007, p.73.

[3] Anne Dickson, *Women at Work: Strategies for Survival and Success,* Kogan Page Ltd, London, Dover 2000, p.1.

[4] Quoted by Rosie Ward, *Growing Women Leaders: Nurturing Women's Leadership in the Church*, The Bible Reading Fellowship, Abingdon, p.172.

[5] Lois Frankel, *Nice Girls Don't Get the Corner Office: 101 Unconscious Mistakes Women Make that Sabotage their Careers,* Warner Business Books, New York and Boston 2004, p.98.

[6] Eleanor Roosevelt, *This is My Story,* Garden City Publishing Co., Inc., New York, 1937. Eleanor was the wife of 32nd President of the US Franklin Roosevelt, niece of Theodore Roosevelt and a social activist & reformer in her own right.

[7] 'Fluke theory' is my definition for the belief that some women hold that their very real accomplishments brought about by sheer hard work are little more than fluke i.e. good luck at best or accidental at worst.

[8] See Mary Ellen Ashcroft, *Temptations Women Face: Honest Talk About Jealousy, Anger, Sex, Money, Food, Pride*, Kingsway Publications, Eastbourne 1992, p.25.

[9] Sally Helgesen quotes Nancy Badore in, *The Female Advantage: Women's Ways of Leadership,* Currency and Doubleday, New York 1990, p.163.

[10] Anne Dickson, *Women at Work,* p.125–126.

[11] Rosie Ward, *Growing Women Leaders,* pp.159–160.

[12] Jeanne Porter, *Leading Lessons: Insights on Leadership from Women of the Bible,* Augsburg Books, Minneapolis 2005, p.31.

[13] Ibid, p.30–31.

[14] Lois P. Frankel, *See Jane Lead,* p.18.

[15] Liz Cook and Brian Rothwell, *The X and Y of Leadership: How Men and Women Make a Difference at Work*, The Industrial Society 2000, p.3.

[16] Joan Raymond, *Newsweek* Web Exclusive, 23 January 2008, **www.newsweek.com/id/101079**.

[17] Liz Cook and Brian Rothwell, *The X and Y of Leadership,* p.158.

[18] Gordon Bailey, *Stuff and Nonsense: A Collection of Verse and Worse,* Lion Publishing plc, Oxford 1989, p.35.

[19] A people group is an ethnic group or group of humans whose members identify with each other, through a common heritage that is real or assumed.

[20] Sylvia Walby and Jonathan Allen, Home Office Research Study 276 Domestic Violence, Sexual Assault and Stalking: Findings from the British Crime Survey Home Office Research, Development and Statistics Directorate March 2004. See also World Health Organisation, Women and Health: Today's Evidence Tomorrow's Agenda, November 2009. Available at **www.who.int/gender/documents/9789241563857/en/index. html**, pp.55, 56.

[21] Peter Brierley, *Pulling Out of the Nosedive A Contemporary Picture of Churchgoing: What the 2005 English Church Census Reveals,* Christian Research, London 2006.

[22] This applies to both role models and paradigms related to strategy and approaches to ministry and mission.

[23] Rosie Ward, *Growing Women Leaders,* p.204.

[24] Ibid p.45. However, much of this thinking originated with scholars such as Mary Evans, see *Woman in the Bible: An Overall View of all the Crucial Passages on Women's Roles*, IVP, Nottingham 1983.

[25] Liz Cook and Brian Rothwell, *The X and Y of Leadership*, p.ix.

[26] Jurgen, Moltmann, *Theology of Hope: On the Ground and the Implications of a Christian Eschatology,* New Harper and Row, New York 1967, p.22. Also online at **www.pubtheo. com/theologians/moltmann/theology-of-hope-0b.htm**.

[27] Rosie Ward, *Growing Women Leaders,* p.181.

[28] In an article written for *The Times* online, 19 March 2009. Professor Nick Wilson, Professor of Credit Management at Leeds University Business School (LUBS), revealed exclusively to *The Times*, 'that women can make the difference between success and bankruptcy… In the financial services industry, about one director in five is female. "That sector, which includes banking, is a bit of a boys' network. It has one of the lowest proportions of female directors," Professor Wilson notes. "Having more women could well have made a difference."' **http://women.timesonline.co.uk/tol/life_and_style/ women/the_way_we_live/article5934200.ece**.

[29] Walter Wink, *Engaging the Powers: Discernment and Resistance in a World of Domination*, Fortress Press, Minneapolis 1992, p.133.

[30] Harlan, Louis R. *Booker T. Washington, The Making of a Black Leader, 1856-1901, vol 1*, Oxford University Press, Oxford 1972.

[31] See Dolly Parton post on Facebook **www.facebook.com/DollyParton/ posts/101457817659** 20 July 2009, checked 6 June 2010.

2nd Deadly Sin

[1] Adapted from a lecture by Rebbetzin Chana Rachel Schusterman see **www.inspirational-motivational-quotes.com/giving-quotes.html**.

[2] Dr Henry Cloud and Dr John Townsend, *Boundaries: When to Say Yes, How to Say No, to Take Control of Your Life*, Zondervan Publishing House, Michigan 1992, p.32.

[3] Ibid, p.38.

[4] Ibid, p.38.

[5] Karen Casey, *Codependence and the Power of Detachment: How to Set Boundaries and Make Your Life Your Own*, Conari Press, San Francisco 2008, p.14 (See also Karen Casey at **www.womens-spirituality.com**).

[6] *New Internationalist*, November 2004. 79 million girls who would otherwise be expected to be alive are 'missing' from various populations, mostly in Asia, as a result of sex-selective abortions, infanticide or neglect. Domestic violence is widespread in most societies but tends to be perpetrated largely against women. The victims of rape and other forms of sexual violence are largely women. Two million girls between the ages of 5 and 15 are introduced into the commercial sex market each year. An estimated 4 million women and girls are bought and sold worldwide each year, either into marriage, prostitution or slavery. At least 130 million women have undergone female genital mutilation or cutting; another 2 million are at risk each year.

[7] Claire Shipman and Katty Kay, *Womenomics: 1. Write Your Own Rules for Success 2. How to Stop Juggling and Struggling and Finally Start Living and Working the Way You Really Want*, Harper Business, New York 2009, p.104.

[8] Karen Casey, *Codependence and the Power of Detachment*, p.14.

[9] Parker Palmer, *Let your Life Speak: Listening for the Voice of Vocation*, Jossey-Bass, San Francisco 2000, pp.30–31.

[10] Karen Casey, *Codependence and the Power of Detachment*, p.15.

[11] Ibid, p.14.

[12] A major focus of the Greek and the Hebrew words for 'discipline' in both the Old and New Testament is 'training, correction and instruction'.

[13] Adapted from a lecture by Rebbetzin Chana Rachel Schusterman see **www.inspirational-motivational-quotes.com/giving-quotes.html**.

3rd Deadly Sin

[1] Stephen R. Covey, *The 7 Habits of Highly Effective People: Powerful Lessons in Personal Change*, Simon & Schuster UK Ltd, London 2004, p.98.

[2] Andy Stanley, *Visioneering: God's Blueprint for Developing and Maintaining Personal Vision*, Multnomah Publishers, Oregon 1999, p.15.

[3] Ibid, p.13.

[4] Andy Stanley, *Visioneering*, p.14.

[5] Kate Coleman in 'Woman, Single, Christian', pp.10–23 in *Sisters with Power,* Continuum, New York 2000, p.10.

[6] Paraphrased from Kate Coleman in 'Woman, Single, Christian', pp.10–23 in *Sisters with Power,* Continuum, New York 2000, p.10.

[7] Rick Warren, *The Purpose Driven Life: What on Earth am I Here for?* Zondervan, Grand Rapids, Michigan 2002, pp.17–18.

[8] Ibid, p.18.

[9] See **www.nextleadership.org**.

[10] See Frank M. Biro et al, 'Self-esteem in Adolescent Health', *Journal of Adolescent Health* vol 39, issue 4, October 2006, pp.501–507. Researchers report, 'Self-esteem began to decline at age 11 years in white girls, but appeared to be stable in black girls between 9 and 14 years of age; these differences were attributed to greater satisfaction in physical appearance. A recent meta-analysis noted greater self-esteem in Blacks, as contrasted to Whites, and observed increased differences in effect size with increasing age, as well as with lower socioeconomic status.'

[11] Kara L. Kerr, 'Sociocultural influences on Body Image and Depression in Adolescent Girls' in Priscilla Papers, pp. 21–22, vol 24, number 2, Spring 2010, (Christians for Biblical Equality, Minneapolis), p.22.

[12] Dale Galloway, *Leading with Vision,* Beacon Hill Press, Kansas, Missouri 1999, p.11.

[13] Andy Stanley, *Visioneering: God's Blueprint for Developing and Maintaining Personal Vision*, Multnomah Publishers, Oregon, 1999, p.8.

4th Deadly Sin

[1] See this definition at **www.yourdictionary.com/rhythm**.

[2] See 'A Day in the Life of a West African Woman' A WOW! e-Brief Work of Women @ World Neighbors, April 2008, **www.workofwomen.org**.

[3] See Richard H. Robbins, *Global Problems and the Culture of Capitalism,* Boston, Allyn and Bacon, 1999, p.354. The United Nations Decade for Women took place between 1976–1985.

[4] **www.peoplemanagement.co.uk/news**, 12 June 2008, p.9.

[5] Mark Greene, *Thank God it's Monday: Ministry in the Workplace,* Scripture Union Publishing, UK 2001, p.75.

[6] Family Friendly Working Arrangements in the UK 1996, DfEE Research Series RR16.

[7] Myron Rush, *Burnout: Practical Help for Lives Under Pressure,* Alpha, Wheaton, Illinois 1997, p.13.

[8] Mark Greene, *Thank God it's Monday*, p.27.

[9] My emphasis.

[10] Mark Greene, *Thank God it's Monday,* p.106.

[11] Steve and Mary Farrar, *Overcoming Overload: Seven Ways to Find Rest in Your Chaotic World,* Multnomah Publishers, Oregon 2003, p.37.

[12] Mark Greene, *Thank God it's Monday*, p.31.

[13] **www.answers.com/topic/recreation**.

[14] See Gary Thomas, *Sacred Pathways: Discover Your Soul's Path to God,* Zondervan, Michigan 2000.

[15] Internet Collections: 20th Century Quotations: From Kevin Harris: 'A collection of famous, thought provoking and humorous quotations of the 20th century'. About 300 quotes total. Kevin Harris 1995 see at **www.quotationspage.com/quote/11226.html**.

5th Deadly Sin

[1] Anne Morrow Lindbergh. (n.d.). BrainyQuote.com. Retrieved 6 June 2010, from BrainyQuote.com **www.brainyquote.com/quotes/quotes/a/annemorrow161675.html**.

[2] Dr Jan Yager, *Friendshifts: The Power of Friendship and How it Shapes Our Lives*, Hannacroix Creek Books, Inc, Connecticut 1999, p.162.

[3] Reggie McNeal, *Practicing Greatness: 7 Disciplines of Extraordinary Spiritual Leaders*, Jossey-Bass, San Franscisco 2006, p.136.

[4] Dr Jan Yager, *Friendshifts*, p.164.

[5] David Gergen, in Linda Coughlin et al, *Enlightened Power: How Women are Transforming the Practice of Leadership*, Jossey-Bass, San Francisco 2005, pxxi.

[6] Liz Cook and Brian Rothwell, *The X and Y of Leadership: How Men and Women Make a Difference at Work*, The Industrial Society, London 2000, p.69.

[7] Ibid, p.141.

[8] Lois Frankel, *See Jane Lead: 99 Ways for Women to Take Charge at Work*, Warner Business Books, New York 2007, p.122.

[9] Harriet B. Braiker, *The Disease to Please: Curing the People Pleasing Syndrome*, McGraw-Hill, New York 2001, p.77.

[10] Lois Frankel, *See Jane Lead*, p.xvii.

[11] Niccolo Machiavelli (1469–1527) is considered one of the main founders of modern political science. He promoted the idea that cunning and deceitful tactics in politics are to be expected.

[12] Deborah Tannen, *That's Not What I Meant: How Conversational Style Makes or Breaks Your Relations With Others*, Virago Press, London 1986, pp.109–112.

6th Deadly Sin

[1] Emmanuel Lartey, *In Living Colour: An Intercultural Approach to Pastoral Care and Counselling*, Cassell, London 1997, p.12. Emmanuel Lartey *In Living Color: An Intercultural Approach to Pastoral Care and Counselling*, Jessica Kingsley Publishers, London and Philadelphia 2003. Reproduced with kind permission of Jessica Kingsley Publishers.

[2] Ibid, p.12

³ Reported by *BBC News Magazine*, 16 May 2008, **http://news.bbc.co.uk/1/hi/ magazine/7402907.stm**.

⁴ Jessica Tuchman Mathews, *A Woman's Lens on Global Issues*, Aspen Institute, 2001 quoted in Marie C. Wilson, *Closing the Leadership gap: Add Women Change Everything*, Penguin Books, New York 2007, p.90.

⁵ Marie Wilson, *Closing the Leadership Gap*, p.89.

⁶ Tara Klena Barthel & Judy Dabler, *Peace Making Women: Biblical Hope for Resolving Conflict*, Baker Books, Grand Rapids, Michigan 2005, p.21.

⁷ Coretta Scott King Ed, *The Words of Martin Luther King*, Fount, London, p.65.

⁸ Sevi Regis, see on **http://schools-wikipedia.org/wp/p/Peace.htm**.

⁹ Strong's Number H7965 see at **www.blueletterbible.org/lang/lexicon/Lexicon.cfm? strongs=H7965**.

¹⁰ Coretta Scott King Ed, *The Words of Martin Luther King*, p.83.

¹¹ See Luke 13:29 'People will come from east and west and north and south, and will take their places at the feast in the kingdom of God.'

¹² Some women also provided funds for Jesus' work (Luke 8:3) and remarkably became the first to witness his resurrection (Mark 16:9).

¹³ Tara Klena Barthel & Judy Dabler *Peace Making Women*, p.21.

7th Deadly Sin

¹ See the articles on Demography in RTD info Magazine on European Research: The Changing Face of the Family, Issue 49, European Commission, May 2006.

² For example, the birth of a child tends to reduce a woman's involvement in the world of work, whereas the same event appears to increase a man's involvement in work. See online article 'Great Britain – Family Roles: Men's Work, Women's Work' at **http:// family.jrank.org/pages/738/Great-Britain-Family-Roles-Men-s-Work-Women-s-Work. html**, checked 15 June 2010.

³ John C. Maxwell, *The 21 Irrefutable Laws of Leadership*, Thomas Nelson Inc, Nashville, Tennessee 2002.

[4] See article entitled, 'Social Cohesion and Demographic Challenges' in Demography & Family: The Changing Face of the Family RTD info Magazine on European Research, no. 49, European Commission, May 2006, pp.4-5. Further examples of such contexts include France and Nordic countries, such as Sweden, Finland, Iceland and Norway. See Avivah Wittenberg-Cox & Alison Maitland, *Why Women Mean Business*, Wiley, West Sussex 2009, p.14 and pp.193–234.

[5] Although David lived almost 1000 years earlier than Jesus, the term 'son of David' is used to denote that Christ was the fulfilment of the prophecy that the Messiah would be the 'seed of David' and a direct descendant (2 Samuel 7:14–16).

[6] This term is used to describe the nations of Africa, Central and Latin America, and most of India and Asia – collectively. Most of these nations have severely limited resources and face challenges related to political, social, and economic upheaval.

[7] **http://balancing-career-mothering.suite101.com/article.cfm/strategies_for_work_life_ balance** Naomi Rockler-Gladen, 3 May 2007, checked 6 June 2010.

[8] Alice H. Eagley and Linda L. Carli, *Through the Labyrinth: The Truth About How Women Become Leaders*, Harvard Business School Press, Boston, Massachusetts 2007, p.54.

[9] Ibid, p.54.

Afterword

[1] This is a paraphrase of a popular African children's story, it is also retold by Christopher Gregorowski, *Fly Eagle Fly: An African Tale*, Margaret K. McElderry Books, Simon and Schuster, New York 2000.

Bibliography

Ashcroft, Mary Ellen, *Temptations Women Face: Honest Talk About Jealousy, Anger, Sex, Money, Food, Pride* (Eastbourne: Kingsway Publications, 1992)

Ashcroft, Mary Ellen, *Balancing Act: How Women Can Lose Their Roles and Find Their Callings* (Downers Grove, Illinois: InterVarsity Press, 1996)

Bailey, Gordon, *Stuff and Nonsense: A Collection of Verse and Worse,* (Oxford: Lion Publishing plc, 1989)

Barthel, Tara Klena & Dabler, Judy, *Peace-Making Women: Biblical Hope for Resolving Conflict* (Grand Rapids, Michigan: Baker books, 2005)

Beach, Nancy, *Gifted to Lead: The Art of Leading as a Woman in the Church* (Grand Rapids, Michigan: Zondervan, 2008)

Braiker, Harriet B., *The Disease to Please: Curing the People Pleasing Syndrome* (New York: McGraw-Hill, 2001)

Brierley, Peter, *Pulling Out of the Nosedive A Contemporary Picture of Churchgoing: What the 2005 English Church Census Reveals,* (London: Christian Research, 2006)

Carter, S. and Shaw, E., *Women's business ownership: recent research and policy developments* (London: Small Business Service, 2006)

Casey, Karen, *Codependence and the Power of Detachment: How to Set Boundaries and Make Your Life Your Own* (San Francisco: Conari Press, 2008)

Chin, Jean Lau, Lott, Bernice, Rice, Joy K. and Sanchez-Hucles, Janis (ed.s), *Women and Leadership: Transforming Visions and Diverse Voices* (Oxford: Blackwell Publishing, 2007)

Cloud, Dr Henry and Townsend, Dr John, *Boundaries: When to Say Yes, How to Say No, to Take Control of Your Life* (Michigan: Zondervan Publishing House, 1992)

Comiskey, Joel, *Planting Churches that Reproduce* (Moreno Valley, California: CCS Publishing, 2009)

Cook, Liz and Rothwell, Brian, *The X & Y of Leadership: How Men and Women Make a Difference at Work* (London: The Industrial Society, 2000)

Coughlin, Linda, Wingard, Ellen and Hollihan, Keith, *Enlightened Power: How Women are Transforming the Practice of Leadership* (San Francisco: Jossey-Bass, 2005)

Covey, Stephen R., *The 7 Habits of Highly Effective People* (London: Simon & Schuster Ltd, 2004)

Croft, Steven, *Focus on Leadership: A Theology of Church Leadership* (London: Church Leadership Foundation, 2005)

Crowley, Katherine and Elster, Kathi, *Working with You is Killing Me: Freeing Yourself from Emotional Traps at Work* (New York: Warner Business Books, 2006)

Cuthbert, Nick, *How to Survive (and Thrive) as a Church Leader* (Oxford: Monarch Books, 2006)

Dickson, Anne, *Women at Work: Strategies for Survival and Success* (London: Kogan Page Limited, 2000)

Eagly, Alice H. and Carli, Linda L., *Through the Labyrinth: the truth about how women become leaders* (Boston, Mass.: Harvard Business School Press, 2007)

Elnaugh, Rachel, *Business Nightmares: When Entrepreneurs Hit Crisis Point...* (Richmond: Crimson Publishing, 2008)

European Commission, Demography & Family: The Changing Face of the Family RTD info Magazine on European Research, no. 49, May 2006

Everett, Lesley, *Walking Tall: Key Steps to Total Image Impact* (Bracknell, UK: Walking Tall Publishing, 2004)

Farrar, Steve and Mary, *Overcoming Overload: Seven Ways to Find Rest in Your Chaotic World* (Oregon: Multnomah Publishers Inc., 2003)

Fernando, Ajith, *Reclaiming Friendship: Relating to Each Other in a Fallen World* (Leicester: Inter-Varsity Press, 1991)

Frankel, Lois P., *Nice Girls Don't Get the Corner Office: 101 Unconscious Mistakes Women Make That Sabotage Their Careers* (New York: Warner Business Books, 2004)

Frankel, Lois P., PhD, *See Jane Lead: 99 Ways for Women to Take Charge at Work* (New York: Warner Business Books, 2007)

Galloway, Dale (compiled by), *Leading With Vision* (Kansas City: Beacon Hill Press, 1999)

Grady, Lee, *10 Lies the Church Tells Women: How the Bible Has Been Misused to Keep Women in Spiritual Bondage* (Florida: Charisma House, 2000)

Greene, Mark, *Thank God it's Monday: Ministry in the Workplace* (UK: Scripture Union Publishing, UK, 2001)

Gregorowski, Christopher, *Fly Eagle Fly: An African Tale* (New York: Margaret K. McElderry Books, Simon and Schuster, 2000)

Helgesen, Sally, *The Female Advantage: Women's Ways of Leadership* (New York: Currency and Doubleday, 1990)

Hybels, Bill, *Courageous Leadership* (Grand Rapids, Michigan: Zondervan, 2002)

Jackson, Bob, *The Road to Growth: Towards a Thriving Church* (London: Church Publishing House, 2005)

King, Coretta Scott Ed, *The Words of Martin Luther King* (London: Fount, 1983)

Kouzes, J. M. and Posner, B.Z., *The Leadership Challenge (4th Edition)* (San Francisco: Jossey-Bass, 2007)

Lartey, Emmanuel , *In Living Colour: An Intercultural Approach to Pastoral Care and Counselling* (London: Cassell, 1997)

Lawrence, James, *Growing Leaders: Reflections on Leadership, Life and Jesus* (Oxford: The Bible Reading Fellowship/CPAS, 2004)

Lopez-Claros, Augusto and Zahidi, Saadi, 'Women's Empowerment: Measuring the Global Gender Gap', World Economic Forum, Switzerland, 2005

Maxwell, John C., *The 21 Irrefutable Laws of Leadership: Follow Them and People Will Follow You* (Nashville, Tennessee: Thomas Nelson, Inc., 2002)

McIntyre, Valerie J., *Sheep in Wolves' Clothing: How Unseen Need Destroys Friendship and Community* (Grand Rapids, Michigan: Baker Books, 1999; orig. pub. Pastoral Care Ministries, 1996)

McNeal, Reggie, *Practicing Greatness: 7 Disciplines of Extraordinary Spiritual Leaders* (San Francisco: Jossey-Bass, 2006)

Meyer, Joyce, *Approval Addiction: Overcoming Your Need to Please Everyone* (London: Hodder & Stoughton, 2007)

Moltmann, Jurgen, *Theology of Hope: On the Ground and the Implications of a Christian Eschatology* (New York: Harper and Row, 1967). See also online at **www.pubtheo.com/theologians/moltmann/theology-of-hope-0b.htm**

Morse, MaryKate, *Making Room for Leadership: Power, Space and Influence* (Illinois: Inter-Varsity Press, 2008)

Ortberg, Nancy, *Unleashing the Power of Rubber Bands: Lessons in Non-Linear Leadership* (Carol Stream, Illinois: Tyndale House Publishers, 2008)

Owen, Grace, *The Career Itch: 4 Steps for Taking Control of What You Do Next* (London: og publishing, 2009)

Palmer, Parker, *Let your Life Speak: Listening for the Voice of Vocation* (San Francisco: Jossey-Bass, 2000)

Porter, Jeanne, *Leading Ladies: Transformative Biblical Images for Women's Leadership* (Philadelphia, PA: Innisfree Press, Inc., 2000)

Porter, Jeanne, *Leading Lessons: Insights on Leadership from Women of the Bible* (Minneapolis: Augsburg Books, 2005)

Pue, Carson, *Mentoring Leaders: Wisdom for Developing Character, Calling, and Competency* (Grand Rapids, Michigan: Baker Books, 2005)

Robbins, Richard H., *Global Problems and the Culture of Capitalism* (Boston, Allyn and Bacon, 1999)

Roosevelt, Eleanor, *This is My Story* (New York: Harper & Brothers, 1937)

Rush, Myron, *Burnout: Practical Help for Lives Under Pressure* (Wheaton, Illinois: Alpha, 1997)

Sanford, John A., *Ministry Burnout* (Louisville, Kentucky: Westminster/Kohn Knox Press, 1982)

Scazzero, Peter with Bird, Warren, *The Emotionally Healthy Church: A Strategy for Discipleship that Actually Changes Lives* (Grand Rapids, Michigan: Zondervan, 2003)

Sealy, Dr Ruth; Vinnicombe, Professor Susan (OBE) and Doldor, Elana, *The Female FTSE Board and Report 2009* (UK: Cranfield University School of Management)

Shipman, Claire and Kay, Katty, *Womenomics: Write Your Own Rules for Success* (New York: HarperCollins, 2009)

Stanley, Andy, *Visioneering* (Sisters, Oregon: Multnomah Publishers Inc., 1999)

Strong, Joyce, *Instruments for His Glory: Releasing Women to Minister in Harmony With God and Man* (Florida: Creation House, 1999)

Strong, Joyce, *Leading with Passion and Grace: Encouraging and Mentoring Women Leaders in the Body of Christ* (Florida: Xulon Press, 2003)

Tannen, Deborah, *That's Not What I Meant: How Conversational Style Makes or Breaks Your Relations With Others* (London: Virago Press, 1986)

Thomas, Gary, *Sacred Pathways: Discover Your Soul's Path to God* (Michigan: Zondervan, 2000)

Thomson, Peninah and Graham, Jacey with Lloyd, Tom, *A Woman's Place is in the Boardroom* (Basingstoke: Palgrave MacMillan, 2005)

Thomson, Peninah and Graham, Jacey with Lloyd, Tom, *A Woman's Place is in the Boardroom: The Roadmap* (Basingstoke: Palgrave MacMillan, 2008)

Valerio, Anna Marie, *Developing Women Leaders: A Guide for Men and Women in Organisations* (West Sussex, UK: Wiley-Blackwell, 2009)

Walby, Sylvia and Allen, Jonathan, Home Office Research Study 276 Domestic Violence, Sexual Assault and Stalking: Findings from the British Crime Survey, Home Office Research, Development and Statistics Directorate March 2004. World Health Organisation, Women and Health: Today's Evidence Tomorrow's Agenda, November 2009 available at **www.who.int/gender/ documents/9789241563857/en/index.html.**

Ward, Rosie, *Growing Women Leaders: Nurturing Women's Leadership in the Church* (Abingdon: The Bible Reading Fellowship/CPAS, 2008)

Warren, Rick, *The Purpose Driven Life: What on Earth am I Here for?* (Grand Rapids, Michigan: Zondervan, 2002)

Weeks, Holly, *Failure to Communicate: How Conversations go Wrong and What you can do to Right Them* (Harvard: Harvard Business Press, 2008)

Wilson, Marie C., *Closing the Leadership Gap (Revised Edition)* (New York: Penguin Books, 2007)

Wink, Walter, *Engaging the Powers: Discernment and Resistance in a World of Domination* (Minneapolis: Fortress Press, 1992)

Wittenberg-Cox, Avivah & Maitland, Alison, *Why Women Mean Business* (West Sussex: John Wiley and Sons Ltd, 2009)

Wright, Walter C., *Relational Leadership: A Biblical Model for Leadership Service* (Carlisle: Paternoster Press, 2000)

Yager, Dr. Jan, *Friendshifts: The Power of Friendship and How It Shapes Our Lives (2nd Edition)* (Stamford: Hannacroix Creek Books, Inc., 1999)

Online Resources

www.yourdictionary.com
www.workofwomen.org
www.peoplemanagement.co.uk
www.newsweek.com
www.women.timesonline.co.uk
www.worshipteamtraining.com/ShowNotes/Leadership_Flattened_
   World_Morgenthaler.pdf
www.brainyquote.com
http://balancing-career-mothering.suite101.com/article.cfm/strategies_
   for_work_life_balance

About the Author

Kate Coleman is founder and director of Next Leadership and a former President of the Baptist Union of Great Britain.

She was the first black woman Baptist minister in the UK and is widely recognised as 'one of the most influential black Christian women leaders in the UK' (*Keep the Faith* magazine). She has extensive experience of mentoring, advising and supporting pastors, churches and leaders from across all sectors. Kate is a popular speaker and leadership consultant. A published author, her media contributions include press, radio and tv.

Kate has a dangerous interest in shortbread biscuits, not quite matched by her enthusiasm for the gym!